Continental Theory Buffalo

SUNY series, Humanities to the Rescue

Continental Theory Buffalo

Transatlantic Crossroads of a Critical Insurrection

Edited by
David R. Castillo, Jean-Jacques Thomas,
and Ewa Plonowska Ziarek

Published by State University of New York Press, Albany

© 2021 State University of New York

All rights reserved

Printed in the United States of America

No part of this book may be used or reproduced in any manner whatsoever without written permission. No part of this book may be stored in a retrieval system or transmitted in any form or by any means including electronic, electrostatic, magnetic tape, mechanical, photocopying, recording, or otherwise without the prior permission in writing of the publisher.

For information, contact State University of New York Press, Albany, NY
www.sunypress.edu

Library of Congress Cataloging-in-Publication Data

Names: Castillo, David R., 1967– editor. | Thomas, Jean-Jacques, editor. | Ziarek, Ewa Płonowska, [date]– editor.
Title: Continental theory Buffalo : transatlantic crossroads of a critical insurrection / David R. Castillo, Jean-Jacques Thomas, and Ewa Plonowska Ziarek.
Description: Albany : State University of New York Press, [2021] | Series: SUNY series, Humanities to the rescue | Includes bibliographical references and index.
Identifiers: LCCN 2021039920 (print) | LCCN 2021039921 (ebook) | ISBN 9781438486451 (hardcover : alk. paper) | ISBN 9781438486444 (pbk. : alk. paper) | ISBN 9781438486468 (ebook)
Subjects: LCSH: Continental philosophy. | Critical theory, | General Strike, France, 1968. | Social change.
Classification: LCC B804 .C575 2021 (print) | LCC B804 (ebook) | DDC 190—dc23/eng/20211007
LC record available at https://lccn.loc.gov/2021039920
LC ebook record available at https://lccn.loc.gov/2021039921

10 9 8 7 6 5 4 3 2 1

—Bon, tout ça est parfait, la France rayonne dans le monde et on avance vers le Grand Soir. (Hervé avait retrouvé son sourire). Si on plongeait là ?

Well, it's all perfect, France shows the way to the entire world and we're moving towards the Grand Soir. (Hervé smiled again). Why don't we take a swim right here?

—Julia Kristeva, *Les Samouraïs*

Contents

Acknowledgments	ix
Introduction: Humanities to the Rescue *David R. Castillo*	1
Continental Theory and Graphic Narrative: A Long Yet Missed Encounter *Jan Baetens*	7
When Poetry Talks Theory: Language Poetry and New Narrative's Dialogue with Continental Critical Theory and Philosophy *Vincent Broqua*	23
OulipoHack *Peter Consenstein*	39
Poststructuralist Turn? *Jonathan Culler*	53
France, 1968, and the Radical Politics of 1970s Film Theory *Jane M. Gaines*	65
Postscriptum on the Master's Tools *Lucile Haute*	81
Return to Form? Expanded Formalism and the Idea of Literature *Alison James*	93

Not Reading Blanchot: Theory and Practice 109
Émile Lévesque-Jalbert

Politics and Life Are Not Coextensive: Nancy, Badiou, Balibar,
and General Equivalence 119
Alberto Moreiras

Is Love Revolutionary? Lacan and Duras after '68 145
Fernanda Negrete

May '68 and *SubStance* 157
Michel Pierssens

May '68 and the Crisis of Philosophy of History: Georges Bataille,
Furio Jesi, and Latin America 167
Sergio Villalobos-Ruminott

Afterword: Ends of Thinking in Computational Age 187
Ewa Plonowska Ziarek

Contributors 203

Index 209

Acknowledgments

In the Fall of 2018, the Humanities Institute at the State University of New York co-organized with the Melodia E. Jones Chair the "North American International Colloquium on Continental Theory (and Its Future) as the last Global Western Epistemology." This North American Colloquium encouraged a dialogue between invited guests, who brought testimony of the many aspects of the "Continental invasion," and participants to discuss both the historical beginnings of this new epistemological trend in US intellectualism and the current version, the twentieth-century avatar of the new progressive and liberating Humanism.

In 2018, all over the world, French and Francophone scholars celebrated the official fiftieth anniversary of the "May '68 Events," a student and popular uprising that marked the coming of age of the baby boomers and the transformation of postwar France from a mostly rural and agricultural traditional society to one that is modern, urban, and consumer-oriented.

In the 1970s and '80s, aspects of this movement progressively found their way to the United States and Canada under the general label of "Continental Theory." The continental invasion was not limited to the two coasts. As a matter of record, the traditional Ivy League schools resisted this continental invasion, and the main propagandists of this new French humanism were found in the Midwest at the University of Wisconsin, the University of Nebraska, the University of Michigan, and the University of Minnesota, to name only a few key locations.

The University at Buffalo (UB) was a great place for this generation of French intellectuals to visit; traces are found in our local archives of the extended visits by writers, poets, philosophers, filmmakers, and feminist intellectuals, including Michel Foucault, Michel Serres, Louis Marin, Michel Deguy, Max Milner, Danièle Huillet, Michel Butor (*Mobile* ends "at home: Buffalo!"), René Girard, and Hélène Cixous. The present volume acknowledges the central role played by the State University of New York at Buffalo in the establishment of this new intellectual trend and its elaboration and influence.

Among the sponsors of the original Colloquium, we wish to thank the UB Humanities Institute, the Departments of Comparative Literature, English, and Romance Languages and Literatures, as well as the Eugenio Donato Chair of Comparative Literature, and the Melodia E. Jones Chair in French. Additionally, we wish to acknowledge the office of the Vice President for Research and Economic Development for its generous sponsorship of this edited volume. Finally, we are especially grateful for the work of Ashley Byczkowski, the research assistant of the Melodia E. Jones Chair, who supervised the preparation of the essays included in this volume.

Introduction

Humanities to the Rescue

DAVID R. CASTILLO

The Humanities to the Rescue book series is a public humanities project dedicated to discussing the role of the arts and the humanities today. As we reflect on the current "crisis of the humanities" in the context of the multifaceted and profound challenges we face in the twenty-first century, the first obvious question we might ask is: What can we do to rescue the arts and humanities from the failing funding model of higher education and the perils of the market university? Yet, Humanities to the Rescue seeks to answer an even bigger and potentially more pressing question: *What can the arts and humanities do to rescue our communities from the antismarts epidemic that has taken hold of public discourse in the post-truth age?* This new book series will explore the different ways in which humanistic disciplines can help us interpret and navigate our rapidly changing environment in the current age of media saturation and informational silos.

As we are inundated 24/7 with a barrage of fake news, demagoguery, hate speech, and self-interested denialisms that are threatening our democratic institutions (not to mention our planetary survival), it is more urgent than ever for the humanities to reclaim a central place in public discourse; to bring evidence-based analysis, ethics, imagination, and creativity to bear on the big challenges of our time. In the current social environment dominated by *attention merchants* who trade in misinformation and divisiveness, the arts and humanities must continue to point the way forward.[1] While the erosion of our civic and political institutions has accelerated with the rise of entrenched media silos, coming to grips with the current crisis of democracy and reclaiming a viable democratic future will require a sense of history and a collective reinvestment in humanistic education, dialectical inquiry, public ethics, and political imagination.

A locally and globally engaged and engaging humanities must help us break through the walls of the media bubble that treats intellectualism with impatience and suspicion while offering cover to the special interests invested in ignoring or actively denying such uncomfortable realities as global warming and structural injustice. Humanists and artists can bring crucial skills to address the current resurgence of authoritarianism, fundamentalism, racism, and misogyny, as well as the cynical posturing that continues to justify destructive economic and environmental policies.[2]

Speaking as the UB Silver's Visiting Professor in the Humanities as part of the inaugural 2018 "Humanities to the Rescue" event that inspired the creation of this book series, fiction writer Margaret Atwood challenged her audience to reflect on the seminal questions that drive the humanities. She made a key point about the need to revisit these historically humanistic questions as we ponder the future we would want to inhabit: "Here is a question that is at the core of the humanities [. . .] Where and how do we want to live? Is it in a society that strives to right ancient wrongs, to search for balance and equality, and to respect truth and fairness, or do we want to live in some other place in some other way? It will be up to you to decide that, to question values, to explore the nature of truth and fairness. It will be up to you to understand the stories and to create better ones."[3]

The Humanities to the Rescue book series seeks to deepen our understanding of the stories that make sense of our world and to help us envision better ones (as Atwood urged us to do). In the process, we will examine the cultural, economic, and political structures that bind us while fostering regenerative ways of thinking and reimagining the past, the present, and the future. The contributors to this inaugural volume deal directly with these matters as they revisit, reclaim, and reassess the "revolutionary" legacy of May '68 in light of the urgency of the future in true Benjaminian fashion.[4]

As indicated in the Acknowledgments, this essay collection grew out of a 2018 UB Conference organized and sponsored by the Humanities Institute and the Melodia E. Jones Chair and cosponsored by the Department of Comparative Literature, the Department of English, the Department of Romance Languages and Literatures, and the Eugenio Donato Chair of Comparative Literature. In 2018, French and Francophone scholars and cultural theorists memorialized and celebrated the fiftieth anniversary of May '68 all over the world. Using these commemorative events as context, the conference organizers asked a distinguished group of international scholars working on both sides of the Atlantic to retrace the transcontinental seeding(s) of May '68 and to help us rekindle their unfulfilled utopianism. The resulting symposium turned out to be every bit as stimulating as we had hoped: "Buffalo: Transcontinental Crossroads of a Critical Insurrection."

Our invited speakers take on that same charge with renewed commitment in this collaborative volume. They bear witness to the radical *multivocality* and *multilocality* of May '68 as a seminal *place of memory* (to refer to Philip Sheldrake's conceptualization) that continues to inspire progressive utopianisms.[5] As Ewa Ziarek notes in her afterword in dialogue with Alain Badiou and Hannah Arendt, *Transcontinental Crossroads* is ultimately a collaborative *act of renewal* that transcends notions of origin and "fidelity to the event" in favor of "new beginnings" (Ziarek).

This idea of a new or "other beginning" of thought is precisely what guides Alberto Moreiras's journey through the multivocal ferments of May '68 in Alain Badiou's *communism*, Etienne Balibar's *citizen-subject*, and Jean-Luc Nancy's *non-equivalential democracy*. Moreiras's essay is as much an exploration of the critical legacy of May '68 as it is a sustained effort to *think anew*, outside and against the dominant Hegelian paradigm. If Moreiras's vision for a new beginning of thought expresses itself through the multivocality of Badiou's, Balibar's, and Nancy's political philosophies, Sergio Villalobos-Ruminott underscores the multilocality of the legacy of May '68 in discussing what he calls the French and the Latin American '68s. He describes the historical "revolt" and its aftermath as the momentous withering away of the relationship between philosophy and politics that would lead to transcontinental interrogations of the categorical order of thought (the Hegelian paradigm in particular), starting with the philosophical writings of French theorist Georges Bataille and the interdisciplinary and multifaceted work of Italian historian Furio Jesi.

While Villalobos-Ruminott looks South to the Latin American '68, others focus on the North American crossroads of this critical insurrection going back to—as Jane Gaines reminds us—*Columbia Revolt* (1968), the documentary shot by the radical collective New York Newsreel. Gaines notes that the events of May '68 and the sustained intellectual movement that followed produced a storm in the US academy, as the philosophical foundations laid in the journals *Tel Quel, Positif, Cinéthique*, and *Cahiers du Cinéma* arrived via the British journal *Screen*, where they were hotly debated and reformulated, first as reengagement with Marx and Freud and later with Foucault and Derrida. The question for Gaines is whether the legacy of May '68 has been disavowed in the US academy in the aftermath of the historical "turn" of the late twentieth century or whether it has taken on new forms.

In his own retracing of the post-'68 reception of French theory in the US, Jonathan Culler underscores the American invention of poststructuralism, a term that has had little currency in France. Culler pinpoints Derrida's critique of Lévi-Strauss in "Structure, Sign, and Play" as a foundational text leading to the poststructuralist turn. Culler reengages Derrida's key text in a broad-ranging discussion involving structuralism and poststructuralism, as well as the paradigm-shifting French theory of the 1980s and the New Criticism.

For his part, Vincent Broqua traces the appropriation of poststructuralist theory in the US through the lens of the Language Poetry and New Narrative movements. Broqua notes that while few French philosophers are to be found in the short-lived *L=A=N=G=U=A=G=E* journal, this does not mean that French theory was absent from the thinking apparatuses of the Language poets. He argues that the West Coast writers associated with the New Narrative movement distinguished themselves from the Language poets in their programmatic attempts to bring back the "gendered subject." According to Broqua this may be interpreted as an effort to achieve in the realm of writing what postminimalism and postconceptualism had accomplished for minimalist and conceptual art.

Peter Consenstein traces another transcontinental literary thread around the experimental work of *Oulipo* going back to the 1960s and '70s. Consenstein reframes the work of the group as a radical form of *collective hacking* that he links to game strategies. He builds on McKenzie Wark's "gamer theory" to offer a class-oriented alternative to the feminist, American, and political critiques of Oulipo. Jan Baetens also goes back to the 1960s to illuminate the historical links between certain strings of French theory and emerging forms of cultural experimentation in the fields of graphic art and photography, including the photo stories known as *fumetti*. He examines the background of emerging scholarship in visual mass culture with a focus on the many thresholds that had to be crossed, and the promises it offered for a fruitful encounter between new forms of critical theory and the field of graphic narrative. His historical retrospective registers a subsequent period of "missed encounters" before the recent revival of critical interest in graphic narrative in French theory circles.

Fernanda Negrete also explores the link between French philosophy and experimental literature. She focuses on the centrality of the notion of love (*amour*) in post-'68 intellectual circles, especially in the work of Jacques Lacan and Marguerite Duras. Negrete notes that both Lacan and Duras are keenly interested in the potential of love to generate a transformative space beyond the orders of self- and group-identities that would include (or actively embrace) the disruptive force of the unconscious. Negrete is particularly interested in a dimension of *the letter* that Lacan and Duras located beyond the purview of the signifier, in the domains of literature and the psychoanalytic clinic. She underscores the potential of this radically inclusive notion of love to foster new modes of relation today.

Emile Lévesque-Jalbert discusses the deconstructive reading of community performed by Maurice Blanchot. Borrowing from the bipartition of Blanchot's *La Communauté inavouable*, he traces the theme of community through two important readings of Blanchot's work, Nancy's *La Communauté affrontée* and Derrida's *Politiques de l'amitié*. In dialogue with these seminal interpretations and in light of Blanchot's later works (and keeping in mind the orientation of his political activism of the 1960s), Lévesque-Jalbert argues for a "constructive" reading of Blanchot that would underscore the potential of "literature" to build a community for those without community.

For her part, Alison James assesses the recent wave of "new formalisms" in Anglophone literary criticism (e.g., the work of Caroline Levine), which prolongs the legacy of French philosophy—especially with reference to Foucault. James argues that these approaches rehabilitate form only by emphasizing formal disruption, conflict, and inadequacy, often reinforcing the incommensurability of the literary and the social. She notes that contemporary theorists in France, in the meantime, seek alternatives to the idea of form by reconceptualizing rhythm and style.

In her essay, James makes an important point about the mediating function of style, which will reappear in Ziarek's critique of "algorithmic thinking" apropos the emerging aesthetics of data presentation. As Ziarek writes: "Defined by Alison James as the mediation between singular expression and the generality of meaning, the matters of artistic style can be deployed to question the new aesthetic practices of visual presentation of data" (Ziarek). Following this argumentative thread, Ziarek insists on the enduring value of the humanities beyond quantifiable, market-driven notions of instrumentality. As a multifaceted set of interpretive traditions, the humanities would thus offer—according to Ziarek—a much-needed reprieve from (and resistance against) what she calls "the datafied world."

In this sense, one could read the essays included in this volume as effective illustrations of the potential of such interpretive traditions as philosophy, literature, and cultural criticism to run interference with (and offer alternatives to) the instrumental logic that reduces the world to a collection of quantifiable and tradable resources. The present book would thus provide a broad multivocal response to Lucile Haute's invitation to interrogate our current uses of technologies (in the dual sense captured by the French term *dispositifs*, i.e., devices and apparatuses) and to reflect on their cultural and political implications. While Michel Pierssens is certainly right to point out that the historical conditions that resulted in the "rupture of May '68" are unique in nature and scope, it is also true (as he himself suggests) that the legacy of that rupture could and should inspire new calls to "enthusiastic" action. This is indeed one way to reclaim the legacy of May '68 and to reissue its insurrectional utopianism: Humanities to the Rescue!

Notes

1. I am borrowing the concept of "attention merchants" from Tim Wu's insightful history of the commodification and monetization of attention in *The Attention Merchants: The Epic Scramble to Get inside Our Heads* (New York: Vintage, 2017).

2. William Egginton and I make this point about the renewed urgency of the Humanities today in dialogue with an earlier age of media saturation in *Medialogies: Reading Reality in the Age of Inflationary Media* (London: Bloomsbury, 2017).

3. Quoted in Julia Beck, "During Speech at UB, Atwood Stresses the Importance of the Humanities." Buffalo News, March 19, 2018, buffalonews.com/2018/03/19/during-speech-at-ub-atwood-stresses-the-importance-of-the-humanities.

4. I am referring here to Walter Benjamin's notion that "to articulate the past historically does not mean to recognize it 'the way it really was' [. . .] but to seize hold of a memory as it flashes up at a moment of danger," in "Thesis on the Philosophy of History," in *Illuminations*, ed. Hannah Arendt, trans. Harry Zohn (New York: Schocken Books, 1969), 255.

5. In Philip Shelldrake, *Spaces for the Sacred: Place, Memory and Identity* (Johns Hopkins University Press, 2001), Shelldrake argues that our symbolic places of memory are not only multivocalities but also multilocalities.

Continental Theory and Graphic Narrative
A Long Yet Missed Encounter

JAN BAETENS

In the call for papers of this conference, the list of suggested topics ended with a symbolical "etc.," actually the symptom of a real lack in our thinking on Continental Theory, that of popular culture, by which I mean image-based or image-oriented mass cultural production and consumption forms and patterns. For clarity's sake, I will limit myself in this essay to a singular type of popular culture, namely, graphic narrative or visual storytelling in print—comics and photo-novels in the first place, but also film novels, drawn novels, and film photo-novels. I do, of course, not claim that this aspect of popular and media culture is more important than others, such as television, design, food, fashion, or music—all clearly more present in the public sphere than the graphic narrative, which has however the advantage of being seen as typically French.

The 1960s have witnessed an exceptional creative outburst in the field of graphic narrative, which radically breaks with the no less radical contempt or demonization of this form of popular culture. As far as comics are concerned, everybody knows the Law of 16 July 1949 regarding publications intended for children—the French equivalent of the American Comics Code. Even more violent was the anti–photo-novel crusade of the early 1950s, which singled out this specific case to more generally stigmatize the new forms of women's romance magazines (presse du coeur) that had appeared after the War. The criticism of the photo-novel escapism often also leads to a condemnation of the economic interests in power of the magazine market and the mass media in general.

The fights against comics and photo-novels have many characteristics in common. First of all, it clearly results from a strong patriarchal stance, which reduces women and children to helpless victims who have to be saved from the dangers of hidden seducers. This remains the case when anticomics and anti–photo-novel groups will eventually use these media for their own propaganda.[1] Second, the antigraphic narrative stance exceeded the conventional divide of left and right. Both the Catholic Church and the Communist Party enthusiastically joined forces to keep this kind of nonliterature out of the newsstands. Third, there is also a systematic anti-Americanism: Comics are framed in terms of crime, violence, and racism, whereas photo-novels and women's magazines are accused of poisoning healthy girls and women with the illusions of Hollywood's dream factory and its individual pursuit of happiness. Fourth, the economic, that is protectionist dimension of the discussion is crystal clear: The rejection of immoral comics comes down to the censorship of American comics, a decision that liberates the local production from a nasty competitor, while the attacks against the photo-novel explicitly point at the bad quality of the Italian import (in its first years, the photo-novel was mainly translated from the Italian).

Yet the most important and overarching common feature is the fact that this rejection of these two forms of graphic narrative was definitely and stereotypically French, its roots being in the obsession of the Vichy regime with the notion of "education"—an obsession that was taken over, if not reinforced by all political currents and tendencies in the post-War years, as convincingly suggested by Wendy Michallat in her work on the key magazine *Pilote* (2018).[2]

Granted, outside the center of mainstream culture, other things are happening that demonstrate a vital shift, such as for instance the attempts of Chris Marker to introduce visual and popular culture in the editorial policy of the rapidly growing Éditions du Seuil or the first Situationist appropriations of comics and photo-novels. The most striking example is the two-way encounter of comics and cinema around Godard's *À bout de souffle*, with Belmondo reading the comics pages of the newspaper in the opening scene of the film (release: March 16, 1960) and the French romance comics soap opera *13, rue de l'Espoir*, serialized in the Parisian newspaper *France-Soir*, which includes an episode (July 3–4, 1960) directly inspired by the shooting of the movie.[3]

But the times do also change in academia: 1957 is the year of Barthes's *Mythologies*, written between 1954 and 1956, the missing French link between Adorno and Horkheimer's work on the culture industry (1947)[4] and Richard Hoggart's seminal book *The Uses of Literacy* (1957).[5] In 1960, sociologist Georges Friedmann creates the *Centre d'études des communications de masse* at the *École pratique des Hautes Études*. One year later he cofounds, with Roland Barthes, the journal *Communications*, and still one year later, in 1962, Edgar Morin publishes another classic, *L'Esprit du temps* (1962),[6] also very critical of the a priori rejection of mass culture by more elitist voices. Finally (but the list is certainly not exhaustive), from the same group also comes Évelyne Sullerot's *La Presse feminine* (1963).[7]

As these dates already indicate, the 1960s will continue and strengthen this growing interest for mass and popular culture, including in the field of graphic narrative. This is the decade that "adult comics" come to the fore, to the point that it will become one of the principal channels of counterculture, with Gébé's *L'An 01* (1972) as a late, but extremely representative example, cocreated with the comics' readers and adapted on screen by Jacques Doillon (1973). A similar opening can be observed on the side of the photo-novel, which is being discovered by various avant-garde poets and storytellers such as Franck Venaille, some of them inspired, perhaps, by Chris Marker's mythical "photo-roman" movie, *The Jetty* (1993). Scholarly and institutional backing will equally arrive. Francis Lacassin, for instance, a well-known specialist and promoter of popular fiction cofounds in 1964, with Alain Resnais and Évelyne Sullerot, the CELEG group ("Centre d'études des littératures d'expression graphique"). Among other things, Lacassin and CELEG, mainly interested in the history of vintage American comics of the 1930s and '40s, also publish a magazine, *Giff Wiff*, and organize the 1967 conference on paraliterature in Cerisy-la-Salle, a clear sign that the interest in comics, although still fraught with fan culture, is moving toward academic acceptation. Francis Lacassin himself would start teaching comics at the Sorbonne in 1971, and eventually become a key editor of popular fiction. Next to these changes in academia, in 1967 a large exhibition of comics art was hosted by the Musée des Arts Décoratifs in Paris, organized by Claude Moliterni, president of Socerlid (Société civile d'études et de recherches des littératures dessinées), a group that had seceded from CELEG. In the meantime, a vital dialogue had started between the previously unrelated fields of comics and visual arts.[8] Yet the most visible sign of recognition was the incorporation of comics into the new look literary textbook *La Littérature en France depuis 1945*,[9] and, of course, a couple of years later, Luc Boltanski's seminal paper on the construction of the field of comics, strategically published in the first issue of Bourdieu's home journal, *Actes de la recherche en sciences sociales*.[10]

However, this is only the bright side of the story. For culture at large as well as academic research continue to be extremely despising of graphic narrative. Critics and theorists share a condescending and patronizing stance that can take three different forms.

First of all, there is silence. Not in the sense of active censorship, but as a reflection of the prevailing idea that graphic narrative is so silly or uneventful that it is simply not worth mentioning it. The examples given above, such as Sullerot for the photo-novel or *Giff Wiff* for comics, should not dissimulate the fact that in most cases theory and criticism simply ignored the very existence of graphic narrative. Barthes's *Mythologies* seem to address nearly every aspect of contemporary mass culture, but graphic narrative is an aspect they have clearly overlooked. Another revealing case is the complete silence that surrounds the film photo-novel, a subgenre of the photo-novel that reedits existing films in photo-novel format, an exceptionally popular format around 1960, with dozens of magazines and thousands of issues.[11] As noted by Serge Ghera, there is only one known example of a film journal, *Midi-Minuit Fantastique* (1962–1972), that acknowledged the existence of this kind of publications and that used it for a review in spite of the fact that, in the large majority of the cases, film photo-novels were the only possible way to have and to keep a substantial visual trace of a certain movie[12] (not to speak of the fact that these film photo-novels sometimes even happened to contain material that did not made it into the final cut).[13] Things have changed today, as shown by the carefully edited republication of some of this material,[14] and the current explosion of publications on graphic narrative, both comics and photo-novels, makes the silence even more audible. It does however not suffice to notice the silence, one also has to make sense of it, and perhaps the most cautious way to do so is to link it with the vanishing of "realism" in high art—a point strongly made by Kristin Ross in *Fast Cars, Clean Bodies*.[15] According to this author, the ideology of modernization involved a critique of historical narrative, which prevented Modern writers (the New Novelists) and Modern thinkers (all those relying on Structuralism) to face the complexities of reality, hence their turning away from any attempt to address "ordinary" life—an attempt they abandon to minor voices such as Christiane Rochefort. To a certain extent—but this is a minor critique to a really major study—Ross's book does not completely escape the same problem: while she foregrounds the central position of the "magazine"—the new hegemonic print format, between book and newspaper—and mentions very explicitly the place taken by romance in women's press, among others, by referring to an early text by Ménie Grégoire,[16] Ross's *Fast Cars, Clean Bodies*, unfortunately, never addresses romance comics or photo-novels (I suppose because their stories were considered dramatically unrealistic).

A second posture, next to silence, is frontal attack. Here are Roland Barthes's infamous words, which date from 1970 and significantly mix up comics and photo-novels.

> There are other "arts" that combine the still (or at the least the drawing) and the story: they are the photo novel and the comic strip. I am convinced that these "arts," born in the lower depths of high culture, possess a theoretical qualification and afford a new signifier (related to the obtuse meaning); this is now acknowledged with regard to the comic strip; but I myself experience that minor trauma of signifying [significance] when looking at certain photo novels: "*their stupidity touches me*" (which might be a certain definition of the obtuse meaning); hence, there would be a future truth (or truth from a very remote past) in these absurd, vulgar, stupid, dialogic forms of the subculture of consumption. And there would be an autonomous "art" (a "text"), that of the *pictogram* ("anecdotalized" images, obtuse meanings placed in a diegetic space); this art would cut across historically and culturally heteroclite productions: ethnographic pictograms, stained-glass windows, Carpaccio's *Legend of Saint Ursula*, *images d'Épinal*, photo novels, comic strips. The innovation represented by the movie still (in relation to these other pictograms), would be that the filmic (which it constitutes) is *doubled* by another text, the film.[17]

A few years later, he even seems to raise the bid: "*Nous Deux*—the magazine—is more obscene than Sade,"[18] but it would be big mistake to quote this statement without further reference to its context, which aims at redefining the notion of the obscene (in modern culture it has moved away from the representation of sexuality to that of sentimentality—hence the conclusion that romance is more obscene than the Marquis de Sade). This is however how Barthes's sentence actually functions: as a stand-alone claim that displays another condemnation of the photo-novel.

On the comics front, nothing is quiet either, as shown by the scorning remarks of many critics. The complete file of the anticomics stereotypes has been discussed by Thierry Groensteen in a study that the author fundamentally revised two years ago.[19] Here as well, the revision shows how radically the situation has changed today.

A third posture could be labeled "reframing" or "upscaling" and is perfectly accountable in terms of cultural capital. It refers to the fact that graphic narrative is accepted, provided it manages to accept the remediating and upwardly mobile influences of "real," that is "good" literature. The point is well made by Sullerot, who insists on the quality shot given by literary adaptations of canonical works.

> But the decisions made during the drawing up of the adaptations were held up and the works produced by these periodicals were, from the outset, of a higher degree than the first Italian, then French, photo-novels. This contamination of the genre, which won gradually from the most crude magazines to periodicals concerned with a certain behavior and by addressing themselves no longer to a strictly popular audience but to the middle class, was one of the causes of the amelioration of the content in photo-novels,—of which one of the aspects was the adaptation of classical works.[20]

This idea matches the underlying current of most work on comics of the period, which strongly positions comics as a narrative genre and equally foregrounds the unbridgeable gap between "bad" (read: American) comics and "good" (read: French) *bande dessinée*, the former thematically limited to superhero stuff and commercially linked with the culture industry, the latter open to real life and in sync with the then dominating *auteur* theory.

As well analyzed by Beaty and Woo, another road could have been taken for the disciplinary pigeonholing of graphic narrative, that of visual arts for instance (after all, the 1960s and 1970s were the heyday of a certain narrative tendency in painting and photography, the so-called narrative art, but something went definitely wrong in the possible encounter of comics and art).[21]

Yet what are the principal motivations behind these three postures? The contrast is strong with the dynamism and very visible presence of the field in terms of reading and creation, and it does not suffice to simply describe this difference, one also has to rethink some of the already mentioned tendencies it from a broader point of view.

First of all, one should not underestimate the continuing impact of anti-Americanism, despite popular mass culture being principally seen as US culture (and vice versa, all culture made in US being primarily seen as crass commercialism). Comics and photo-novels are among the usual suspects in this regard, in spite of the complete absence of photo-novels in the US (photo-novels are a homegrown European cultural form), as well as in spite of the huge difference between *bande dessinée* and superhero comic books. This anti-Americanism is reinforced by the joint influence of iconophobia, on the one hand, and *auteur* theory, on the other hand.

A good example of iconophobia, a permanent thread in modern French thinking, may be given by Debord's *The Society of the Spectacle*,[22] a book written against images and media, more precisely against television, a book that also manages to avoid not only illustrations but also, to a large extent, concrete examples.[23] There could be no stronger opposition between France and North America than that between *The Society of the Spectacle* and *The Medium Is the Massage*,[24] both published the same year, the former the epitome of antivisual theory, the latter the epitome of visual thinking in theory. Debord's stance is complex and ambivalent, though, for many Situationist publications make room for the image, more particularly very popular images, while he himself will make a filmic translation of his book that is not afraid of doing what he denounces in theory. This brings the iconophobic position of *The Society of the Spectacle*—the book—even more to the fore, as if Debord wanted to keep his practical fascination with the popular image at as large of a theoretical distance as possible. The 1960s are full of examples of what I would like to call sophisticated iconophobia or second-degree iconophobia. Think, for instance, of the New Novel's active resistance to *illustration* or Barthes's decision to study fashion not as a cultural practice but as a *discourse* on fashion.[25] Initially rooted in a phenomenological *Zeitgeist* and strongly oriented toward almost behaviorist description, the New Novel will very soon turn to a radical denunciation of all forms of referential illusion and actively exclude all kinds of illustrations of the text as well as the book ("good" New Novel covers are blank covers—also a strong traditional marker of literary quality in French). And Barthes's choice to study captions instead of images is not only motivated by purely scientific reasons. Structuralism's focus on linguistics as pilot science of the humanities has played a role in this move, but certainly does not suffice to explain the shift from image to word (poststructuralism will remain globally text-centered as well).

Auteur theory points into the same direction: At first sight it aims at increasing the prestige and symbolic capital of a new medium that endangers the traditional position of literature, but the French interpretation of the concept, as is well documented by Antoine de Baecque in his study on cinephilia made in France,[26] quite explicitly reintroduces the privileges of the pen, not only via the camera-pen aesthetics but also, and more importantly, via the observation that the horizon of the movie director remains the book (hence the success of self-novelization, the interview book, and the published screenplay, which all tend to suggest that the director, often a former critic, is also—eventually—a writer).

Next to anti-Americanism, iconophobia, and auteurism, aestheticization and intellectualization are two other aspects of the reluctance to graphic narrative and mass culture in general, and both stances are clearly linked. The first element refers to the attempt to reposition mass cultural phenomena, which cannot be separated from fun, pleasure, and excitement within culturally better-received, that is, more serious contexts, in this case the context of narrative, more precisely the well-made narrative as one usually expects from literature. Certain comics, those that tell "real" stories by "real" authors in "real" books published by "real" publishers, are not yet labeled graphic novels, but the implicit tendency is clear: If comics cannot find their place within the field of visual arts, they can at least be integrated as examples of narrative and be studied with the same tools as written narrative.

Tintin is here a good point in case. First, because the place taken by this series is beyond comparison. Seen from a certain distance, the emerging comics scholarship in French may have looked like another term for Tintin scholarship, and this overlap undeniably reveals a will to endorse a certain type of comics that is both highly narrative and socially acceptable. Second, because the Tintin reading heavily promotes literary frames and tools—the first years of visual semiotics will be years of narrative semiotics applied to a visual corpus—while concealing other, more visual and more popular aspects of Hergé's work, such as for instance the sometimes direct influence of a less educative if not vulgar comic such as *Les Pieds nickelés*.[27]

Aestheticization of comics is a long-standing feature which continues even today. There is not in France a real equivalent of the a priori defense of "ugliness," "violence," and "bad taste" in comics, as is powerfully articulated in the recent work by Christoper Pizzino, who makes a strong plea for the study of comics as popular and mass culture, yet definitely not in the depoliticized sense of the US Bowling Green tradition of American popular studies.[28] The French silence on this aspect is all the more surprising given the warm welcome given to the "bête et méchant" or "foolish and nasty" humor (in comics as well as in photo-novels).

Similar remarks apply to the photo-novel. Hence the aspirations of critics such as Serge Saint-Michel and Jean-Claude Chirollet, who are among the first to take the photo-novel seriously and who both dream of a radical upgrade, for instance via an adaptation of New Novel authors.[29] Saint-Michel even quotes one of the major directors of the photo-novel, Hubert Serra, who is said to be dreaming of "a photo-novel filmed by David Hamilton on a screenplay by Marguerite Duras."[30] In his posthumously published memoir, Serra himself, an author who has never been ashamed of delivering romance on command, has given the following reading of this project.

Having been put in contact with Marguerite Duras by his business partner Georges Figon, he writes (we are in the early sixties):

> I saw a small woman arrive, simply dressed, all covered-up, and who wasn't much to look at. She had a soft voice and seemed to really take her time composing her sentences as she would pause in her speech. Behind her thick glasses, her gaze had something singular about it. A persistent certain something that seemed to be searching through my soul. What she did say was always concise, there was never anything to add. Naturally, we spoke about photo-novels. She didn't have anything against them, on the contrary, she would have really liked if I adapted one of her books set in Italy, *Les Petits Chevaux de Tarquinia*. I promised her that I would read it right away. It was difficult to talk about literature without discussing the imaginary rivalry invoked by she and Françoise Sagan. I remarked to her that Sagan certainly had some large print runs but that she didn't have the same audience as Duras.
>
> "Your audience, I said, is more selective or, more informed. Essentially, your admirers are recruited from the elite."
>
> She was silent.
>
> *What you are saying pleases me,* she said.
>
> Another silence.
>
> *But still, larger print runs would fulfill me.*
>
> I suddenly understood the power of the "durassien" silence.[31]

Intellectualization is the flip side of aestheticization and is best observed in the move away from fan culture. The first impulse to study graphic narrative was given by fans (in this case: US comics and popular fiction fans), but the attempts to introduce this kind of study to academia and theoretical reflection were triggered by a different agenda, far away from fan culture, but also from journalism and more essayistic writing. Semiotics and sociology take the lead, as shown by the table of contents of the special issue of *Communications* on comics (no. 24, 1976). There is a strong difference with the more anthropological and autobiographical tendencies of the emerging UK cultural studies. The impact of intellectualization—and the refusal of fun, of "only entertainment" as Richard Dyer[32] has called it—is a sign of the times. It can also be deduced from the nonpublication of Henri Lefebvre's book *Toward an Architecture of Enjoyment*,[33] written in 1973 and strongly marked by the libertarian dimension of the student revolts and its foregrounding of pleasure, individual freedom, and the body, but apparently incompatible with the official leftist positions the author was supposed to defend. In his book Lefebvre analyzes modern and modernist architecture of the 1960s, which he does not automatically reject as the result of capitalist speculation. More specifically, he interprets the savage, but actually perfectly planned, transformation of Spain's coastline into a gigantic touristic resort with new forms of architecture that seem to be the apparent negation of all possible ideals of urban life and shared experience in a much more ambivalent way. Places meant to be devoted only to entertainment and thus reproducing straightforwardly the existing boundaries and dichotomies between labor and leisure, are seen by him not only as instruments of mass deception but also as windows to forms of enjoyment that other types of architecture do not always allow. The "absence" of this research, which didn't get into print in spite of the prestige of its author, is another symptom of the importance of gaps and silences in the history of a period. In the case of graphic narrative, the silence is overwhelming during the 1960s. As clearly argued by Kristin Ross, this intellectualization is definitely something that becomes increasingly visible and powerful at the end of the 1950s, under the aegis of Structuralism—and the divide of Barthes's *Mythologies* in two parts—the mythologies themselves, very focused on ordinary life, and the highly theoretical afterword—may be a symptom of this shift. In the field of graphic literature as well, one will have to wait for the rise of *l'histoire culturelle du contemporain*, or cultural history of the contemporary—a typically French form of cultural studies, to observe an interest in the relationship between graphic storytelling and daily life.

All these observations—anti-Americanism, iconophobia, auteur theory, aestheticization, intellectualization—bear strong ideological markers, but they also hint at more concrete and historical institutional aspects. In this regard, two elements should be mentioned, let's call them *strategy* and *bureaucracy*. First of all, the relative absence of graphic narrative in the new forms of theory that emerge in the 1960s is probably due to strategic reasons: In comparison with television and the state control of this new medium or in comparison with cinema, which raised similar issues of censorship, it does of course not come as a surprise that graphic narrative remains in the background, if not simply behind the curtain. Second, and this is crucial, there is also a kind of institutional mismatch between the French academic system and the kind of objects and practices that come to the fore via the various types of graphic narrative. The UK-US cultural studies paradigm is heavily relying on French Theory—actually, it would not be absurd to describe cultural studies as a way of "doing" French Theory—but cultural studies as such, that is, as a recognized field of research, is a rather recent phenomenon in France, where the barriers between institutionalized disciplines remain very strong, as demonstrated by the sacrosanct list of "groups" and "sections" at the CNU or *Conseil national des universités*. The difficulty in giving graphic narrative a place in this centralized classification means that it can only be marginalized in favor of topics and approaches that are closer to the core business of each section or that it will have to be addressed from a different point of view. Interdisciplinarity is not a real solution either, for this supposes of course the previous existence of independent disciplines, and this is where the shoe pinches.

Today, the situation is fairly altered. Both the visual turn and globalization have made a radical difference. The visual turn has shifted our priorities from word to image. Globalization has opened French research to work in other languages. The impact of both changes can be easily seen in the study of graphic narrative, less text-centered and more open to historical, political, and institutional concerns and debates. Yet as a final remark I would like to argue that the most fundamental change has to do with digitization—perhaps a somewhat surprising remark given to the commonly accepted resistance of much graphic narrative to the digital turn (very few graphic novelists, for instance, are willing to abandon paper and ink). The spread of digital communication systems and networks has had a dramatic impact on the graphic narrative field. Given the long-standing importance of status and legitimacy issues in graphic narrative, what digitization mainly produced was the supersession of the divide of fan culture and academic research, more specifically at the level of legitimization mechanisms.

In the digital world, the traditional gatekeepers (publishers, critics, librarians, academics) lose their traditional monopoly (directly linked with the technology of print culture), which is now challenged by audience participation, on the one hand, and commercial algorithms, on the other hand.[34] This radical shift is accompanied by no less far-reaching changes at the level of publication itself, the traditional forms of academic publication being defied by fan-based publication formats, such as the "rogue archives" studied by Abigail De Kosnik.[35] Rogue archives are created bottom-up, by sometimes untrained and generally unpaid amateurs and volunteers sharing a special interest in a certain, often marginal or marginalized field, and whose ambition is less to transmit a certain idea of things past to future generations in a well-structured and tightly controlled way than to make possible the very survival of ignored or censored experiences as well as to generate a community life around an archive where all roles and functions become and remain blurred. Rogue archivists are almost always activists, and the driving force of their work is passion and commitment. Rogue archivists are in many cases not interested at all in technical or scientific standards and reliability and ignore or willfully break the current rules of copyright and intellectual property rights. In addition, a rogue archive often has a transformative agenda. The idea is not only to gather existing material, but to rework it and to stimulate the production of new material.

To conclude, I don't think it is exaggerated to present the place of graphic narrative in modern (that is: pre-postmodern in US terminology) thinking as that of a missed encounter. Around 1960, everything seemed ready to allow the development of a new take on this kind of popular culture. In practice, however, the encounter between low-brow cultural production and consumption and high-brow theory did not take place. It is only when one of the UK-US versions of French theory, namely, cultural studies, was striking back that France could really welcome critical thinking on graphic narrative.

Notes

1. Paola Bonifazio, "Political Photoromances: The Italian Communist Party, *Famiglia Cristiana*, and the Struggle for Women's Hearts," *Italian Studies* 72, no. 4 (2017): 393–413.

2. See Wendy Michallat, *French Cartoon Art in the 1960s and 1970: Pilote hebdomadaire and the Teenager* Bande dessinée (Leuven, Belgium: Leuven University Press, 2018).

3. For a detailed discussion of this intermedial network, see Nicolas Labarre, "À bout de souffle et son adaptation fantôme," Picturing it! Carnet de recherche sur la bande dessinée, October 17, 2014, accessed December 21, 2018, https://picturing.hypotheses.org/100.

4. Theodor W. Adorno and Max Horkheimer, *Dialectic of Enlightenment*, trans. Edmund Jephcott (Stanford: Stanford University Press, 2007 [1947]).

5. Richard Hoggart, *The Uses of Literacy* (London: Penguin Modern Classics, 2009 [1957]).

6. Edgar Morin, *L'Esprit du temps* (Paris: Grasset, 1962).

7. Évelyne Sullerot, *La Presse féminine* (Paris: Colin, 1963).

8. Bart Beaty, *Comics Versus Art* (Toronto: University of Toronto Press, 2012).

9. Jacques Bersani, et al. *La Littérature en France depuis 1945* (Paris: Larousse, 1970).

10. Luc Boltanski, "La Constitution du champ de la bande dessinée," *Actes de la recherche en sciences sociales* 1 (1975): 37–59.

11. Jan Baetens, *The Film Photonovel* (Austin: Texas University Press, 2019).

12. Serge Ghera, "Ciné-romans," 2006, accessed December 21, 2018, http://bmania.pagesperso-orange.fr/index.html.

13. Roberta Bassano, "Cineromanzi per giganti. Senso e La Strada," in *Gianni Amelio presenta Lo Schermo di Carta. Storia e storie dei cineromanzi*, ed. Emiliano Morreale (Torino: Museo Nazionale di Cinema/Il Castoro, 2007), 87–95.

14. Pierre Pinchon and Marie-Charlotte Calafat, *Contrebandes Godard 1960–1968* (Montreuil: Matière, 2018).

15. Kristin Ross, *Fast Cars, Clean Bodies: Decolonization and the Reordering of French Culture* (Cambridge, MA: MIT Press, 1995).

16. Ménie Grégoire, "La Presse féminine," *Esprit* (July–August 1959): 17–34.

17. Roland Barthes, "The Third Meaning," in *The Responsibility of Forms*, trans. Richard Howard (New York: Hill and Wang, 1985), 60. Originally in "Le Troisième Sens," in *L'Obvie et l'obtus* (Paris: Seuil 1982), 59–60, "Il est d'autres 'arts' qui combinent le photogramme (ou du moins le dessin) et l'histoire, la diégèse: ce sont le photo-roman et la bande dessinée. Je suis persuadé que ces 'arts,' nés dans les bas-fonds de la grande culture, possèdent une qualification théorique et mettent en scène un nouveau signifiant (apparenté au sens obtus); c'est désormais reconnu pour la bande dessinée; mais j'éprouve pour ma part ce léger trauma de la signifiance devant certains photos-romans: '*leur bêtise me touche*' (telle pourrait être une certaine définition du sens obtus); il y aurait donc un vérité d'avenir (ou d'un très ancien passé) dans ces formes dérisoires, vulgaires, sottes, dialogiques, de la sous-culture de consommation. Et il y aurait un 'art' (un 'texte' autonome, celui du *pictogramme* (images 'anecdotisées,' sens obtus placés dans un espace diégétique); cet art prendrait en écharpe des productions historiquement et culturellement hétéroclites: pictogrammes ethnographiques, vitraux, *la Légende de sainte Ursule* de Carpaccio, images d'Épinal, photos-romans, bande-dessinées. La novation représentée par le

photogramme (par rapport à ces autres pictogrammes), ce serait que le filmique (qu'il constitue) serait en double avec un autre texte, le film."

18. Roland Barthes, *Fragments d'un discours amoureux* (Paris: Seuil, 1977), 211, "*Nous Deux*—le magazine—est plus obscène que Sade."

19. Thierry Groensteen, *Un objet culturel non identifié* (Angoulême: éditions de l'an 2, 2006), and *La bande dessinée au tournant* (Bruxelles: Les Impressions Nouvelles, 2017).

20. Évelyne Sullerot, "Photoromans et œuvres littéraires," *Communications* 2 (1963): 79, "Mais les résolutions prises dans les rédactions au moment de la reconversion furent tenues et les œuvres réalisées par ces périodiques ont été d'emblée d'un niveau supérieur à ce qu'avaient été les premiers photoromans italiens puis français. Cette contagion du genre, qui gagna de proche en proche, après les magazines les plus primitifs, des périodiques soucieux d'une certaine tenue et s'adressant non plus à un public strictement populaire mais bien aux couches moyennes, fut une des causes de l'amélioration des contenus des photoromans, — dont l'un des aspects fut l'adaptation d'œuvres classiques."

21. Bart Beaty and Benjamin Woo, *The Greatest Comic Book of All Time: Symbolic Capital in the Field of American Comics Books* (London: Palgrave Macmillan, 2017). See also, Hugo Frey and Jan Baetens. "Comics Culture and Roy Lichtenstein Revisited: Analyzing a Forgotten 'Feedback Loop,'" *Art History* 42-1 (2019): 126–153.

22. Guy Debord, *The Society of the Spectacle*, trans. Donald Nicholson-Smith (New York: Zone Books, 1994 [1967]).

23. For an analysis of the "abstract" character of Debord's book, see Jan Baetens, "L'exemple, un mal nécessaire?," *MéthIS* 4 (2012): 135–48.

24. Marshall McLuhan and Quentin Fiore, *The Medium Is the Massage* (New York: Bantam, 1967).

25. Roland Barthes, *The Fashion System*, trans. Mathew Ward and Richard Howard (New York: Farrar, Straus and Giroux, 1983 [1967]).

26. Antoine De Baecque, *La cinéphilie. Invention d'un regard, histoire d'une culture, 1944–1968* (Paris: Fayard, 2003).

27. Jean-Yves Puyo, "'Vive le général Alcazar! C'est un lascar!," in *Les Géographies de Tintin*, ed. Paul Arnould (Paris: CNRS éditions, 2018): 179–92.

28. Christopher Pizzino, *Arresting Development. Comics at the Boundaries of Literature* (Austin: Texas University Press, 2016). Similar remarks can be found in books such as Charles Hatfield, *Alternative Comics* (Jackson, MS: University Press of Mississippi, 2006), Jared Gardner, *Projections: Comics and the History of Twenty-First-Century Storytelling* (Stanford: Stanford University Press, 2012), and Eddie Campbell, *The Goat Getters: Jack Johnson, the Fight of the Century, and How a Bunch of Raucous Cartoonists Reinvented Comic*s (San Diego, CA and Columbus: IDM and Ohio State University Press, 2018).

29. Serge Saint-Michel, *Le Roman-photo* (Paris: Larousse, 1979), and Jean-Claude Chirollet, *Esthétique du photoroman* (Paris: Edilig, 1983).

30. *Le Roman-photo*, "un roman-photo filmé par David Hamilton sur un scénario de Marguerite Duras," 87.

31. Hubert Serra, *Voyage au cœur du roman-photo. Autobiographie* (Paris: Les Indes savantes, 2017), "Je vis arriver une petite femme très couverte, habillée simplement et qui ne payait pas de mine. Elle avait une voix douce et semblait prendre le temps de composer ses phrases car elle marquait des temps d'arrêt dans son débit. Son regard, derrière ses lunettes épaisses, avait quelque chose de singulier. Un je ne sais quoi de persistant qui semblait vous fouiller l'âme. Ce qu'elle disait était toujours concis, il n'y avait jamais rien à rajouter. Naturellement nous parlâmes de romans-photos. Elle n'avait rien contre, au contraire, elle aurait bien aimé que je réalise un de ses romans qui se déroulait en Italie, *Les Petits Chevaux de Tarquinia*. Je luis promis de le lire très vite. Il était difficile de parler de littérature sans évoquer la concurrence imaginaire qu'évoquaient Françoise Sagan et elle-même. Je lui fis remarquer que Sagan avait certes de gros tirages mais qu'elle n'avait pas le même public qu'elle-même. 'Votre public, dis-je, est plus choisi ou plus averti. Au fond, vos admirateurs se recrutent dans l'élite. // Elle eut un silence. // *Ce que vous me dites me fait plaisir*, me dit-elle. // Re-silence. // *Mais tout de même, des tirages plus importants me combleraient.*' Je compris soudain la puissance du silence 'durassien,'" 86.

32. Richard Dyer, *Only Entertainment* (London: Routledge, 1992).

33. Henri Lefebvre, *Toward an Architecture of Enjoyment*, ed. Łukasz Stanek (Minneapolis: University of Minnesota Press, 2014).

34. Benoît Epron and Marcello Vitali-Rosati, *L'Édition à l'âge numérique* (Paris: La Découverte, 2018), 73–91, and Jim Collins, *Bring on the Books for Everybody: How Literary Culture Became Popular Culture* (Durham, NC: Duke University Press, 2010). See also, from an economic point of view, Joel Waldfogel, *Digital Renaissance* (Princeton, NJ: Princeton University Press, 2018).

35. Abigail De Kosnik, *Rogue Archives* (Cambridge, MA: MIT Press, 2016).

When Poetry Talks Theory

Language Poetry and New Narrative's Dialogue with Continental Critical Theory and Philosophy

VINCENT BROQUA

> [Language writing] was a poetry conversant with Continental Theory.
>
> —Dodie Bellamy and Kevin Killian,
> *Writers Who Love Too Much*

What happens when poetry talks theory? Does this question make any sense at all? By "talking theory," I mean engaging with theory, conversing about and through theory as well as using theory as a language. I want to focus on two movements of US poetry that both talked theory and talked to each other through theory. The two movements are the so-called Language movement and the New Narrative movement, to whom, for different reasons, theory was crucial in their aesthetic development. It served as a propulsive force for poetics and as a contentious point conducive to an oppositional dialogue. The Language movement emerged in the 1970s on the West Coast and the East Coast; its main representatives were Barrett Watten, Ron Silliman, Lyn Hejinian, Charles Bernstein, and Bruce Andrews. Other figures such as Steve McCaffery, Rosmarie Waldrop, Susan Howe, and David Antin were also part of the movement or associated with it without fully identifying as Language. The New Narrative movement emerged in the late 1970s on the West Coast, in San Francisco, as a self-avowed response to

Language poetry. Theory was key to Language poets in their exploration of the constituting power of language.

I want to study how both movements talked and talked about theory in order to define themselves, and in so doing, I will attempt to look at how New Narrative took continental theory as a strategic space in which they would both follow and question Language writing: it is my contention here that theory acted as an instrument of differentiation. I will demonstrate this by focusing on and analyzing their discourse—which will bring me to consider the legacy of Language writing's investigation of theory for both their generation and generations to come. I will not be able to cover everything but will give a sense of situations, positions, discourses, and retroactive discourses, in what I would like to call "provisional genealogies."

Although the term *theory*, and specifically *French Theory*, gained traction in the humanities as a word describing the influx of continental thinking into the US,[1] it has many disadvantages, such as that of creating the false illusion that such "theory" is an undifferentiated mass of thinking, whereas it is composed of the thinking of discrete thinkers, as different sometimes as Derrida and Foucault. Moreover, as in the case of Deleuze, Derrida, and Barthes, not only was the thinking rather different from one thinker to the other, but their disciplines were also not the same. Deleuze insisted on defining his discipline, philosophy, as that which pertains to the elaboration of concepts, whereas Barthes's work was chiefly that of a semiotician and a literary critic. Of course, part of the difficulty lies in the fact that each of these thinkers and readers attempted to go beyond the boundaries of their original discipline, and as Anthony Easthope and John O. Thompson argue, "these powerful theoretical movements were themselves belated responses and theoretical reorientations made necessary by a previous artistic movement."[2] I therefore wish to stress that although I'll be using the term *theory* throughout this article for reasons of brevity, it would be better to distinguish between "philosophy" and "critical theory" at least. Charles Bernstein (poet and coeditor of *L=A=N=G=U=A=G=E* magazine, and cocreator of the Poetics program at Buffalo), insisted on speaking not of "what is mistakenly called theory" but of philosophy and critical theory: "I would call Derrida a philosopher, not a theorist."[3] Bernstein's view is no doubt influenced by the fact that he was a philosophy major at Harvard and had studied with Stanley Cavell, but, more crucially, as I will show below, the distinction is more profound and has to do with the very definition of poetry, as he sees it.

New Narrative's Discourse about Theory

New Narrative started in the late 1970s and early 1980s as a response to Language writing. The general understanding is that writers Steve Abbott, Bruce Boone, and Robert Glück created New Narrative in 1977 in a series of workshops that they ran at Small Press Traffic bookstore and art center in San Fransisco.[4] It was a community-based movement that was first mainly local and became transnational, incorporating Canadian authors such as Gail Scott and East Coast writers such as Kathy Acker, with resurgences or associations in France via Dennis Cooper, for instance. The movement was marked by the lower-class background of some of its writers, and by the emphasis on the redefinition of the sexual subject—particularly as AIDS was spreading in the 1980s—together with the reintroduction of narrative into experimental writing, although poetics and poetry was always the starting point. Indeed, its founding members had strong links to poetry. Robert Glück, for instance, describes how he started out as a poet and how, in his early days, "with the zealousness of a convert [he] became Frank O'Hara."[5] Although he then went on to write fictional prose, poetry remained a vantage point from which he rethought questions of narrative. Moreover, younger members of the New Narrative movement such as Kevin Killian and Rob Halpern are poets in their own right.

New Narrative felt that Language writing—here they mostly meant West Coast Language—viewed narrative as something akin to heresy. And this is partly true, as the Language writer Lyn Hejinian states in her 2013 introduction to *A Guide to Poetics Journal*:

> A number of the terms that Language writing had generated were being productively (and sometimes contentiously) challenged by members of the loosely constructed New Narrative group [. . .]. The central argument concerned the status of narrative itself—a mode that a number of Language writers (but most definitely *not* Carla Harryman) had dismissed as ideologically suspect.[6]

In his contribution to this two-part introduction, prominent then–Bay Area Language writer Barrett Watten refers to "the prison house of narrative" as well as to the "resistance to dominant narratives."[7]

Theory was an integral part of the development of New Narrative: To them, embracing narrative didn't amount to a conservative return to the mastery of bourgeois novel writing, and theory (mainly continental theory) allowed them to make this clear. Their relation to theory though was mixed, both because, given the social background of some of the New Narrative writers, it was a language they felt they were not supposed to own,[8] and because it had to be kept at a distance. Thus, Dodie Bellamy in her text "Incarnation" says,

> as a matter of principle I am opposed to theory. Whenever I read anything theoretical that strikes me I try to forget it before I write in order to avoid contamination. One might say that I'm theoretically opposed to theory, a paradox, perhaps, but fitting since conflicting drives attract me.[9]

This paradox or even downright contradiction is well encapsulated in her novel *The Letters of Mina Harker*, a rewriting of *Dracula*, where she "litter[s] the texts with scraps of text, whole sentences, paragraphs and jargon from the theorists that fueled [New Narrative], Kristeva, Lévi-Strauss, Elisabeth Grosz, Avital Ronell."[10]

Theory was both a driving force and something to hold in check, particularly the notions of the death of the author that seemed, to them, to go hand in hand with a more abstract form of literature encapsulated in *l'écriture blanche* or in the *nouveau roman*.

> Bruce recommended Stephen King (in the mid-1980s, still a writer to be reckoned with) and in a famous New Narrative legend had written a position paper in which he had crowned King's huge novels as the answer to Blanchot's call for an "écriture blanc" [*sic*], a blank writing, what Bruce called "wallpaper writing," in which every page was the same, interchangeable.[11]

This is a misreading of *écriture blanche* and the *nouveau roman*: Barthes's theorization of écriture blanche or écriture littérale never amounted to saying that pages were interchangeable. Neither in Camus's *L'Etranger* nor in Marguerite Duras's work are pages intended to be the same.[12] In "Littérature littérale," his seminal article about Alain Robbe-Grillet's novel *Les gommes*, Barthes never even remotely suggested that one page is equal to the other.[13] I will not comment further on those misinterpretations; sometimes misunderstandings are fruitful and perhaps even needed for one's aesthetic development.[14] Although theory had to be checked (by that I mean examined, surveyed, and mastered to keep it in check), it was also seen as a powerful tool to check narrative—it was on a par with porn, for instance, seen as a tool to mine and undermine traditional narrative, as Bruce Boone says in an interview with Charles Bernstein[15]—and to legitimize some of the experiments New Narrative was exploring around the questions of the body and transgression. So, theory was inherently tied to the conceptual frame of New Narrative, almost out of *necessity*, as is perceived in Kevin Killian's recollection.

> Small Press Traffic offered a fifteen week theory workshop with Steve Abbott running it. [. . .] One week we mastered Kristeva, another W. E. B. Dubois; we raced through Lacan, Benjamin, Roland Barthes; another week Derrida; another Deleuze and Guattari, Hannah Arendt, Frantz Fanon.[16]

The way theory is introduced and discussed in retrospective texts by New Narrative writers (texts where they discuss New Narrative and theory) doesn't do justice to the place and function of theory in their movement, because it seems that the way they talk about theory amounts to seeing it as a mere toolbox. Consider the style used in two texts below that mention theory. In his manifesto-like essay, "Long Note on New Narrative," published in 2004, Glück lists theoreticians they read (Lukács, Althusser, Bataille) and juxtaposes them, without attempting to link them together:

> Five more critics. Walter Benjamin: *for* lyrical melancholy (which reads as autobiography) and for permission to mix high and low. V. N. Voloshinov: *for* discovering that meaning resides within its social situation and that contending powers struggle within language itself. Roland Barthes: *for* a style that goes back to autobiography, for the fragment and for displaying the constructed nature of story—'baring the device.' Michel Foucault: *for* the constructed nature of sexuality, the self as collaboration and the not-to-be-underestimated example of an out gay critic [. . .]. Julia Kristeva: *for* elaborating the meaning of abjection in *Powers of Horror*.[17]

The genre of the catalog is used here, creating the false impression that these theoreticians are used as tokens rather than as integral to the concerns of New Narrative. This same sense of juxtaposed references emerges at the end of an essay by Steve Abbott: "subway violence, graffiti art, Derrida and Kristeva, Judy Grahn's feminism, the return of Benjamin's disappearing storyteller, rap singing and break dancing, Boy George, pastiche in film and New Narrative writing."[18] Once again, this could be derided as a reified conception of theory, as if the writer was grappling with it through a *reader*; it could also be said that theory in this case is taken as a fixed entity composed of particles that one may pick and choose from as he or she pleases. Yet there is an element of comedy here, and another reading of these two quotes must be proposed: By being both serious and casual about references to theory, New Narrative writers probably wanted to escape the pompous quotes and the professional tone, as is made clear by Robert Glück in his article on expertise: "most experimental writing has an adversarial relation to professionalism, to work-ethic mentality; a resistance to fetishizing the 'expert,' or whatever is authoritarian."[19] Maybe, as in Dodie Bellamy's case, this was a way to use theory and yet undermine it at the same time, to use its legitimizing force and yet undermine that authority by revoking some of its power. Or as Glück seems to confirm in his "Long Note on New Narrative": "Frankly, Bruce and I pillaged critical theory for concepts that gave us access to our experience."[20] Such piracy was also advocated by Kathy Acker as coextensive of her conception of gender,[21] and indeed she would pastiche, parody, and plagiarize texts ranging from literary classics to theoretical books. In fact, pillaging amounted to a compositional strategy for some New Narrative writers.

Theory as Agonistic Conversation

In fact, theory is one of the many entry points into an agonistic conversation that shaped the poetic scene in the US—the ancient Greek word *agon* means a gathering or assembly, especially for public games, or for a contest for a prize at the games, and by extension, any contest or struggle, battle, action at law, mental struggle, and, of course, *anxiety*. This conversation happened between New Narrative and Language writers via fora, study groups, reading series, journals, much later listservs and, more elusively even, in unrecorded conversations.[22] In all of these, theory was talked about and discussed.[23] If their recollection is to be trusted, New Narrative members such as Kevin Killian and Dodie Bellamy viewed Language writing as intrinsically *speaking* theory just like a bilingual child might speak both his languages: "It was a poetry conversant with Continental Theory, and that was scary, repellent even, to the ideologies that had dominated the poetry world for the previous forty years."[24] That Killian and Bellamy should use the term *conversant*, from the French *converser*, meaning "to talk" or literally "to engage in conversation," is certainly telling. The prevalent argument is usually that Language writing was not just embracing theory as a toolbox to be pillaged but as *poetics*. And this is partly true. Barrett Watten shows the kinship between the language turn in continental theory and the turn to language in poetry.

> While the turn to language in poetry took place, first and foremost, as a development of literary and artistic possibilities (in experimental modernism, after Gertrude Stein and Louis Zukofsky; the New American poetry; and new developments in conceptual and interdisciplinary art), it also took many of its cues, even central assumptions, from the rise of neopragmatist and poststructuralist theory in the 1960s and 1970s [. . .]. It is significant that the turn to language in poetry was so immediately identified with the turn to theory.[25]

Moreover, in his article on "Philosophy and Theory in US Modern Poetry," Michael Davidson describes how Language writing embraced theory as poetics.

> Poets were among the combatants in the culture wars, often deploring but occasionally defending the linguistic turn in theory.
> Among the latter were Language Writers who took the premises of post-structural linguistics and Russian Formalism to heart and aligned these theories with European avant-garde movements such as Surrealism and Dadaism. [. . .] These poets developed a critique of the expressivist premises that dominated so much poetry of the 1950s and 1960s.[26]

To give a more precise example of the inherent link between poetics and theory in Language or Language-related writers: On October 13, 2018, at a "Poets and Critics" symposium organized at the Pratt Institute in Brooklyn, with and on the work of US poet and former Buffalo professor Susan Howe (often associated with the Language movement, but not strictly speaking a Language poet), Howe said that at that time when a poet entered a bookshop he or she would not go to the poetry section first but to the philosophy section (she called it the theory section). Speaking of philosophy and critical writing, she added, "It's in me," testifying to the importance of theoretical notions and modes of writing, which the Language writer Lyn Hejinian also confirms, saying that "poetics as a contemporary genre of writing and artistic-intellectual practice was [. . .] just beginning to discover its possibilities."[27] In addition, Peter Middleton shows that the relation with theory was so deep that not only did Susan Howe read theory, but her work *converses* with theory, namely, that of Kristeva, in that Howe's poetry calls into question some of Kristeva's "assumptions about linguistic order."[28] And indeed, the boundaries between theory and poetry became extremely porous in the work of Language writers, and testifies to a nonreified use of theory. In the collective interview quoted above in which he makes the distinction between theory and philosophy, Bernstein adds,

> As philosophy becomes systematized into literary theory, taught outside the context of philosophical history in English departments, where there is often little interest in philosophy, you get a highly reductive conception of philosophy (call it applied philosophy)—just as in many creative writing programs you get a highly reductive conception of poetry (call it applied poetry).[29]

This is a claim that he had made a decade before in "Writing and Method," published in the 1983 issue that *Poetics Journal* devoted to poetry and philosophy: In this essay, he goes against the forced distinction between poetry and philosophy. He shows that philosophy is often restricted to expository discourse, consistency and system building and that on the other hand poetry is often misleadingly seen as having to do with the beauty of language and emotions: "I would characterize as sharing a political project both a philosophical practice and a poetic practice that refuse to adopt expository principles as their basic claim to validity."[30] For him, "poetry and philosophy share the *project of investigating the possibilities (nature) and structures of phenomena.*"[31]

As Tyrus Miller says,

> theories do work in important and highly effective ways at a remove from this kind of direct contact, by shaping and sharpening the writer's and the reader's heuristic repertoire. Theories may shape our heuristic approaches in ways that open up new ways of seeing, hearing, and reading.[32]

Yet I would argue that in the case of Language writers, it didn't just amount to an opening up. There was a much more coextensive relationship between theory and writing, theory and poetry—it is not just a dialectical relationship, but a constant blurring of lines, within the understanding that poetry is never dissociated totally from the modes of thinking, writing, and conceptualizing that also characterize theory. In short, for Language writing, theory was not just a way to conceptualize the nontransparency of language, the constructedness of the poem or the sociological stakes of the poetic community (these poets could have equally arrived at those understandings via the modernist poetry they were reading and promoting, namely, that of Stein, Zukofsky, Williams, and the Objectivists); but theory was also a language that allowed for the examination of language, just like poetry did.

It thus seems to me that at their best, Language writers did not *braid* poetry and theory, nor did they pick and choose from a toolbox, but instead they *talked* theory; it was a constitutive part of their language and their exploration. The intense correspondence between Lyn Hejinian and Susan Howe, for instance, held at the Mandeville Special collections library at the University of California at San Diego and at the Beinecke Library at Yale, shows the extent to which, to recall Howe's phrase, it was *in them*. In a much more fundamental way than other poets using theory, their mode of reading it and talking it was a radical undercurrent of thought-processes that not only facilitated but matched their poetic endeavors. Although not a Language poet, but strongly associated to the Language writers, David Antin encapsulated this in his talk poems, as these improvised poems intricately wove together personal stories, linguistic considerations, and often theoretical musings from Wittgenstein to Roland Barthes and Paul Ricoeur.

Language writers talked and practiced theory; it gave language writing an authority, and it also made Language writers subject to accusations of hegemony, notably by the New Narrative. It is precisely in relation to this great familiarity that the New Narrative writers tried to position themselves by both embracing and rejecting Language writing's traffic with theory and with what New Narrative saw as their lack, so New Narrative thought, of engagement with life or what Kevin Killian calls "fun." To give a sense of New Narrative's agonistic relationship to Language writers, let me just quote the following two fragments from a long article about Language writing that Bruce Boone published in *Soup* magazine in 1982.

> It's not that the current Language Writing movement doesn't succeed on its own terms. It excels on that terrain—abstraction,

language experimentation and so on. But it isn't what you would call an *engaged* writing and as a movement it suffers from some serious defects for this reason. And for the same reason, it gives you the feeling of being rather distant from life. It's as if the genuine intelligence you feel there ends up eluding life, not participating in it or embracing it.[33]

Besides, criticizing what he calls Barrett Watten's abstractions, Boone argues,

the once acclaimed linking of modernist cultural forms with leftism now appears as a historical vestige instead of a current solution to problems in the United States. [. . .] Theoretical people, in my view, should be looking toward what is actually happening here in our own time.[34]

This was by no means a criticism of all the Language poets, Bob Perelman and Ron Silliman, for instance, are viewed more positively in his article. However, New Narrative's position is both a conversation with Language writing's endeavors and at the same time an attempt to shift the theoretical and social framework. Indeed, as Robert Glück argues,

If I could have become a Language poet I would have; I craved the formalist fireworks, a purity that invented its own tenets [. . .] I craved the community the Language poets made for themselves [. . .] I experienced the poetry of disjunction as a luxurious idealism in which the speaking subject rejects the confines of representation and disappears in the largest freedom, that of language itself. My attraction to this freedom and to the professionalism with which it was purveyed made for a kind of class struggle within myself. Whole areas of my experience, especially gay experience, were not admitted to this utopia, partly because the mainstream reflected a resoundingly coherent image of myself back to me.[35]

Beyond the question of narrative, which the Language writers were said to disavow (at least a form of conventional narrative that appeared manipulative and not critical enough of fiction, of authenticity, and of the supposed transparency of language), what the New Narrative seemed to identify as problematic in Language writing was the writers' insistence on the dissolution of the self, on the consequences of the death of the author, and the desexualized subject positions. This last point is chiefly where they found their difference, like rival brothers. Among other criticisms addressed to Language writing, they felt that something was not addressed in Language writing, and they thus strove to reintroduce a sexualized conception of the body into the body of the text, for which the Bataillian notion of transgression was fundamental. Indeed, Bataille is often referred to and quoted directly in a number of New Narrative texts. As Robert Glück recalled in 2008, Bataille was crucial for them in that his theorization of transgression was not so much espoused for its catholic proclivities as for what it allowed in terms of the transformation of narrative and the representation of homosexual relationships.

> In Bataille's novels [. . .] transgression is certainly wedded to sex [. . .]. Here in one stroke is a self at once grander and more porous than the pallid, ironized being who inhabited stories in the *New Yorker*, or the character of the wronged innocent in my own community. Here is a series of chance ruptures rather than a coherent system or an autonomous being.[36]

So, New Narrative's dialogue with Language writing through theory was very similar to what postminimalism and postconceptualism did to minimalism and conceptualism in art, as Hal Foster says in "The Crux of Minimalism," where he argues that postminimalism, just like postconceptualism, took on and yet criticized minimalism for its failure to de-universalize the subject of perception.

> As we have seen, this narrative leaves out a crucial concern: the sexual-linguistic constitution of the subject. For the most part this concern is left out of the art as well, for again, even as minimalism turned from the objective orientation of formalism to the subjective orientation of phenomenology, it tended to position artist and viewer alike not only as historically innocent but as sexually indifferent, and the same holds for much conceptual and institution-critical work that followed minimalism. This omission is addressed in feminist art from the middle 1970s through the middle 1980s, and in the investigation such disparate artists as

Mary Kelly and Silvia Kolbowski, Barbara Kruger and Sherrie Levine, Louise Lawler and Martha Rosler turned to images and discourses adjacent to the art world, especially to representations of women in mass culture and to constructions of femininity in psychoanalytical theory. This is the most productive critique of minimalism to date, and it is elaborated in practice.[37]

It seems that from the point of view of New Narrative, their contention with Language writing was close to what Foster is describing for art. It should be noted, though, that such questions were not altogether absent from the writings of Language poets or Language publications. Lyn Hejinian and Rae Armantrout, for instance, were always attentive to questions relative to women, and Hejinian further remarks in her description of the "Women and Language" issue of *Poetics Journal* that questions such as those revolving around the body, gender, identity, performativity, and sexuality were covered.[38] One could also add that Rosmarie Waldrop, who was not strictly speaking a Language poet but was associated to the movement, certainly addresses those questions in her poetry, such as in *A Key into the Language of America*.[39] One of the ways that two movements differed in their treatment of the body and of sexuality is that New Narrative strove for more explicit and direct representations of these issues. Be that as it may, it was crucial for New Narrative to reintroduce the self, however plural, through autobiography, notably, and what they were doing was certainly different from Language writing in that regard.

> The New Narrative practice of interrogating the subject by exposing its simultaneous self-effacement and self-aggrandizement, by representing event or identity or experience while taking apart the materials of representation, looked like a counterpoint to Language Poetry, which interrogated the semiotics of meaning and the materiality of language at the level of the sentence, the word, the phoneme.[40]

Camille Roy's introduction to "Biting the Error" claims that New Narrative was trying to go against a *void* left by Language writing, or rather that New Narrative writers were essentially critiquing what they took to be the subjectless, universal "author is dead" paradigm.[41] If the author dies, doesn't that amount to an easy erasure of female authors into a huge universal notion of "author," albeit absent, that doesn't exist? Along similar lines, Gail Scott speaks about "a queer response to the absent author of late-century avant-garde poetics [. . .] to French formalism's death of the author."[42]

The Argument

As I said in my introduction, these are provisional genealogies. Currently, new research done by Rob Halpern and Robin Tremblay-McGaw is trying to take a different look and casts New Narrative in a new light, that of a set of practices rather than a movement. Yet, what I hope to have shown is that both the writers identifying as Language and as New Narrative were part of an argument that I have just begun to examine, a conversation that involved a conflicting togetherness and, more precisely even, an argument in left-wing literary milieus that involved the role and uses of what some will call theory, and continental theory at that. To the Language writers, philosophy and critical writing were part of an effort to think about the politics of poetic form whereas for New Narrative the politics of poetic form was elusive, and if theory was valid, it was for rethinking the present conditions of writing and for channeling their experience into forms that were both experimental and transgressive. It is this argument that emerges retrospectively and retroactively from the documents of the time as well as from later retrospective accounts of the period. This argument, it seems to me, was propulsive both in the case of Language writing and in the case of New Narrative and its futures. Indeed, one of the consequences of taking theory as one of the focal points of the argument is that younger generations of poets such as Jena Osman, Juliana Spahr, and Rob Halpern, to name a few, have managed to pursue careers as poets and to talk theory themselves without its being a hindrance. For instance, Jena Osman incorporates Roland Barthes's and Walter Benjamin's writings into the fabric of her essay-poem *Public Figures*,[43] and Juliana Spahr is a theoretical critic in her own right; her latest theoretical investigation is *Du Bois's Telegram, Literary Resistance and State Containment*.[44] It should also be added that more senior writers weave theory to their poetry, be they post-Language poets such as Lyn Hejinian or postbeat and post–New York School poet Anne Waldman. In her latest book to date, *Tribunal*, Lyn Hejinian quotes from Julia Kristeva.[45] In her 2013 book-length poem *Gossamurmur*, Anne Waldman begins a litany by the at once funny, ironical, and serious, "I know this from Derrida," from which she develops a poem made from her reading of Derrida's *Archive Fever*.[46] It thus seems to me that for all the talk of the institutionalization of experimental poetry, the argument with theory that I've tried to touch on electrified the field of American poetry and still does.

Notes

1. See François Cusset's famous description of "French Theory" in *French Theory, Foucault, Derrida, Deleuze & Cie et les mutations de la vie intellectuelle aux Etats-Unis* (Paris: La Découverte, 2003).

2. Anthony Easthope and John O. Thompson, eds., *Contemporary Poetry Meets Modern Theory* (Hemel Hempstead, UK: Harvester Wheatsheaf, 1991), vii.

3. Charles Bernstein, Bob Perelman, Jonathan Monroe, and Ann Lauterbach. "Poetry, Community, Movement: A Conversation," *Diacritics* 26, no. 3 (1996): 197.

4. For a description of the origins of the movement, see for instance Rob Halpern and Robin Tremblay-McGaw's introduction to their edited volume *From Our Hearts to Yours: New Narrative as Contemporary Practice* (Oakland, CA: On Contemporary Practice, 2017), 7–15. See also Dodie Bellamy and Kevin Killian's introduction to their anthology of New Narrative writing: *Writers Who Love Too Much: New Narrative 1977–1997* (New York: Nightboat Books, 2017), i–xx.

5. Robert Glück, "My Community," in Robert Glück, *The Communal Nude* (South Pasadena, CA: Semiotext(e), 2016), 33.

6. Lyn Hejinian and Barrett Watten, "Introduction," in *A Guide to Poetics Journal: Writing in the Expanded Field 1982–1998*, eds., Lyn Hejinian and Barrett Watten (Middletown, CT: Wesleyan University Press, 2013), 4.

7. Hejinian and Watten, "Introduction," 20 and 19.

8. Bellamy and Killian, *Writers, Who Love Too Much*, xv.

9. Bellamy and Killian, *Writers Who Love Too Much*, 265.

10. Bellamy and Killian, *Writers Who Love Too Much*, xii.

11. Bellamy and Killian, *Writers Who Love Too Much*, x.

12. See Roland Barthes's definition of "écriture blanche" in *Le degré zéro de l'écriture* (Paris: Seuil, 1972 [1953]), 54–57. On questions of "écriture blanche," see Rabaté Dominique and Dominique Viart, *Écritures blanches* (Saint-Étienne, France: Publications de l'Université de Saint-Étienne, 2009).

13. Roland Barthes, *Essais critiques* (Paris: Seuil, 1964), 63–70.

14. On fruitful misunderstanding see Philippe Forest, *La Beauté du contresens et autres essais sur la littérature japonaise* (Nantes, France: Cécile Defaut, 2005).

15. Bruce Boone interviewed by Charles Bernstein, in Bellamy and Killian, *Writers Who Love Too Much*, 158–62. For porn, see also Glück, "Caricature," in *The Communal Nude*, 87–89.

16. Bellamy and Killian, *Writers Who Love Too Much*, xv.

17. Robert Glück, "Long Note on New Narrative," in *Biting the Error: Writers Explore Narrative*, eds., Mary Burger, Robert Glück, Camille Roy, and Gail Scott (Toronto, ON: Coach House Books, 2004), 31.

18. Bellamy and Killian, *Writers Who Love Too Much*, 221.

19. Glück, "Who Speaks for Us: Being an Expert," in *The Communal Nude*, 54.

20. Glück, "Long Note on New Narrative," in *Biting the Error*, 30.

21. Kathy Acker, "Seeing Gender," *Bodies of Work* (London: The Serpent's Tail, 1997), 158–68.

22. Among many other journals and fora, *Poetics Journal* tried to move beyond its language-marked editorship. Poets Lyn Hejinian and Barrett Watten created the journal in 1982 as a way to "articulate the linkages between th[e] multicentered Language writing movement and parallel developments in other avant-garde poetics," such as New Narrative. Hejinian and Watten, "Introduction," *A Guide to Poetics Journal* 1. For examples of discussion groups gathering Language and New Narrative, see Kaplan Harris, "The Small Press Traffic School of Dissimulation: New Narrative, New Sentence, New Left," *Jacket 2* (April 7 2011), https://jacket2.org/article/small-press-traffic-school-dissimulation.

23. See the transcripts of countless debates and panels—such as at the end of Bernstein's *Content's Dream* where critical theory, philosophy and ideology are discussed at length by members of the Language writing group and others (Tom Mandel, Ron Silliman, Barrett Watten, Michael Palmer, Bob Perelman, Larry Eigner, Carla Harryman, Robert Grenier, Stephen Rodefer, Lyn Hejinian, Susan Bee, and Charles Bernstein) in relation to modernist poetry. Charles Bernstein, "Introduction," in *Content's Dream* (Evanston, IL: Northwestern University Press, 1986), 428–62.

24. Bellamy and Killian, *Writers Who Love Too Much*, viii.

25. Hejinian and Watten, *A Guide to Poetics Journal*, 17.

26. Michael Davidson, "Philosophy and Theory in US Modern Poetry," in *A Concise Companion to Twentieth-Century American Poetry*, ed., Stephen Fredman (Oxford, UK: Wiley-Blackwell, 2005), 245.

27. Hejinian and Watten, *A Guide to Poetics Journal*, 1.

28. Peter Middleton, "Julia Kristeva, Susan Howe and Avant-Garde Poetics," in *Contemporary Poetry Meets Modern Theory*, 82.

29. Charles Bernstein, Bob Perelman, Jonathan Monroe, and Ann Lauterbach, "Poetry, Community, Movement: A Conversation," *Diacritics* 26, no. 3 (1996): 197.

30. Charles Bernstein, "Writing and Method," in *A Guide to Poetics Journal*, 49.

31 Bernstein, "Writing and Method," 48.

32. Tyrus Miller, "Avant-Garde and Theory: A Misunderstood Relation," *Poetics Today* 20, no. 4 (1999): 564.

33. Bruce Boone, "Language Writing: The Pluses & Minuses of the New Formalists," *Soup* 2. For an accessible version online see: http://jacketmagazine.com/39/perelman-halpern.shtml#soup-large.

34. Boone, "Language Writing."
35. Glück, "Long Note on New Narrative," *Biting the Error*, 25–26.
36. Glück, "Bataille and New Narrative," *Communal Nude*, 115.
37. Hal Foster, *The Return of the Real* (Cambridge, MA: MIT Press, 1996), 49.
38. Hejinian, "Introduction," *A Guide to Poetics Journal*, 5.
39. Rosmarie Waldrop, *A Key into the Language of America* (New York: New Directions, 1994). See Vincent Broqua, "Never-at-Home: Notes on Gender in the Work of Rosmarie Waldrop and Caroline Bergvall," *How2* 3, no. 1 (Summer 2007), http://www.asu.edu/pipercwcenter/how2journal/vol_3_no_1/inconference/broqua.html.
40. Mary Burger, "Introduction," in *Biting the Error: Writers Explore Narrative*, 9.
41. Camille Roy, *Biting the Error*, 8.
42. Gail Scott, *Biting the Error*, 11.
43. Jena Osman, *Public Figures* (Middletown, CT: Wesleyan University Press, 2012).
44. Juliana Spahr, *Du Bois' Telegram, Literary Resistance and State Containment* (Cambridge, MA: Harvard University Press, 2018).
45. Lyn Hejinian, *Tribunal* (Oakland, CA: Omnidawn, 2019).
46. Anne Waldman, *Gossamurmur* (New York: Penguin, 2013), 67–69.

OulipoHack

PETER CONSENSTEIN

The Oulipo hacked the system. They did so consciously and intentionally. As François Le Lionnais declared in the first Oulipo manifesto, the members of the group did what literature would have done anyway by accelerating literary evolution according to their specific methods. They broke into the writing codes that structure literary genres (try to imagine them as programs or algorithms for the purposes of this essay), codes that grid novels, history, narration, poetry, and theater. They also hacked language itself, breaking into that code by forcing language, a combinatorial system, through the grids of other combinatorial systems, such as word games, mathematical equations, or configurations sourced elsewhere. They left no writing system behind and felt free to borrow and mix systems that structure academic writing, law, directions for using machinery, manuals for appliances, medical and scientific language, anything from any era, from any culture. Theirs was a hack.

In addition, I am postulating that the Oulipo has been hacked. Whether referring to The French National Research Agency's 2013–2015 project, titled " 'Differences of Potential' DifdePo History, Poetics and Aesthetics of Oulipo," to which a number of authors in these proceedings contributed; to Jacques Roubaud's latest book,[1] in which he expresses deep frustration with the group's evolution and his own role within it; to Anne Garréta's call for social parity in the recruitment of new members; or to a diminishing number of attendees at their Jeudi's (a play on words, because *jeu* means game in French) at the French National library, the group's initial clandestine existence and its goals have been hacked. Such hacks are not necessarily negative, in fact, there is no problem with subversion being subverted, the dynamics of history are nonlinear.

The group's goal is the creation of potential literature. The road to potential that the Oulipo follows the road to potential according to specified principles (not always, of course): (1) they apply either newly invented or modified preexisting constraints to the creation of literary texts; (2) said constraints must have "potential," which means, quite simplistically, that they can be used by other writers who may make further modifications; (3) to build potential, the members of the Oulipo freely exploit "anticipated plagiarism," a sort of atemporal voyage in literary time and space that allows for borrowing future constraints from past authors, or past constraints from future (or contemporary) authors. Another original member of the group, Claude Berge, sees the group's goals as resulting from Oulipian constraints that (1) "replace traditional constraints," (2) perform "research into methods of automatic transformation of texts," and (3) "the transposition of concepts existing in different branches of mathematics into the realm of words."[2] Paul Fournel, another original member, hoped to produce "algorithmic literature,"[3] based on Paul Braffort's work, a fellow Oulipian, on what they termed the Centre Pompidou Experiment. In the third and final Oulipian manifesto, François Le Lionnais targets the oeuvre[4] in a three-phase program that promises to bring forth "future literature." In the first phase, all possible mathematical theorems are categorized and all possible chemical substances are composed; the second phase extracts from math and chemistry all structures deemed valuable and efficacious. When these extracted structures become the building blocks of artistic creations, we arrive at the third phase, the threshold of the "l'OEuvre" (799). The "Oeuvre" encompasses not only literature and writing, but the sciences (at least mathematics and chemistry), as well, it resounds with what Mallarmé called the "musicality of all things" in his *Crise de vers*. These goals are all hacks: replacing traditions, automatic transformations, transpositions of mathematical concepts into the realm of words, and the building of literary relationships between computers, readers, and writers.

Further, the Oulipians "hack" literature by employing strategies inspired by games—they're gamers. A game is a way to collaborate (a fundamental practice of the Oulipo) that tests and exercises skills, all while exorcising personal limits thanks to the various sets of neutral, neural, and raw strategies that games provide. In 1967 Jacques Bens, another of the group's founding members, authored the *Guide des jeux d'esprit*[5] ("mind games" or "games of wit"), and in which he defines and provides a list of such games, highlights their attributes, spells out their rules and determines their levels of difficulty. Examples of integrating games into literature by members of the Oulipo are numerous: in *Life A User's Manual*, Georges Perec employs certain strategies of the chessboard to design the chapters of his novel. Further, in 1968 he wrote, with Jacques Roubaud and Pierre Lusson, a manual for the game of Go, *Petit traité invitant à la découverte de l'art subtil du jeu de GO*.[6] Not only did such a manual represent the prevalent and rebellious spirit of 1968 that challenged traditional European politics, policies, games and strategies, but the authors make it quite clear that the centuries-old strategies practiced by Go players can be compared to literary forms. The group embraces the game playing spirit by rewriting proverbs according to game-like rules, creating "perverbs" and rewriting classical poetry and novels with their famous S + 7 constraint. At the end of his guide to games, Bens concludes that "All literary or musical creations are mind games"[7] that have the potential to reveal who one is: "Tell me what you play and I'll tell you who you are," he writes. A good hack is one that contributes to either self-awareness or the discovery of systemic incoherencies. Game playing does the same by building agency, a notion to which I will return.

There are so many examples of Oulipian hacks, let's just review a couple: Raymond Queneau attempted to hack the French language by modifying its orthography, turning spoken French into written French, creating neo-French. He hacked into the *I Ching* and the Italian ritornello, constructing a poetic form that is now used by other poets, the form *morale élémentaire*. Anne Garréta's novel *La Décomposition* hacked into Proust, killing off one character at a time of *In Search for Lost Time* and in *Sphinx*, she created a character whose gender is unknown, quite a feat in a gendered language. Georges Perec undid the French language in *La Disparition*, writing an entire novel without the letter *e*, and constructed the intricate *La Vie mode d'emploi* by using logarithm-type programming inspired by his professional activities in gathering and analyzing sociological information. In her latest text *Comme une rivière bleue*, Michèle Audin hacked into the nineteenth-century Paris Commune, bringing to life the day-to-day existence of everyday *citoyens* and *citoyennes* of historical Paris, thanks to newspapers and other historical sources of the era. Michelle Grangaud hacks both the French language and French civil code. In *Memento-fragments* and in *Stations* she crafts endless, sensitive, and expansive anagrams and in *État civil*, another of her creations, she reconceptualizes the French citizen's civil status. Jacques Roubaud intertwined the sonnet, ancient Japanese anthologies, and the game of Go in ϵ (*Appartenance*), creating a collection of French poetry with multidimensional possibilities that reach beyond the confines of the physical book. The list of Oulipian hacks does not end here.

These social-, cultural-, historical-, formal-, and language-based hacks attracted American writers hungry for methodical means to upend and uproot culture—to shake it up from below, at its roots, through artistic inventiveness, experimentation, and intelligence. American writers and critics have both enthusiastically praised the work of the Oulipo and have also expressed frustration, sometimes confusing the group's social organization and its collaborations with its formal cornerstones. Their critics don't see that while much of the experimental literature produced by the authors of the Oulipo hacks the literary system, the group's approach to creating such literature is based on quasi-scientific premises. The group's members take responsibility for their premises that are rooted in mathematics, game strategies, and notions of constraint but do not make claims on the political, ideological, or social outcomes that readers or other authors might read into them. There is a lot of criticism of the Oulipo and many reactions to it, more than can be summarized here, but what follows traces its main lines, all while aiming to connect them to the notion of hacking put forth by McKenzie Wark.

The Verbivoracious Press published a 500-page volume containing many responses to criticism of the Oulipo in 2017, an indication of worldwide recognition of the group and the scrutiny and admiration that it continues to attract.[8] In 2013, Lauren Elkin and Scott Esposito published *The End of Oulipo? An Attempt to Exhaust a Movement*,[9] a text to which many have responded. And earlier, in 2007, the *The noulipian Analects*, a book of texts and discussions that took place at a CalArts conference in Los Angeles in 2005 was published.[10] In her article "Transatlantic Oulipo: Crossings and Crosscurrents," Alison James also studies such criticism, choosing to trace "transformations of constraint," a term she borrows from Jean-Jacques Poucel and Jan Baetens, "that both vindicate the Oulipian concept of potentiality and reveal its divergent meanings in different contexts."[11] How these "divergent meanings in different contexts" manifest themselves leads to the contentious, political, feminist, and ideological "Foulipo" and "Noulipo" discussions, which Kenneth Goldsmith, the avant-garde poet and 2013 MoMA poet laureate, has called "nostalgic."[12] The impetus behind the "Foulipo" and "Noulipo" critique is a sense that women writers are left out of the methods that the group promotes and practices. Juliana Spahr, Stephanie Young, and Bruna Mori express frustration with the fact that constraint-based experimentation has received more critical attention, followers, and practitioners than "body-based feminist performance art." Bruna Mori asks, "why in our social/literary/generational scene, only process-based art methods seemed to have any continuing lineage or practitioners" [in comparison to] body-based feminist performance art, though they evolved at the same time?"[13] In general terms, the Oulipo has influenced the avant-garde practices of procedural and conceptual writing, but it has not attracted practitioners of more social/political-minded experimental writers who explore questions of identity and subjectivity. Kenneth Goldsmith, who called the Foulipo-Noulipo discussions "nostalgic" in a dismissive fashion, did so because highly engaged, political and feminist writing and performance seem so 1960s to him, a take on the debate that lacks in empathy and is full of self-importance. At the same time, the American critique of the Oulipo is advanced by a group of authors who project on to the group their own vision of experimental writing that is tied to social and political critique. There is validity to the critique accusing the members of the Oulipo of avoiding responsibility for the social, political, or ideological implications that results from their particular form of literary experimentation. If they were to take responsibility for what their experiments imply, they would be obliged to stake out political, ideological, or social positions and defend them to all comers. On the one hand, avoiding responsibility could be considered cowardice or an act of simple convenience, which would deserve healthy criticism; on the other hand, avoiding social, political, and ideological stances represents a methodical approach to formal experimentation that prioritizes setting parameters to which the writers must adhere, like any other serious group of scholars, scientific or otherwise.

Another take on the Oulipo's work belongs to Christian Bök who, in his version of conceptual writing, interprets Oulipian methods by implementing difficult constraints and exploiting the relationship between literature and science; he views the group's experimental methods as a challenge to which he must rise. Like other examples of conceptual writing, he too has been criticized for avoiding both subjectivity and the development of an overt political consciousness. Bök is known for his *Eunoia*,[14] *Crytallography*,[15] and the "Xenotext Experiment," all of which are driven by literary constraints inspired by other sciences as well as by games. In his postface text explaining *Eunoia*, he calls the Oulipo an "avant-garde coterie," renown for "extreme formalistic constraints," and views his own text as exercising a "Sisyphean spectacle of its labour," thanks to constraints that put language under "conditions of duress," actually "crippling" it. For the most part, the members of Oulipo are less dramatic and do not consider themselves "avant-garde," a position that needs a little explanation. Two results of skirting the avant-garde label are that (1) the term avant-garde implies a limited and finite time period; (2) as a corollary, their methods ensure that their experimentalism can be implemented endlessly and will not be limited to literature and writing. They resemble scientists experimenting in a lab, they are practitioners of gaming and of constraints, who simply expect language to exceed the boundaries of its day job. Bök's take on the group may express a theoretical misunderstanding of it, but his work is praiseworthy. Marjorie Perloff celebrates *Eunoia*, indicating that it "recalls such classic poems as Keats' 'Eve of St Agnes,' a poem that, like *Eunoia*, dramatizes the inextricability of pain and pleasure—an inextricability carried through, of course, on the sound and visual level as well," just as she celebrates Bök's success at highlighting how vowels express "semantic overtones."[16] Bök is inspired by the work of the group and takes their cross-hybridization of science and writing to new levels.

Bök's "Xenotext Experiment" received the most attention. Contemporary North American experimental poets Ron Silliman and Steve McCaffery, journals such as the *Guardian* and the *New Scientist*, and the BBC have all addressed it. The experiment involved Bök teaching himself biochemistry and then, as Isabel Waidner, an avant-garde Queer writer puts it, biologically encoding "a poem (called 'Orpheus') into the genome of a microbe so that, in reply, the cell builds a protein that encodes yet another poem (called 'Eurydice')."[17] In her analysis of Bök's experiment, Waidner critiques the Oulipo as well as both conceptual and procedural writing. She suggests that by connecting his poetry to biochemistry, Bök effectively answers the well-discussed theoretical questions "who writes?" or "who is the author?" by stating that it is the genome, not the poet, who generates the poem, that the poet responds "entirely" to the organism's rules in order to discover its "singular potential."[18] In other words, Bök surrenders not only his own agency, but also the agency and influence of any and all other writers and poets who may have informed his writing. He surrenders his poetic language to that of an "organism," thus pursuing, states Waidner, "a version of positivism."[19] As such, Bök shirks responsibility for his choices and hands it over to a genome, going so far as to qualify those choices as "both beautiful and meaningful," aesthetic determinations that are relative and not positivist.

In general, the various critiques of procedural or conceptual experimental writing by authors interested in constraints or in science arrive at similar conclusions: experimental writers, including the members of the Oulipo may, and often do, avoid taking political or social positions. As such, these writers take advantage of the unspoken privilege and the societal norms that are accorded to them as recognized writers. This is the crux of the debate; often the erudition or difficulty of the self-imposed task or constraint predominates, drawing attention away from the text's social, subjective, political, or ideological content and its repercussions. Critics express frustrated disappointment in the eschewing of such responsibilities that they believe to be inherent in experimental writing, without allowing for the possibility that the task of the experimental writer may be (self)limited to the formalities of experimentation. The results are up to others to decipher.

McKenzie Wark's two books, *A Hacker Manifesto*[20] and *Gamer Theory*[21] are theoretical texts that form a bridge between experimentalism and responsibly engaged political and socially conscious writing. I am proposing that this bridge may offer connecting points between the opposing viewpoints of the debates outlined above and that are currently affecting the group Oulipo. One of Wark's approaches to writing forms that bridge: "It seemed to me self-evident that one should [. . .] apply avant-garde techniques to the writing of theory itself. Hence *A Hacker Manifesto* uses Situationist *détournement* and *Gamer Theory* uses Oulipo-style constraints."[22] Wark's writing does not focus primarily on the Oulipo, but his input is germane and contingent to the critiques of the group because he emphasizes the intersection between hacking, gamers, agency, and experimental writing. In *Gamer Theory* (2007), a text that avoids expressly the term *game theory*, Wark "wonders how the agency of the gamer comes into being as something distinct in the first place."[23] By developing a unique nomenclature related to the building of space and of stories, Wark builds a foundation for discussing the agency of gamers. For example, he emphasizes the difference between topography and topology and invests these notions of space with such terms as "allegorithm," "atopia," and "gamespace."[24] *Gamer Theory*, a book written in numbered single paragraphs without pagination, analyzes video games such as the Sims, Vice City, Sim Earth, State of Emergency, Civilization III, Katamari Damacy, and Deux Ex, all driven by algorithms. The games create a space that appears to proffer agency to the gamer, but in fact they actually usurp that agency by confusing the topographic with the topological. The gamer believes that he or she is confronting and interacting with topological questions related to demographics, environmental issues, natural phenomena, and the building of economies, but in reality, the gamer is navigating in space generated and limited by algorithms, the gamer is only redesigning coded topographical images. The space created is neither dystopic or utopic, it is "atopic"; it is what Wark calls a "gamespace." The atopia Wark describes is disquieting in its globality; atopia aptly describes contemporary society, in which people stroll about fixated on smartphone screens. Atopia promises,

> the digital—a real of absolute, impersonal equity and equanimity. The game opens a critical gap between what gamespace promises and what it delivers. What is true is not real; what is real is not true. This is what the double movement of allegorithm and allegory have to report. The game is true in that its algorithm is consistent, but this very consistency negates a world that is not.[25]

Literary history presents us with a similar relationship between what is real and what is true. Traditional literary forms promised, thanks to their mimetic whiff, a "real" that was inconsistent with what was true. Innovative Oulipian constraints expose that long-standing artifice and replace it with others. They reveal for all to see the layers of artifice's onion or the historical evolution of literary forms and structures; the constraints demystify the artifices that uphold a mimetic literature. Always at issue for those who create is the next step, the need to see beyond the boundaries of traditional structures as well as any form of innovative positioning. The difficulty is in getting beyond atopia.

Wark reminds readers that the story line driving video games is not morally grounded or probing, it is not an allegory because it too is algorithm-driven, the choices appear infinite but are in fact the opposite, they are finite; the stories are what Wark terms "allegorithms." He writes: "Uncritical gamers do not win what they desire; they desire what they win. The score is the thing. The rest is agony."[26] He then refers to the Oulipian writer Georges Perec and the space he created in *W or The Memory of Childhood* (1975), calling that space a "heterotopian marginality," thus a more poignant and realistic dystopia, fearless of human depravity and therefore "a more enduring gameplan for gamer theory."[27] It has been a long time since the Oulipo has produced such a far-reaching experimental novel; it has been a long time since the authors have reinvented the game to the point of creating an artifice that spills into the real; it has been too long since the members of the Oulipo have determined to hack the hackers. It may be that their current status gives them no reason to do so. The methods that drive the invention of Oulipian constraints or the theoretical premises that drive conceptual art and writing do not necessarily communicate literary depth and meaning. Wark's notions of allegorithm and atopia are warning signs, indicators that there is danger in an artistic creativity that depends on recycling or that promotes an infinity that is actually finite.

Yes, Perec hacked the novel's formal, might we say, abstract structures and he did so in ways that update the novel's multiple artifices in order to produce a more probing reflection on the contemporary. Wark decries the fact that algorithms have undermined gaming, inspirational to the constraints at work in Perec's constructs. In *A Hacker Manifesto* (2004) Wark recalls how endless and ongoing the process of hacking is, how hacking resets the algorithms that undermine numerous social interactions, from banking to social media. By linking hacking to video games, he reminds us just how foundational gaming is to building a society. At the same time, Wark considers hacking fundamental to the building of Western economics, suggesting that our economy is born of an initial hack on nature itself, transforming it into property and dividing people into haves and have-nots. Nature is our source, it is our first nature, whereas land ownership, or ownership of nature, in Wark's terms, is second nature. The third nature, the main focus of Wark's analysis and central to his hacker manifesto, is populated by those who Wark terms "Vectoralists." The Vectoralists control the vectors—the highways along which information flows; they have "appropriated" it and like capitalists of old, they control it. They have blocked access to information that, like land, belongs to those who produce (on) it; the Vectoralists deprive what Wark calls the "productive" classes access to what is theirs. The use of the word *class* is central: hackers are a class that resists the Vectoralists. Using language reminiscent of Marx and the class struggle historicizes the present theoretical quagmire in which capitalism and the Internet and its information highways break down the borders of the nation-states. Economies now bleed together without much oversight. The word "class," Wark admits, "has become just another in a series of antagonisms and articulations, [. . .] because it has become the structuring principle of the vectoral plane which organizes the play of identities as differences."[28] He underlines how facile it is to capitalize on identity politics by playing groups off of one another and how vulnerable society is to such manipulation. By controlling and manipulating "identities as differences," the Vectoralists use them for their own purposes, which is why Wark's version of the hack is more class-based than identity based. Identities become vulnerable because those who manipulate information do so to divide then conquer. Wark argues the following:

> the productive classes get caught up in representations that have nothing to do with class interest. They get caught up in nationalism, racism, generationalism, various bigotries. There is no representation that confers on the producing classes an identity. There is nothing around which its multiplicities can

unite. There is only the abstraction of property that produces a
bifurcated multiplicity, divided between owning and non-owning
classes. It is the abstraction itself that must be transformed, not
the representations that it foists upon its subaltern subjects as
negative identity, as a lack of possession.[29]

Clearly, Wark defines the role of hackers as those willing, like the members of Oulipo of old, to reveal the artifices that have a stranglehold on the producing classes: the means of production, pitting identities against one another, producing a real that is not true. Clearly, only abstractions can combat abstractions. Vectoralists who purport that there is not enough of something—food, material goods, riches—maintain the myth perpetrated by ruling classes so that they can continue to control the means of production for their own enrichment. Therefore, the hacker class is a theoretical body being called on to dismantle control of the vectors by abstracting, or hacking into, information, at which point both virtuality and potential are freed, those being the hack's ultimate goal. Contemporarily, hackers disseminate disinformation and deserve the attention of the hacker class.

McKenzie Wark's theories and critique offer up possibilities for the group Oulipo. The group's methods of experimentation produce texts that make political and social commentary; this is inescapable. If, however, they were to consider the political prerogatives of the "hacker class," as put forth in Wark's manifesto, they could exercise their excellent methods of experimentation to free information and wrest it from the hands of those controlling it simply by adhering to and honing their original and foundational skills. Wark contends that the "hacker class frees the hack by hacking class itself,"[30] to hack class includes innovating on past structures, an activity well-known to the members of the Oulipo. Further, since the Vectoralists control the means of production and often do so by creating the sense that there is not enough to go around, that we are verging on a general lack (of goods, food, medicine, justice), they are also fueling a general sense of precarity and desire. Hackers are those performing that desire by returning production to the "productive" class. Wark writes [. . .],

But what is "real desire" if not the hack—the desire to release the
virtual from the actual? Desire itself calls for hacking, to release
it from false representation as lack, opening its expression with
the knowledge that it lacks only the absence of lack. Hack the
lack that lacks the hack.[31]

Convinced to desire what we believe we lack is a con game, the ultimate hack of human desire. To hack the lack would identify, produce and release that which is "virtual," and the virtual "is not just the potential latent in matter, it is the potential of potential,"[32] or another version of the "po" in the Oulipo, another version of what François Le Lionnais made reference to in the third Oulipian manifesto, "future literature," produced by linking the arts and sciences, the oeuvre. Wark views hacking as "a pure, free experimental activity [that] must be free from any constraint that is not self-imposed,"[33] a description that fits into the particularly conscious forms of writing espoused by the Oulipo.

Just by existing the Oulipo invites hacks and critique. Is the group prepared to fight off hackers or do they welcome them? Parity within the group would demonstrate the integrity of a social class that sees beyond destructive struggles of identity and agency, since parity would simply provide the group with a wider variety of inputs beyond its dominant white male European formation. Tools from any and all of the sciences are necessary to fight off hackers who have already adopted and romanticized the group's experimentation, whether that be France's Bibliothèque nationale or its Centre National de la Recherche Scientifique, institutions to which they have conceded. Writers from a wider variety of backgrounds offer a wider variety of creative constraints. "Science and Literature" is the title of an article Raymond Queneau, one of the group's founders, published in the *Times Literary Supplement* on September 28, 1967, in which he states expressly that one aim of the Oulipo is to employ mathematics to found a "new rhetoric," an excellent and abstract tool for rebuking a hack and reacquiring, reinventing, even producing language. Looking to "science" to inspire the creation of new innovative literary constraints is intermodal, contemporary, and abstract enough to provide another view of the truths science supposedly advances.[34] The prowess of the Oulipo's members is well-known and is most apparent when they integrate games into literary texts. Games are inherent, Queneau has written, to devising techniques for building artistic potential and the members of the Oulipo are well-aware of the powerful strategic position and social attributes of games they play well. To ward off a hack into their brand of literary experimentation, useful game strategy delivers both technical strength and agency that are threatened, Wark reminds us, by the dominance of algorithms and Vectoralists. To conclude, let's listen to Perec describe how Bartlebooth, a main character of *Life A User's Manual*, experiences the reassembling of jigsaw puzzles.

> Fortunately, it was more usual for Bartlebooth, at the end of such hours of waiting, having gone through every stage of controlled anxiety and exasperation, to reach a kind of ecstasy, a stasis, a sort of utterly oriental stupor, akin, perhaps, to the state archers strive to reach: profound oblivion of the body and the target, a mental void, a completely blank, receptive, and flexible mind, an attentiveness that remained total, but which was disengaged from the vicissitudes of being, from the contingent details of the puzzle and its maker's snares. In moments like that Bartlebooth could see without looking how the delicate outlines of the jigsawed wood slotted very precisely into each other, and taking two pieces he had ignored until then or which perhaps he had sworn could not possibly join, he was able to fit them together in one go.[35]

Perec fully understood the power of the relationship between gaming and agency. But the Oulipo has been hacked and it is time to return the favor. Reinvigorating the relationship between gaming and creativity is a means to return a powerful experience of agency to writers and readers alike. If they'd like, the members of the Oulipo could consider the impetus of the theoretical premises of the hacker class and restore gaming and information back to those producing them, an act of potential if there ever was one.

Notes

1. Jacques Roubaud, *Peut-être ou la nuit de dimanche* (Paris: Seuil, 2018).

2. Claude Berge, "For a Potential Analysis of Combinatory Literature," in *Oulipo: A Primer of Potential Literature*, ed. and trans. Warren F. Motte Jr. (Lincoln: University of Nebraska Press, 1986), 115–25. From the French "Pour une analyse potentielle de la litterature combinatoire." *La Littérature potentielle* (Paris: Gallimard, 1973), in "Six Selections from the Oulipo," accessed August 16, 2018, https://nickm.com/classes/the_word_made_digital/resources/12-oulipo-p.pdf.

3. Paul Fournel, "Computer and Writer: The Centre Pompidou Experiment," in *Oulipo: A Primer of Potential Literature*, ed. and trans. Warren F. Motte Jr. (Lincoln: University of Nebraska Press, 1986), 140–52. From the French "Ordinateur et écrivain." *Atlas de littérature potentielle* (Paris: Gallimard, 1981), in "Six Selections from the Oulipo," accessed August 16, 2018, https://nickm.com/classes/the_word_made_digital/resources/12-oulipo-p.pdf.

4. François Le Lionnais, "Prolégomènes à toute littérature future," in *Anthologie de l'Oulipo*, eds. Marcel Benabou et Paul Fournel (Paris: Gallimard, 2009), 798–801.

5. Jacques Bens, *Guide des jeux d'esprit* (Paris: Éditions Albin Michel, 1967).

6. Georges Perec, Jacques Roubaud, and Pierre Lusson, *Petit traité invitant à la découverte de l'art subtil du jeu de GO* (Paris: Christian Bourgois, 1969).

7. Bens, *Guide des jeux d'esprit*,14.

8. G. N. Forester and M. J. Nicholls eds., *The Oulipo—Festschrift Volume Six* (Great Britain, Singapore: Verbivoracious Press, 2017).

9. Lauren Elkin and Scott Esposito, *The End of Oulipo? An Attempt to Exhaust a Movement* (Alresford, UK: Zero Books, 2013).

10. Matias Viegener and Christine Wertheim eds., *The noulipian Analects* (Los Angeles, CA: Les Figues Press, 2007).

11. Alison James, "Transatlantic Oulipo: Crossings and Crosscurrents," *Formules* 16 (2012): 249–62.

12. Kenneth Goldsmith, "A Response to Foulipo," accessed September 8, 2018, http://d7.drunkenboat.com/db8/oulipo/feature-oulipo/essays/goldsmith/response.html.

13. Bruna Mori, "Noulipo's Oulipoed Foulipo," accessed September 8, 2018, http://d7.drunkenboat.com/db8/oulipo/feature-oulipo/essays/mori/noulipo.html.

14. Christian Bök, *Eunoia* (Toronto, ON: Coach House Books, 2009).

15. Christian Bök, *Crytallography* (Toronto, ON: Coach House Books, 1994).

16. Marjorie Perloff, "The Oulipo factor: the procedural poetics of Christian Bök and Caroline Bergvall," *Textual Practice* 18, no. 1 (2004): 23–45.

17. Isabel Waidner, "Christian Bök's *Xenotext Experiment*, Conceptual Writing and the Subject-of-No-Subjectivity: "Pink Faeries and Gaudy Baubles," *Configurations* 26, no. 1 (Winter 2018): 27–46. See also Jean-Jacques Poucel's discussion of the Xenotext Experiment here: https://vimeo.com/117661089.

18. Waidner, 32, quoting Bök from Ron Silliman, *Silliman's Blog*, May 10, 2011, http://ronsilliman.blogspot.co.uk/2011/05/deinococcus-radiodurans-future-of.html.

19. Waidner, "Christian Bök's *Xenotext Experiment*," 33.

20. McKenzie Wark, *A Hacker Manifesto* (Cambridge, MA: Harvard University Press, 2004).

21. McKenzie Wark, *Gamer Theory* (Cambridge, MA: Harvard University Press, 2007).

22. "Alexander R. Galloway: — An Interview with McKenzie Wark," *boundary 2* (April 7, 2017), accessed September 28, 2018, https://www.boundary2.org/2017/04/alexander-r-galloway-an-interview-with-mckenzie-wark/.

23. *Gamer Theory*, 124. Numbers for the quotes from *Gamer Theory* and *A Hacker Manifesto* refer to the numbered paragraphs and not the page numbers of this text, which is nonpaginated.

24. Wark, *Gamer Theory*, 067.

25. Wark, *Gamer Theory*, 032.

26. Wark, *Gamer Theory*, 021.
27. McKenzie Wark, *Gamer Theory*, 116.
28. Wark, *A Hacker Manifesto*, 033.
29. Wark, *A Hacker Manifesto*, 217.
30. Wark, *A Hacker Manifesto*, 196.
31. Wark, *A Hacker Manifesto*, 293.
32. Wark, *A Hacker Manifesto*, 014.
33. Wark, *A Hacker Manifesto*, 197.
34. In 2017, there was a one-day conference dedicated to the Oulipo and Knowledge. View the list of papers here: https://calenda.org/403949?formatage=print&lang=es. An edition of the journal *Formules* is dedicated to the same subject: http://www.ieeff.org/formulessitenewhome.html.
35. Georges Perec, *Life: A User's Manual* (Verba Mundi Book #18), trans. David Bellos (Boston, MA: David R. Godine, Kindle Edition), Kindle Locations 6298–6304.

Poststructuralist Turn?

JONATHAN CULLER

We are invited to reflect on the consequences of French theory in America, and on transatlantic divergences. The most obvious divergence is the so-called poststructuralist turn, alleged to have begun not in Buffalo, alas, but at Johns Hopkins, at the famous conference organized in 1966 by Richard Macksey of Hopkins and Eugenio Donato, who from 1968 to 1976 directed the Program in Comparative Literature in Buffalo. The conference, they wrote, was to explore "the impact of contemporary 'structuralist' thought on critical methods."[1] But the paper that came largely to define the legacy of the conference was Jacques Derrida's "Structure, Sign and Play in the Discourse of the Human Sciences," which offered an exposition and critique of the methods and theoretical framework of Claude Lévi-Strauss. So much so that while the conference proceedings were originally published as *The Languages of Criticism and the Sciences of Man*, they were republished two years later with the former subtitle promoted to the status of title, *The Structuralist Controversy*, since they had come to represent a controversy about structuralism and its failings. In *French Theory*, his history of French influences on modern American critical thought, François Cusset writes that this encounter, "which everyone would later reread as a liminal scene, a founding moment," did not have immediate effects and it would be at least ten years before the lines of investigation adumbrated here would be pursued and so-called poststructuralism could be constituted.[2] But the conference was taken, both by those who were there and especially by those who only heard about it, to signal that structuralism was in difficulty.

One could certainly argue that structuralism never got a fair shake in the United States, since just as it was becoming known, news of Derrida's critique of Lévi-Strauss started to spread, so that structuralism no longer seemed even the latest thing. People could then feel that they need not pay attention to it, especially if it was alleged to go wrong in various ways. They could attend to particular works of theory and criticism without concerning themselves with structuralism. The result, in the United States though not of course in France, was to treat what was interesting and innovative in French thinkers as belonging to poststructuralism, which for reasons to be explored, found a readier audience than structuralism ever had. Frank Lentricchia, chronicling the critical scene in 1980 in slapdash fashion, wrote,

> Sometime in the early 1970s we awoke from the dogmatic slumber of our phenomenological sleep to find that a new presence had taken absolute hold over our avant-garde critical imagination: Jacques Derrida. Somewhat startlingly, we learned that, despite a number of loose characterizations to the contrary, he brought not structuralism but something that would be called "post-structuralism."[3]

How could this happen? It is a story worth exploring, for a number of reasons. First, although the major theoretical influences were French, the notion of poststructuralism never caught on in France. In *Why There Is No Poststructuralism in France*, Johannes Angermuller observes that "In France the label 'poststructuralism' as used in international intellectual discourse is unknown," and he reports that a catalog search "for the element *poststru* yields 243 titles, of which 84 percent are English and none are French."[4] This suggests that the differences presumed to be so important in the American account may be the effect of some misprision. Second, even within the United States, there was considerable confusion about what might count as structuralist and what as poststructuralist. This is nicely reflected in two knowledgeable publications by Josué Harari. His 1979 anthology of poststructuralist criticism, *Textual Strategies: Perspectives in Post-Structuralist Criticism*, consists mainly of work by writers who already featured in his 1971 bibliography, *Structuralists and Structuralisms*: Roland Barthes, Gilles Deleuze, Eugenio Donato, Michel Foucault, Gérard Genette, René Girard, Louis Marin, Michael Riffaterre, and Michel Serres.[5] The work of these authors had not changed, only the label under which they were now to be grouped. Harari's articulation of the field effectively makes Claude Lévi-Strauss and Tzvetan Todorov the only true structuralists, since they were not now counted as poststructuralists. In fact, as Angermuller notes, "structuralism was often reduced to a caricature, [as] poststructuralism rapidly became an umbrella term designating various strands coming from continental Europe."[6]

My discussion will concentrate on Derrida's crucial paper, usually cited as a Nietzschean embrace of the infinite play of signification and a damning critique of Lévi-Strauss's use of the notion of structure, and hence of structuralism in general. For instance, even François Cusset, in his generally knowledgeable *French Theory*, writes that Derrida programmatically declares that it is urgent to embrace the Nietzschean option.[7] In fact, we find something quite different: Derrida does not claim to be turning the page on structuralism; on the contrary, he begins with the announcement that an event has occurred in the thinking of structure, which until recently had always been tied to a center, to notion of origin (and hence to a metaphysics of presence), an origin that founds and makes possible the play of substitutions and variation. Structuralism in general and Lévi-Strauss in particular have made it possible, Derrida maintains, to think of the center as a function rather than as a given or an origin; so that we now can conceive of "a system in which the central signified, the original or transcendental signified, is never absolutely present outside a system of differences."[8] For this new thinking of the structurality of structure Derrida cites the legacy of Nietzsche and Freud but his principal exhibit is Lévi-Strauss, and he is manifestly crediting structuralism in general with this advance.

This event in the thinking of structure is momentous and involves a critique of the metaphysics of presence, but Derrida stresses that there is no way of doing without the concepts of metaphysics in order to disrupt metaphysics. We have no categories, syntax, or lexicon that are not caught up in this system of thought.[9] Thus, Nietzsche, Freud, and Heidegger can be shown to be complicit with the metaphysics they seek to evade. Heidegger treats Nietzsche in this fashion: "One could do the same for Heidegger, for Freud, or for a number of others. And today no exercise is more widespread."[10] Derrida is usually thought to have performed this exercise of demonstrating complicity on Lévi-Strauss in turn, but his casual reference to this as a widespread, commonplace exercise certainly suggests that this is not what he sees himself doing and that a demonstration of complicity with metaphysics would certainly not constitute a devastating critique. What, then, are the implications of Derrida's reading of Lévi-Strauss?

Derrida's lengthy discussion of Lévi-Strauss praises ethnology as the privileged example of a structuralist science, based on its self-decentering:

Western culture no longer treats itself as the center, but of course it cannot escape its character as a Western science: "Consequently, whether he wants to or not—and this does not depend on a decision on his part—the ethnologist accepts into his discourse the premises of ethnocentrism at the very moment when he denounces them. This necessity is irreducible; it is not a historical contingency."[11] But there are different ways of yielding to it, and "the quality and fecundity of a discourse are perhaps measured by the critical rigor with which this relation to the history of metaphysics and to the inherited concepts is thought."[12]

In Lévi-Strauss's engagement with the opposition between nature and culture and his discovery of the breakdown of the opposition through the scandal of the prohibition of incest, which is both natural, because apparently universal, and yet obviously cultural, Lévi-Strauss discovers that the language of conceptual categories bears within itself the necessity of its own critique. But, Derrida argues, there are two ways of carrying out this critique. "Once the limit of the nature/culture opposition makes itself felt, one might want to question systematically and rigorously the history of these concepts."[13] This is one option. The other option is to preserve these concepts, treating them as tools within the domain of empirical investigation, while denouncing their limits or inadequacies, "in order to avoid the possibly sterilizing effects" of the first option.[14] Lévi-Strauss adopts the second strategy: he exploits the "relative efficacity" of these categories and uses them to "destroy the old machinery to which they belong. This is how the language of the social sciences criticizes itself." In sum, Lévi-Strauss "preserves as an instrument something whose truth value he criticizes."[15]

Derrida shows that from *Les Structures élémentaires de la parenté* to *Mythologiques*, Lévi-Strauss is committed to this "double intention." But it does not seem too far-fetched to relate this double move to Derrida's own frequent evocation of a double procedure, a double game—formulations with doubling often surface when he explains his own procedure, which cannot simply scrap the old concepts but must operate with them. Deconstruction must, he writes in "Signature Event Context," "through a double gesture, a double science, a double writing put into practice a reversal of the classical opposition and a displacement of the system."[16] It must work within the terms of the system in order to affect it; using the categories of the system in order to displace it. Derrida needs *signifier* and *signified* to critique the notion of sign, for instance—and the same is true for all of the binary oppositions of philosophy and of structuralism that are subjected to deconstructive analysis. There is no doing without them. There is no stepping outside; the systems must be breached from within.

Derrida goes on to characterize what he sees as the inadequacy of Lévi-Strauss's form of self-critique, in *Mythologiques* in particular, where in admitting that his construction may be but a myth of mythology, Lévi-Strauss offers the very seductive "abandonment of all reference to a *center*, to a *subject*, to a privileged *reference*, to an origin."[17] More than anyone else, Lévi-Strauss has "brought to light the play [*jeu*] of repetition and the repetition of play."[18] The lack of center, origin, end, the assertion of the primacy of structure and thus of play, which should be conceived as prior to presence and absence, are nonetheless accompanied in Lévi-Strauss, Derrida argues, by "a sort of ethic of presence, an ethic of nostalgia for origins, an ethic of archaic and natural innocence, of a purity of presence," which is even presented as the motivation of the ethnological project of recovering archaic societies and the lost value they represent or embody.[19] Derrida calls this ethics and this nostalgia "this structuralist thematic of broken immediacy," the "negative, nostalgic, guilty, Rousseauistic, side of the thinking of play," of which the Nietzschean affirmation of the joyful "play of the world and the innocence of becoming" is the other side.[20] It is here that comes a famous passage contrasting two interpretations of interpretation, of structure, sign, and play.

> There are thus two interpretations of interpretation, of structure, of sign, of play. The one seeks to decipher, dreams of deciphering, a truth or an origin which escapes play [*échappe au jeu*] and the order of the sign, and lives the necessity of interpretation as an exile. The other, which is no longer turned toward the origin, affirms play [*affirme le jeu*] and tries to pass beyond man and humanism, the name man being the name of that being who, throughout the history of metaphysics or of onto-theology—in other words, throughout his entire history—has dreamed of full presence, the reassuring foundation, the origin and the end of play.[21]

The implication seems to be—this is how people have interpreted this passage—that Lévi-Strauss and structuralism belong to the guilty, nostalgic side of interpretation, while something new—call it "poststructuralism," as people would come to do—is turned toward the future, affirming play and trying to pass beyond humans and humanism. The choice seems clearly outlined. François Cusset, in his account of the conference, claims that

> between "the two interpretations of interpretation" it is urgent to substitute, Derrida concludes in programmatic tones, for the one that "dreams of deciphering a truth . . . which escapes play," one that, on the contrary, "affirms play and attempts to pass beyond man and humanism." The point is clear: this lofty structuralism with its rarefied stakes, which the American university knew only in its narratological version (Genette and Todorov), was something that should be left behind in order to move toward a more playful [*réjouissant*] *post*structuralism. The word will not make its appearance until the early 1970s, but all the Americans present at Johns Hopkins in 1966 realized that they had attended the live performance of its public birth.[22]

But in fact, as I am not the first to notice, while Derrida deliberately, dramatically, creates the impression of a stark choice between a nostalgic humanism and a forward-looking affirmation of freedom—while he seems to offer this choice between apparently distinct alternatives (calling these two interpretations of interpretation "absolutely irreconcilable, even if we live them simultaneously and reconcile them in an obscure economy")[23]—he then expresses the view that there can be no question of choosing. I cite the French here for this key passage.

> Je ne crois pas pour ma part, bien que ces deux interprétations doivent accuser leur différence et aiguiser leur irréductibilité, qu'il y ait aujourd'hui à *choisir*. D'abord parce que nous sommes là dans une région—disons encore, provisoirement, de l'historicité—où la catégorie de choix paraît bien légère. Ensuite parce qu'il faut essayer d'abord de penser le sol commun, et la *différance* de cette différence irréductible.[24]

> For my part, although these two interpretations must acknowledge and accentuate their difference and define their irreducibility, I do not believe that today there is any question of *choosing*—in the first place because here we are in a region (let's say, provisionally, a region of historicity) where the category of choice seems particularly trivial; and in the second, because we must

first try to conceive of the common ground, and the *différance* of this irreducible difference.[25]

Given these two interpretations of interpretation, one cannot effectively choose: we cannot for instance, embrace the "free play" of meaning since meaning always depends on prior structures or associations; nor can we escape play by fixing on origins; language, with its play, always supervenes. One cannot, for example (to give a bit more concreteness to Derrida's entirely appropriate disclaimer), choose to make meaning either the original intention of the speaker or the creation of the reader, even if one claims to do so. Such claims are very insubstantial, ineffective, masking a reintroduction of the internal division of meaning under some other guise. We cannot just reject one side of this double conception of interpretation and embrace the other. And the essay somewhat grandiloquently concludes with Derrida situating himself not as leading the movement toward a joyful Nietzschean future of free play, but as one among those who

> turn their eyes away when faced with the as yet unnamable which is proclaiming itself and which can do so, as is necessary whenever a birth is in the offing, only under the species of the nonspecies, in the formless, mute, infant, and terrifying form of monstrosity [la forme informe, muette, infante et terrifiante de la monstruosité].[26]

One might have imagined that the evocation of something monstrous on the horizon would have reduced the temptation to embrace "Structure, Sign, and Play" as heralding a new poststructuralism, but no doubt for humanists the appeal of something new can outweigh the fear of the monstrous. But at the very least one has to admit that Derrida's essay is not a repudiation of structuralism and celebration of a future alternative. In "Force et signification," Derrida declares, "Comme nous vivons de la fécondité structuraliste, il est trop tôt pour fouetter notre rêve" (Since we are sustained by the fecundity of structuralism, it is too early to attack our dream).[27] More crucially, his conclusion in the essay is made possible above all by an appeal to the undeniable thematics of nostalgia and of humanism in Lévi-Strauss. If Derrida were writing about other structuralists—Genette, Jakobson, or Todorov, for instance, perhaps even Barthes—he would find it hard to speak of a nostalgia for origins or a guilty, Rousseauistic thematics of immediacy disrupted.

But still, there is a specific critique here that is easily lost sight of in the rhetoric of the conclusion, which has the strange effect of heightening the opposition, even though the evocation of monstrosity ought logically to render the supposed alternative to structuralism less attractive, rather than make structuralism itself seem passé. I noted earlier, along with Derrida's distinction between two different ways of pursing the critique of the categories that organize thought that Derrida himself must use the categories he critiques. But the major difference between the two modes of critique might hinge on a term that comes up a couple of times in his discussion of Lévi-Strauss: *empiricism*. Lévi-Strauss is said to conserve these categories, not because he needs to do so in order to criticize them, but for "la découverte empirique" (empirical discovery).[28] He is studying some particular phenomenon—kinship systems, totemism, mythology, and so on—and wants to understand these systems. The rigorous questioning of the history of concepts, for which Derrida is known, yields a reading of texts—that is the form that Derrida's enterprise takes—but not an account of particular cultural systems. In the end, given Derrida's claim that Lévi-Strauss seeks to dispense with the center, *arche*, and *telos*, but inhabits that quest in the wrong way, the crucial difference may be between a thought that does not seek to study any cultural activity or system but only to produce a critique and displacement of concepts that have been used in such enterprises, through a reading of theoretical texts, and a thought actively seeking to understand cultural phenomena, while subjecting the necessary concepts to critique. We may have here above all a difference between a hermeneutics turned away from center or origin—a transcendental signified—while it reads a text of some sort, in a hermeneutics of suspicion, as we have come to say (Derrida's enterprise could be described in this way), and another enterprise, which is not a hermeneutics nostalgic for an origin or transcendental signified but a poetics, and which is not seeking to interpret at all but to understand the conditions of possibility of signification in a particular cultural domain.

If one is interested in understanding why it is that Derrida's subtle and complex critique of the structuralism he hailed as an event and says we continue to inhabit might have caught on and been taken to inaugurate a so-called poststructuralist turn, it may help to start with this distinction between poetics and hermeneutics. François Cusset claims that with "poststructuralism" America invented an open-ended successor, "a far more malleable one, with two distinct advantages: it had a much looser and therefore more accommodating definition, and it did not exist as a coherent category on the Old Continent."[29] But there are more precise reasons for its success.

Given the underlying presumption in Anglo-American literary studies that the task of the analyst is to produce richer, superior interpretations of texts, Derrida's critique had the attraction of encouraging forms of interpretation that included a critique of fundamental philosophical categories, with a new vocabulary and some new assumptions about the goals of interpretation (no longer was it to be assumed that an interpretation should demonstrate the organic unity of a work, for instance). This sort of critical activity seemed at once more radical and more in keeping with the traditions of literary study than a structuralist enterprise that attempted to advance an understanding of the cultural systems and conventions that make meaning possible and that in principle does not seek to provide interpretations of texts. If this more difficult enterprise of poetics could be represented as in some way deluded, all the more reason to convince oneself that the world had moved beyond structuralism to something else, which turned out to be an all-too-comfortable hermeneutics of suspicion, carried out in the name of poststructuralism.

This distinction between an enterprise devoted to the critique of fundamental concepts and one seeking to use these concepts (while critiquing them) to understand some particular domain also helps to explain why it is that Michel Foucault, despite his disclaimers, was always identified as a structuralist.[30] He sought to reconstruct the underlying systems of disciplinary thought, the conditions of possibility of various historical forms of knowledge, and at one point even claimed to be happy to be called a positivist.[31] On the other hand, once we were thought to have taken a poststructuralist turn, Foucault's critique of the subject and focus on the role of power in the constitution of knowledge enabled him to be treated as a leading poststructuralist devoted above all to the critique of concepts rather than to research into conditions of possibility of various discourses.

The strange result of the American positing of poststructuralism is that the vocabularies, procedures, and results of structuralist thinkers are preserved and celebrated but the frameworks of systematic projects are often bracketed or set aside, as if they had been discredited. But as I have argued, the intervention by Derrida that was seen, retrospectively, as constitutive of poststructuralism, does not in fact call for a movement beyond structuralism but offers two ways of proceeding within this framework, and it is unfortunate that the attractions of a negative hermeneutics have eclipsed the combination of systematizing projects with the necessary critique of the concepts they employ, which might advance our understanding of what is undeniable—the production of meaning in social and cultural activities.

Notes

Some material from this chapter appeared in "1980: Structuralism and Poststructuralism," *Ex-position* 40 (December 2018): 79–94. Reprinted with permission.

1. Richard Macksey and Eugenio Donato, eds., *The Languages of Criticism and the Sciences of Man* (Baltimore: Johns Hopkins University Press, 1970). Reprinted as *The Structuralist Controversy: The Languages of Criticism and the Sciences of Man* (Baltimore: Johns Hopkins University Press, 1972), xv.

2. François Cusset, *French Theory: How Foucault, Derrida, Deleuze, & Co. Transformed the Intellectual Life of the United States*, trans. Jeff Fort (Minneapolis: University of Minnesota Press, 2008), 32.

3. Frank Lentricchia, *After the New Criticism* (Chicago, IL: University of Chicago Press, 1980), 159. It is scarcely clear what Lentricchia has in mind in speaking of "the dogmatic slumber of our phenomenological sleep," as if American criticism had been dogmatically yet unthinkingly phenomenological. In fact, there was little explicitly phenomenological criticism around. In Lentricchia's own chapter on phenomenology the only American critic mentioned is J. Hillis Miller, whose books *The World of Charles Dicke*ns (1958), The *Disappearance of God: Five 19th Century Writer*s (1963), and *Poets of Reality: Six 20th Century Writers* (1965) studied the imaginative world of these authors.

4. Johannes Angermuller, *Why There Is No Poststructuralism in France* (London: Bloomsbury, 2015), 20, 6.

5. Josué Harari, *Structuralists and Structuralisms* (Ithaca, NY: Diacritics, 1971). Josué Harari, ed., *Textual Strategies: Perspectives in Post-Structuralist Criticism* (Ithaca, NY: Cornell University Press, 1979).

6. Angermuller, *Why There Is No Poststructuralism in France*, 16.

7. Cusset, *French Theory*, 31. For further discussion of Cusset's presentation of the issue, see below.

8. Jacques Derrida, "La Structure, le signe, et le jeu dans le discours des sciences humaines," in *L'Ecriture et la différence* (Paris: Seuil, 1967), 411. English translation by Alan Bass: "Structure, Sign and Play in the Discourse of the Human Sciences," in *Writing and Difference* (Chicago, IL: University of Chicago Press, 1978), 280. References to this essay will be given in the form p. 411/280, with the first number corresponding to the French text and the second to the English translation in *Writing and Difference*, which is more accurate than that published earlier in *The Structuralist Controversy*.

9. Derrida, "La Structure, le signe, et le jeu," 412/280.

10. Derrida, "La Structure, le signe, et le jeu," 413/281–82.

11. Derrida, "La Structure, le signe, et le jeu," 414/281.

12. Derrida, "La Structure, le signe, et le jeu," 414/282.

13. Derrida, "La Structure, le signe, et le jeu," 417/284.

14. Derrida, "La Structure, le signe, et le jeu," 417/284.

15. Derrida, "La Structure, le signe, et le jeu," 417/264.
16. Jacques Derrida, "Signature Event Context," in *Margins of Philosophy*, trans. Alan Bass (Chicago, IL: University of Chicago Press, 1982 [1972]), 329.
17. Derrida, "La Structure, le signe, et le jeu," 419/286.
18. Derrida, "La Structure, le signe, et le jeu," 426/292. As in other such passages, *jeu* was originally, in *The Structuralist Controversy*, translated as *freeplay*: "the freeplay of repetition and the repetition of freeplay." *The Structuralist Controversy*, p. 264. I discuss this problem below.
19. Macksey and Donato, *The Structuralist Controversy*, 427/292.
20. Macksey and Donato, *The Structuralist Controversy*, 427/292.
21. Macksey and Donato, *The Structuralist Controversy*, 427/292.
22. Cusset, *French Theory*, 31.
23. Derrida, "La Structure, le signe, et le jeu," 427/293.
24. Derrida, "La Structure, le signe, et le jeu," 427–28.
25. Derrida, "Structure, Sign, and Play," 293.
26. Derrida, "La Structure, le signe, et le jeu," 429/293.
27. Jacques Derrida, "Force et signification," in *L'Ecriture et la différence*, 11/6.
28. Derrida writes the following:

> I have said that empiricism is the matrix of all the faults menacing a discourse which continues, as with Lévi-Strauss in particular, to consider itself scientific. If we wanted to pose the problem of empiricism and bricolage in depth, we would probably end up very quickly with a number of absolutely contradictory propositions concerning the status of discourse in structural ethnology. On the one hand, structuralism justly claims to be the critique of empiricism. But at the same time there is not a single book or study by Lévi-Strauss which does not offer itself as an empirical essay which can always be completed or invalidated by new information. The structural schemata are always proposed as hypotheses resulting from a finite quantity of information and which are subjected to the proof of experience. ("La Structure, le signe et le jeu," 422/288)

It is important to stress, since Derrida is uncharacteristically hasty here, that the structuralist critique of empiricism as traditionally conceived and practiced does not mean that empirical evidence does not work to confirm or invalidate structural analyses. Formulating a grammar of a language, the very model of a structuralist project, is not an empirical activity, but any proposed grammar is a structural analysis that empirical evidence about the language can confirm or put in question.

29. Cusset, *French Theory*, 31.
30. When Michel Foucault's *Les Mots et les choses* became a best-seller, a famous cartoon by Maurice Henry in the *Quinzaine Littéraire* (July 1, 1967) depicted

Foucault, Lacan, Lévi-Strauss, and Barthes as natives wearing grass skirts sitting in a circle in the jungle: the circle of structuralists.

31. Foucault writes that if "by substituting the analysis of rarity for the search for totalities, the description of relations of exteriority for the theme of the transcendental foundation, the analysis of accumulations for the quest of the origin, one is a positivist, then I am quite happy to be one." Michel Foucault, *The Archeology of Knowledge* [1969], trans. A. M. Sheridan-Smith (New York: Vintage, 1972), 125.

France, 1968, and the Radical Politics of 1970s Film Theory

JANE M. GAINES

What was the connection between New York and Paris in Spring of 1968 at the height of the student protest movements? Exploding in April 23, 1968, the Columbia University revolt took over five campus buildings and stopped the construction of a student gym on Morningside Park. Working with the Harlem community, students blocked the bulldozers in the public park where the university had begun to excavate. When New York police moved in to arrest 750 protesters, another group emerged to counter that arrest, reinforcing and sustaining the street activity until graduation in mid-May. This part of the struggle is well known and documented in the film *Columbia Revolt* (1968). (See figure 1.) The connection between New York and Paris, however, is neither part of the film nor part of the official historical narrative of the student revolt.

To repeat, there is no reference to Paris in this film. Yet *Columbia Revolt* (1968), the documentary shot on 16 millimeter film by the radical collective New York Newsreel encourages the afterlife of an idea that many at the 2018 Buffalo conference might have found strange, not to mention historically inaccurate. Bear with me. This is the idea that May 1968 *began* at Columbia University in New York. Here is an idea that circulated on this side of the Atlantic for years, and after the fiftieth-year celebration screenings this May '68 origin story was made available to be picked up again.[1] The connection was even confirmed by a former student, who at one April 2018 *Columbia Revolt* screening described the telegram sent from Paris to New

Figure 1. *Columbia Revolt* (New York Newsreel, US, 1968).

York in May 1968: "We have taken a building in your honor. Now what do we do?" Indeed, the accounts of the 1960s activists at those screenings confirmed that version of events.[2] Now let me say that I have opened with this provocation deliberately, even risking the charge of circulating a falsehood. For, I must confess, I *know* that the idea that the Paris 1968 uprising "began" in New York is somewhat if not completely heretical. After all, there is the case for dating the movement as seen to stir on March 22 at the University of Nanterre and from there spreading to the Sorbonne.[3]

However, since this myth in which May '68 began in New York is an origin myth among other origin myths, we'll let it stand, knowing what we know as poststructuralists about vain searches for origins. Screening *Columbia Revolt* in April 2018, however, offered the chance to retell yet another version of events—the one that drew us together in Buffalo in October 2018. This version was revived as well on the Columbia campus in Spring of 2018. As part of the May '68 events celebration at the Maison Française, the director called on graduate students to testify to the connection between the Paris revolt, the reform of French universities, and the critical tradition of poststructuralism foundational for the Institute for Comparative Literature and Society, founded by Edward Said, as well the Department of French and Romance Philology.[4]

But there is a third version of events that advances still another origin myth, again, despite our rejection of origins and our long-standing critique of "firsts." Much is riding on this other origin myth for my own field, the emerging field of film and media studies. To state it thus: The Golden Era of 1970s film theory "had its origins" in the May 1968 Paris "uprising." This myth cements the association with Continental philosophy, a reputation by association that has done so much to advance the academic standing of a field whose intellectual viability is always endangered by the ill repute of its low culture object of study. Yet the connection between May 1968 and 1970s film theory may come as a surprise to some, for, to be honest, during the 1970s the connection between Paris 1968 and film theory was not a version of events that very many scholars were advancing. A decade later, one book appeared—Sylvia Harvey's *May '68 and Film Culture*—which, although a seminal work, was followed by no groundswell of interest.[5] Over the decades, the English translation of volume II of François Dosse's *History of Structuralism*, with its starting point in 1967, offered a backstory of institutional change and intellectual ferment.[6] More recently, a key resource for connecting Continental philosophy and May 1968 has been Étienne Balibar and John Rajchman's edited *French Philosophy Since 1945*, a compendium of texts that English language readers had first encountered in translation out of chronological order.[7] Reordered and thematized, the canonical philosophical works can now be grasped relative to their "conjunctural" moment.

Thus, "under the thrall," shall we say, of these texts, by March 2018, I had formulated this new mythology of the connection between May '68, 1970s film theory, and Continental thought. In a major address to the Society for Cinema and Media Studies at the annual meeting in Toronto, I tried out my provocation. "Recall," I said to colleagues, "how in the US the concern about legitimation in the academy was resolved by association with Continental philosophy." Then, I made a wildly exaggerated claim: "But we might never have had poststructuralism if it hadn't been for an event that took place in New York City."[8] Softening this somewhat I explained that in preparation for the New York screening of *Columbia Revolt*, we tried to verify the apocryphal story that the May 1968 Paris riots would not have happened if Columbia University students had not first occupied the campus administration building. To give credit for poststructuralism to the New York student antiwar revolt is of course a completely presumptuous rhetorical move on my part, except that, seen another way, it's a "play" with overdetermination, knowing what we know about the multiplicity of causes and the inextricability of events. Thus, I had no qualms about taking entirely too much license in my variation on the story that May 1968 *began* in New York. And no one raised an objection. By the April 2018, Columbia celebration of fifty years since 1968, this account of events was firm in my mind. Or, to put it another way, events in this order, thus linked, came to have a vivid *conceptual existence*—for me, at least. And, after all, was this not an opportunity to reconsider Althusser and Balibar's discussion of "*philosophical events of historical scope*"?[9]

Then again, even after Althusser, Balibar, and Foucault have taught us to refuse an old "history of ideas," we still revert to traditional historical methods, do we not? Let me continue a demonstration of that familiar approach. Returning to the French language journals, so incendiary in their times, we easily find seminal ideas "in embryo." From the new *Cinéthique* and the more established *Cahiers du Cinéma* we can locate materialist analysis, and most importantly, a new theory of ideology more comprehensive than that of Marx and Engels. In the *Cahiers* August 1968 editorial titled "Revolution in/through Cinema" there is reference to "militant practice" as well as "alternative distribution circuits." *Cinéthique*, appearing in January 1969, featured on its cover a photograph of a wall with posters posing "Who Creates? For Whom?," introducing the corollary question as to which class "profits" and proposing alternative production as challenge to the capitalist film industry.[10] Here we see the productive ambiguity in the Marxist-Leninist "signifying practice," applied as it was to a theory of cultural production that became a way of reading film texts as well as a form of radical cinema. Here, too, we find the literary journal *Tel Quel* entering into the debates on cinema. Featured in the third issue of *Cinéthique* is the interview with *Tel Quel* editors Marcelin Pleynet and Jean Thibaudeau, in which Pleynet declares that the majority of films are political because in their "empiricist practice" they are carriers of bourgeois ideology.[11] As he famously lays it out: "The cinematographic apparatus is a strictly ideological apparatus; it disseminates bourgeois ideology before anything else." And he is unsparing, even including revolutionary films which he thinks are unaware of the complicity of the camera itself: "Don't you think that before wondering about their 'militant function,' the filmmakers would do well to look into the ideology produced by the apparatus (the camera) which produces the cinema?"[12] Pleynet goes one step further to connect the camera lens with the fifteenth-century perspective designed to "rectify" any perspectival anomaly and thus reproduce the point of view of Renaissance humanism, referencing here Niépce's invention of photography.[13] Pressed by *Cinéthique* interviewer Gérard Leblanc, Pleynet maintains that even marginal cinema cannot escape since it is not outside the capitalist system. No, he is firm, there is no possibility of a transgression of the cinematic code, no possibility of the "*deconstruction* of the apparatus of ideological production" that is cinema.[14] Thus for *Tel Quel*, not even Jean-Luc Godard's *La chinoise* could qualify as oppositional because of the use of the camera.[15]

Here, then, is early indication of this position of complete ideological saturation as well as "no possibility" of formal reflexivity that figured in debates around the politics of materialist film form. A difference, however, emerged between *Cinéthique* and *Cahiers*. While *Cinéthique* held to the modernism requisite for a proper materialist film practice, *Cahiers* developed a criticism that offered more room for maneuver. Here they offered a political classification of types of films from (a) to (g), although by means of codifications so cryptic that scholars mulled over them for decades.[16]

The post-1968 foundation laid in the journals *Tel Quel*, *Cinéthique* and *Cahiers du Cinéma* arrived in the US via the British journal *Screen*, where Marx and Freud were reinvigorated via Althusser, then shaped by Jacques Lacan as a theorization of gendered film form and spectatorship. On one or two outlying US campuses, however, the 1970s film theory pipeline was direct from France.[17] As the University of Buffalo was a conduit for Continental philosophy, the University of Wisconsin–Milwaukee was the funnel for French philosophical challenges to auteur theory and impressionistic film criticism. At the Center for Twentieth Century Studies "Milwaukee Conferences," on this Midwestern campus far from the Ivy League, 1970s film coalesced further as "apparatus theory."[18] Structural analysis of narrative cinema conjoined with Lacanian psychoanalysis also shaped the infamous theory of the "male gaze," and here the arrival of Continental philosophy in the US hinterlands can be made to explain Laura Mulvey's "Visual Pleasure and Narrative Cinema," first delivered in 1973 as a paper in the Milwaukee French Department.[19] However, the imaginary line from May 1968 to "Visual Pleasure" does not lead only to the "male gaze," but also to the concept of *countercinema*, more precisely, oppositional cinema as counter to patriarchal cinema and, at the time, the only form a feminist avant-garde practice could (theoretically) take.[20]

Thus, if following Pleynet, as we have seen, ideology was perspectivally "built into" the technology, where could film theory, not to forget film practice, go from there? After all, it was Pleynet's dictum that was channeled into the highly influential "apparatus theory."[21] As theorized, ideology saturated all aspects of culture, effective because it appeared as "an unthought, immediate 'reality,'" especially in a representationalism epitomized by cinematic realism, an editing style as well as a narrative trajectory.[22] It did not occur to anyone in 1968 that the *Tel Quel* position, taken to the extreme and making no exception for oppositional practice, would allow for no film production at all, a position that would be played out in British feminist film theory and practice in the 1970s, and later found to be unworkable, as I said. Yet Sylvia Harvey suggests another approach to understanding the *Tel Quel political modernism* that first appeared as a "way forward," only to become, as she says, a "dead end, a graveyard," by which she must mean where it ended up in the UK.[23] Analyzing the evolution of 1970s film theory, she concludes that in the UK and US, theory became disengaged from both the question of the social formation and the May 1968 "mood of political militancy."[24] She reminds us that what came to be called *political modernism* was formulated in the context of the revolutionary project of rethinking the social formation from top to bottom. Also in France, intense debates over the kinds of films that took working-class audiences into account were not immediately carried over into the US and the UK. There, especially after the end of the Vietnam War struggle, the formulation of a revolutionary film practice was hypothetical. Perhaps this is one way of saying that the consequence of divorce from the prerevolutionary project in May 1968 France was a film theory and practice that had lost its imperative political justification. What remained was the implication that a revolutionary film theory and film practice could on its own "overthrow" the capitalist system!

Nevertheless, without French political conditions, post-1968 ideas spread and took root not only in theories of film form but, as countercinema, in theories of film practice. Thinking back to Paris where debates about film form and ideology raged, the one position that all sides—from *Tel Quel* to *Cahiers*—shared was deference to the Soviet film theory and practice model from the postrevolutionary 1920s. Jean-Luc Godard and Jean-Pierre Gorin aligned with the Soviets by naming themselves the Dziga Vertov collective, and their powerful anti–Vietnam War *Letter to Jane* emerged in 1971. (See figure 2.) The aesthetic marker of modernist-materialism is evident in the voice-over interrogation of the photograph of "Hanoi Jane" looking down at a Vietnamese man. At its foundation the Dziga Vertov group was Leftist but critical of the French Communist Party. Committed to film as a "weapon in class struggle," they modeled themselves after the Soviets as a "vanguard organization."[25] But strangely the Dziga Vertov films, although avowedly antirealist, were not edited in Soviet montage style but rather

Figure 2. *Letter to Jane* (Jean-Pierre Gorin and Jean-Luc Godard, France, 1972).

innovated countercinema, an aesthetic defined as whatever was the reverse of the form it opposed, that form the group called "Hollywood Mos-film."

Perhaps the vagueness of this anti-aesthetic explains why so few films claiming to be countercinema were actually produced either in France or in the UK, although the concept of *political modernism* could later provide art historical legitimation to film form. In the long run, however, it was not antirealist film form that had the greatest impact. What had more staying power was analysis, which, as the poststructuralist "critique of realism" challenged an ideology of realist representation in which, as it was said, cinematic signifiers so effectively erased themselves that "what you see is what you get." But 1970s antirealism was scattershot. It was against bourgeois culture, Hollywood continuity editing, fiction, and narrative form as well as the naive realism associated with documentary. The main target—classical Hollywood narrative realism—remained in our sightlines for decades. However, the "critique of realism" leveled against documentary overshot its goal, and in retrospect one could even say that radical documentary was a casualty of "political form/political content," for the political aesthetic party line was a hard line. One couldn't get credit for content—for making films about union organizing or even antiwar protest movements in the style of cinéma vérité documentary. Such films, as they were accused, failed to "criticize the ideological system in which they are embedded," and were found to "unquestioningly adopt its language and its imagery."[26] Ironically, *Columbia Revolt* might have been radical in the context of Students for a Democratic Society recruitment on US campuses, but it was not formally radical enough for the 1970s film theory that followed the historical moment that the film helped to catalyze. Thus, my contrast between *Letter to Jane* and *Columbia Revolt*, two antiwar films, the one canonized as countercinema and exemplary of political modernism, the other too complicit in the bourgeois realism delivered by the recording camera to count as radical.

Now I need to make a confession. The above account is the easy version. One would not be able to tell from it that the theorization of countercinema as antirealism had anything to do with larger philosophical questions underpinning the focus on representational realism as ideological. Neither does this telling give much more than cursory indication of clashes in the French debates or much background to the historical moment that *Cinéthique* and *Cahiers* critics as well as French filmmakers considered a revolutionary moment in which the means of cultural production had to be totally reconceived at the level of artistic practice. Stepping back from my own account, I would also have to say that my return to these ideas and this canonical moving image work is an academic move of the most traditional kind. But also, even asking about the historical context of the post-1968 revolutionary situation, I stand accused of making the tired complaint that events have been suspiciously "left out" of the historical record. Furthermore, while refusing "origins," I keep returning to the *Cinéthique* no. 3 interview with Marcelin Pleynet in 1969. The Buffalo conference, however, is an invitation to think anew about conceptual shifts, or what Althusser and Balibar in 1968 called "*philosophical events.*"[27] And yet we slip into the traditional historian's causal reasoning, whereby we are here because of what came before and thus we are here *not only* because of what they *did* but because of what they thought. Thus, there is unlikely to be an objection if I write something like this: "The radical events of May '68 were kept alive for twenty years, resonant between roughly 1971 and 1991, kept vibrant in the Marxist aesthetics and poststructuralist thought foundational in 1970s film theory and film practice." However, having written this, following the tradition we celebrate, I must also refuse to write this. And conversely, I can as easily write: "In film and media studies, between 1971 and 1991, the connection between the events of May '68 and 1970s film theory was lost." But now that I think of it, it would be best to write: "In 1970s film theory, the connection to the events of May '68 was never really established."

Yet this is not to advocate historical rereading and consequent retelling. Such a case requires recourse to the empirical historian's tools: new evidence in the form of documents, eyewitness testimony, or even visual recording. Here would be evidentiary proof and statement of certainty, the very devices associated with the dread *historicism* so discredited by the poststructuralist philosophers in question. Here, then, is the paradox: the very philosophical tradition that we celebrate has challenged and continues to suspect all attempts to make historiographic connections claiming cause and consequence; all accounts of continuous evolution over time and all efforts to establish origins, legacies, and lines of what is routinely called "influence."[28] On our political double bind, here is Michel Foucault in an interview published in May 1968, just prefatory to the publication of *Archaeology of Knowledge*: "Doesn't the kind of thinking that introduces the constraints of the system and discontinuity into the history of thought undermine the foundations of any progressive political interventions?"[29] Foucault, critiquing the "history of ideas" and posing "discontinuity" as a problematic fifty years ago, had already pulled the rug out from under our political efforts to claim contemporary connection to the events of May '68. But to suggest, as I have done, that May 1968 both *was* and *wasn't* kept alive in 1970s film theory may or may not introject a Foucauldian "discontinuity."[30] And yet, let us admit, we assume some kind of historical "continuity" when we even put the May '68 Paris uprising and Continental philosophy together in the same sentence.

Now to draw these questions into what I call the "critique of the historical turn" in film and media studies.[31] Here I ask why the field turned away from 1970s film theory whose "critique of realism" was also, in my analysis, an adamant "antihistoricism," that concept itself a signifier of a post–World War I philosophical crisis around the question of empirical evidence and objective "truth."[32] Then, I question why in the 1980s an "impasse" was declared, an admission that we had reached a theoretical dead end.[33] And yet, to relitigate the question of *which* events-in-time led to which positions relative to the dead end of 1970s film theory is to forget the philosophical underpinnings of that theory in which the question of "reality" was always doomed to lead to an "impasse." For in Heidegger, where the French had gone before, the "problem of reality," if it entails the question of whether or not the "external world is objectively present," or proof of it can be demonstrated, is finally an "impossible" problem. And this is not necessarily because such questioning could lead to "inextricable impasses" but because the very problematic of "being-in-the-world," as Heidegger says, "repudiates" such inquiry.[34] Thus we have in post-1968 film theory the seeds of redoubled impasse, adding the impossibility of finally accessing the "external world" to the modernist refusal of the image produced by the camera turned on that world.

In my critique of the "historical turn," French philosophical tradition enters again, but with a difference. Louis Althusser and Roland Barthes come back, but not as theorists of either "the subject" or of film form and photographic realism. They come back as sources for theories of history, that is, theories that keep alive the critique of the concept of "history." But here, in the "reality effect," we glimpse the theorization just before the confusion between the aesthetic effect and the philosophical question of existence or "reality itself."[35] Lest I get to my point too quickly, let me pause to illustrate the continued relevance of the Heideggerian-Althusserian theory of ideology, as found even, and perhaps especially, in academic notions of "history" or "historical" relations.

Today we reauthorize an account of events that took place fifty years ago, do we not? In doing so, however, we find causal links "in the wake of" that convulsive moment and imply, as I said, that we are where we are because of what they thought as much as did. In effect, we assume that we wouldn't be here today "if it hadn't been for" those philosophical progenitors, for their reconceptualizations of as well as their attacks on entrenched knowledges. An idea of origination, cause, and consequence then is inadvertent and everywhere in our phraseology: "paved the way," "gave way to," "prepared the ground," or "was instrumental in" and "the product of" something or other. But there is another approach and here is what I mean by the "comeback" of this French philosophical foundation to which I return, although here I take a tack for which I haven't exactly prepared the reader. In yet another return to 1968, I rediscover Althusser's notion of the "peculiarity" of historical time.

Significantly, "Outline of a Concept of Historical Time," is the one chapter from the 1968 *Reading Capital* reprinted in *French Philosophy since 1945*. This is where Althusser and Étienne Balibar argue for levels of historical time, each of which has its own time and history, first referred to as each *peculiar time*, the first of four uses of the word *peculiar* in the essay that draws on two meanings—"particular" and "strange." Among these usages is reference to the "peculiar" time that "never comes back to the same place."[36] I've elsewhere likened this structure to the "never together" of the three modes of historical time, the past "never again" and the future always "to be."³⁷ Neither the past nor the future can be "here" but are always "there," elsewhere. But finally, in the sweep of the refusal of the "ideological continuum of a linear time," there is the contrast. The ideological "this, then, that, and therefore" is juxtaposed with its antithesis, here formulated as that "extremely complex and peculiar temporality," which, the authors exclaim, is "utterly paradoxical."³⁸ Consider, then, the temporality of the May '68 present as "complex and peculiar" relative to the present that was once itself a "future" present relative to 1945, but which, relative to April 2018, is a "former" present, making the current present the "former future" of May 1968.³⁹

No, this is not Hegel's philosophy of history. For some contemporary theorists, this is the terrain of the *deconstructive historian*.⁴⁰ Thus, a useful text for us as we approach the historical problem of how to grasp the peculiarity of "history" in Jacques Derrida's *Heidegger: The Question of Being and History*, unpublished lectures delivered between 1964 and 1965 at the École Normale Supérieure. Here we find early clues to the development of the post-1968 theory of ideology, Derrida crediting Heidegger with destroying the "presence" associated with Hegel and Husserl.⁴¹ Here, phrased differently, is the philosophical problem of the self-evidence of "presence" that would become in film theory the "self-evidence of the seen." Further, the project of critiquing Western thought as a "metaphysics of presence" later made its specific contribution to the "critique of realism" in film and media studies and its prohibition against documentary as promising privileged access to "the real." What would be taken up as the "reality" delivered by the camera (and attendant apparatus) appears here in Derrida as the "point of view of common sense and transcendental idealism of the present, present lived experience . . . the very form of real, authentic, effective, full experience."⁴² But we are interested less in the diagnosis than in the antithesis. For against the self-evidence of "presence" (manifest in the experiential of the historical Present) Derrida proposes a plurality of historicities, multiple levels, each with its own temporal rhythm and "inequality of development."⁴³ In this, he is eerily in agreement with Althusser and Balibar as they posit the paradox of historical temporality, the imbalance in which the absence of one time is the presence of another.

Derrida's diagnosis of Heidegger, finally, is that *he* "cannot get out of the enigma of the origin of historicity." But neither can we, Derrida thinks. And why? He answers: "enigmatic, then is the discourse on history at the moment when we really must speak about the *past*."⁴⁴ But no, in the face of this enigmatic discourse we are not to throw up our hands. Rather we pose the philosophical puzzle alongside the empirical historian's unraveling and pinpointing; contrasting the certainty of the historical event-in-time (as well as its record) with the perplexing enigma of the historical past relative to the present. We are foiled in every attempt to line up "when it was *what it was*" in the past and "when again" it might be in the future, to reference these times to which we have no access yet about which we still confidently say, even of the "philosophical event," that it "was," the infinitive "to be" the problem in a microcosm.[45]

In conclusion, we'll return to *Columbia Revolt* and April 1968, as well as April 2018, a half century later. For French and Francophone scholars worldwide, it may be unthinkable that the events of May '68 could have *begun* in New York City. But since we now know that we can both sustain a critique of origins and posit the origins of "philosophical events," SUNY Buffalo colleagues should be receptive. For there is a way in which May 1968 as a "philosophical event" expands to include Buffalo, New York.

Knowing full well that I am playing the empirical historian's card, I offer this evidence: The radical student newsletter *The Rat* reported the reaction to a screening of newsreel films at the State University of New York, Buffalo in 1969, as follows: "At the end of the second film, with no discussion, five hundred members of the audience arose and made their way to the University ROTC building. They proceeded to smash windows, tear up furniture and destroy machines until the office was a total wreck; and then they burned the remaining paper and flammable parts of the structure to charcoal."[46] Since I quoted *The Rat* thirty years after in an article on the social change legacy of documentary, scholars have wondered about the identity of this second film, which was credited with producing the kind of palpable political effects on the bodies of viewers that the Soviets sought to effect, or what in that article I called an effective "political mimesis."[47] To admit, "political mimesis" was just another attempt to recruit Eisenstein in an effort to reject the proscriptive aesthetics of political modernism. But today the philosophical problem that the French took up from Heidegger seems much more pressing.

In April 2018, at a panel following the *Columbia Revolt* screening, Norm Fruchter, a former student activist who traveled to campuses with Newsreel Films, confirmed the identity of the second film. The documentary that ignited this explosive moment of social activism on the Buffalo campus was none other than *Columbia Revolt*. It does seem strange that the 1968 political moment could produce *both* an incendiary documentary (used so effectively as a political tool to incite overthrow of the system) as well as the renunciation of documentary—the form that it took. This renunciation in the name of the problem of "reality" turns out to have been part of the larger problem of Western philosophy as post-1968 thinkers sharpened the critique of it, finding that philosophical orientation in the privileging of immediacy, proximity, proof, and, of course, origination. And if, to put this orientation in check, we think the differential historicities of "then" and "now," as on no continuum but as uneven and "peculiar," what today do we make of the 1969 burning of the ROTC building? It was, after all, the very next year that Michel Foucault was invited to teach in the SUNY Buffalo French Department.

Notes

1. *Columbia Revolt* (New York Newsreel, 1968) is available on DVD from Third World Newsreel.
2. "Columbia Revolt: 50 Years After," Lenfest Center for the Arts.
3. Paul Cronin, "Preface," in *A Time to Stir: Columbia '68*, ed. Paul Cronin (New York: Columbia University Press, 2018), xxiv.
4. See events at the Columbia University Maison Française and director Shanny Peer.
5. Sylvia Harvey, *May '68 and Film Culture* (London: British Film Institute, 1978).
6. François Dosse, *History of Structuralism, Volume II: The Sign Sets, 1967–Present*, trans. Deborah Glassman (Minneapolis: University of Minnesota Press, 1997).
7. Étienne Balibar and John Rajchman, eds., *French Philosophy since 1945: Problems, Concepts, Inventions*, trans. Arthur Goldhammer et al. (New York and London: The New Press, 2011).
8. "Once More with Feeling," Distinguished Career Award Speech, Society for Cinema and Media Studies, Toronto, Canada, March 2018.
9. Louis Althusser and Étienne Balibar, "The Errors of Classical Economics: Outline of a Concept of Historical Time," in *French Philosophy Since 1945: Problems, Concepts, Inventions*, eds. Étienne Balibar and John Rajchman, trans. Arthur Goldhammer et al. (New York and London: The New Press, 2011), 165–66.
10. *Cahiers du Cinéma* 203 (August 1968): 24–30, trans. Diana Matias, *Screen* 13, no. 4 (Winter 1972–73).
11. *Cinéthique* 3 (1969); reprinted in Harvey, *May '68 and Film Culture*, 149.
12. Harvey, *May '68 and Film Culture*, 158.
13. Harvey, *May '68 and Film Culture* 159.
14. Harvey, *May '68 and Film Culture*, 154.

15. Harvey, *May '68 and Film Culture*, 160.

16. The significant article is Jean-Louis Comolli and Jean Narboni, "Cinéma, ideologie, critique," *Cahiers du cinéma*, no. 216 (1969): 11–15, translated as "Cinema/Ideology/Criticism," *Screen* 12, no. 1 (1971): 145–55. See also Harvey, *May '68 and Film Culture*, 35.

17. See, for example, the first issues of *Camera Obscura*, which came out of the University of California–Berkeley.

18. Papers from "The Cinematic Apparatus," the influential February 1978 conference sponsored by the Center for Twentieth Century Studies, University of Wisconsin–Milwaukee, are published in Teresa de Lauretis and Stephen Heath, eds., *The Cinematic Apparatus* (New York: St. Martin's Press, 1980). For the recent reevaluation of "apparatus theory," see papers from the conference "The Impact of Technological Innovations of the Theory and Historiography of Cinema" in the Canadian journal *Recherches sémiotiques/Semiotic Inquiry* 31, nos. 1–2–3 (2011). In my contribution to the same issue, "The Inevitability of Teleology: From *le dispositif* to Apparatus Theory to *dispositifs* Plural," I also take up the issue of the historical overview in what is effectively a critique of "from . . . to" historical accounts.

19. Laura Mulvey, "Visual Pleasure and Narrative Cinema," *Screen* 16, no. 3 (Autumn 1975): 6–18.

20. Diane Waldman and Janet Walker, "Introduction," in *Feminism and Documentary*, eds. Diane Waldman and Janet Walker (Minneapolis: University of Minnesota Press, 1999), give the best summary of the British feminist critique of documentary as purporting to "capture" the "truth" of women's oppression, p. 7.

21. See Bertrand Augst, "The Apparatus: An Introduction," *Camera Obscura* 1 (1976): 97. Jane M. Gaines, "The Inevitability of Teleology: From *le dispositif* to Apparatus Theory to *dispositifs* Plural," *Recherches sémiotiques/Semiotic Inquiry* 31, nos. 1–2–3 (2011): 101–14.

22. Philip Rosen, "*Screen* and 1970s Film Theory," in *Inventing Film Studies*, eds. Lee Grieveson and Haidee Wasson (Durham, NC: Duke University Press, 2008), 272–73.

23. Harvey, *May '68 and Film Culture*, 82.

24. Harvey, *May '68 and Film Culture*, p. 2. See also David Rodowick, *The Crisis of Political Modernism* (Berkeley: University of California Press, 1994), ix.

25. Harvey, *May '68 and Film Culture*, 30.

26. This is the series (d). See Comolli and Narboni, "Cinema/Ideology/Criticism": *Cinema against Spectacle: Technique and Ideology Revisited*, trans. and ed. Daniel Fairfax (Amsterdam: Amsterdam University Press, 2015) "if they are captured by the system they want to dismantle," 257.

27. Louis Althusser and Étienne Balibar, "The Errors of Classical Economics: Outline of a Concept of Historical Time," in *French Philosophy since 1945: Problems, Concepts, Inventions*, eds. Étienne Balibar and John Rajchman, trans. Arthur Goldhammer et al. (New York and London: The New Press, 2011), 165.

28. Michel Foucault, *Archaeology of Knowledge*, trans. A. M. Sheridan Smith (New York: Pantheon Books, 1972), 21, says of "influence" that it "provides a support—of too magical a kind to be very amenable to analysis—for the facts of transmission and communication; which refers to an apparently causal process (but with neither rigorous delimitation nor theoretical definition)." And yet, "influence" remains everywhere assumed in academic overviews in the humanities, especially those that rely on comparisons over time.

29. As quoted in Dosse, *History of Structuralism*, 161.

30. Paul Ricoeur, *Memory, History, Forgetting*, trans. Kathleen Blamey and David Pellauer (Chicago, IL: University of Chicago Press, 2004,) 202, gently takes him to task: "Should we reproach Foucault for having substituted for the ideology of the continuous the one of the discontinuous?"

31. Jane M. Gaines, "What Happened to the Philosophy of Film History?" *Film History* 25, nos. 1–2 (2013): 70–80.

32. Charles Bambach, "Weimar Philosophy and the Crisis of Historical Thinking,' in *Weimar Thought: A Legacy*, eds. Peter E. Gordon and John P. McCormick (Princeton, NJ: Princeton University Press, 2013), 133–49.

33. Annette Kuhn and Jackie Stacey, "Screen Histories: An Introduction," in *Screen Histories: A Screen Reader*, eds. Annette Kuhn and Jackie Stacey (Oxford, UK: Clarendon Press, 2009), 2.

34. Martin Heidegger, *Being and Time*, trans. Joan Stambaugh (New York: State University of New York Press, 1996), 191.

35. Roland Barthes, "The Discourse of History," in *The Rustle of Language*, trans. Richard Howard (New York: Hill and Wang, 1986), 127–40.

36. Althusser and Balibar, *French Philosophy since 1945*, 163.

37. Jane M. Gaines, "Even More Tears: The Historical Time Theory of Melodrama," in *Melodrama Unbound*, eds. Christine Gledhill and Linda Williams (New York: Columbia University Press, 2018), 332.

38. Althusser and Balibar, *French Philosophy since 1945*, 167.

39. Reinhardt Koselleck, *Futures Past: On the Semantics of Historical Time*, trans. Keith Tribe (New York: Columbia University Press, 2004), echoed here, takes Heidegger in a direction different from Derrida's concerns, although where the two converge in their reading would be as they find the "circularity of historicity," which Koselleck finally takes further.

40. See on the "deconstructive historian," *The Nature of History Reader*, eds. Keith Jenkins and Alun Munslow (New York and London: Routledge, 2004), 12–15.

41. Jacques Derrida, *Heidegger: The Question of Being and History*, trans. Geoffrey Bennington (Chicago, IL: University of Chicago Press, 2016), 256–57.

42. Derrida, *Heidegger*, 256–57.

43. Derrida, *Heidegger*, 208.

44. Derrida, *Heidegger*, 174.

45. Derrida, *Heidegger*, 224.

46. *The Rat*, the radical campus newsletter, State University of New York, Buffalo, as quoted in Michael Renov, "Early Newsreel: The Construction of a Political Imaginary for the New Left," *Afterimage* 14, no. 7 (1985): 14.

47. Jane M. Gaines, "Political Mimesis," in *Collecting Visible Evidence*, eds. Jane M. Gaines and Michael Renov (Minneapolis: University of Minnesota Press, 1999), 89–90.

Postscriptum on the Master's Tools

LUCILE HAUTE

The contemporary context of the society of new media and new technologies of information and communication (social network in particular) renews Deleuze and Guattari's analysis of the modalities of elaboration, encoding, and communication of signs in the capitalist system, of which the concept of lines of flight [*lignes de fuite*][1] is part. Postinternet uprising has driven a diverse pictorial and visual production. Is French Theory still relevant to think about and analyze if and how these online actions initiate new *lignes de fuite*? This chapter aims at following some pathways of thought coming and going through the Atlantic Ocean, starting in Paris in 1969, then traveling to the US, coming back to Europe, and so on.

During the 1968 events in Paris, two regimes of visibility were opposed to each other. On the one hand, political posters popped up everywhere in the public space, from the Ateliers Populaires to the walls of the City. They were the voices of the rebellion. On the other hand, at the climax of the events, social conflicts, and massive strikes interrupted the release of many mainstream publications, particularly weekly news magazines.

The École Nationale Supérieure des Beaux Arts was occupied by students and workers and then renamed Atelier Populaire—the People's Workshop—from May to June 1968. Dozens of political posters were made there, and some of them soon became internationally famous. One of the exhibitions of the 2018 international photography festival of Arles, in the South of France, was dedicated to the commemoration of May 1968 events.[2] Many of the Atelier Populaire's posters where displayed, framed, obviously displaced from their original context. In another part of this exhibition, covers of the weekly French magazine *Paris Match* were shown chronologically, the missing issues managing "holes" in this time line, embodying sociopolitical events powerful enough to interrupt the machinery of mass media production. This confrontation showed a double movement, depending on the mediatic apparatus. First, there was a search for a popular representation, voicing up through its own resources and graphic language. Second, came the unexpected and sudden silence of an offspring of the dominant regime of the cultural industry.

Nowadays, at the age of constant visual flow, we produce ourselves through producing and sharing images on social networks. "Be visible or vanish"[3] is the motto. Both the underground and the mainstream use social networks to meet their audience. How can we inherit from 1968, in terms of resistance in the contemporary era of networked society? How do contemporary (re)claims put contemporary tools and mediatic apparatuses to work?

Allow us . . . temporarily

> The master's tools will never dismantle the master's house. They may allow us temporarily to beat him at his own game, but they will never enable us to bring about genuine change.[4]

The original context of this quote is a talk given by Audre Lorde in a feminist symposium at New York University in 1979, dedicated to De Beauvoir's book *Le deuxième sexe*.[5] Audre Lorde was invited in the only panel dedicated to what wasn't yet named "intersectionality"—a social-political framing explored at the same period by Angela Davis in her book *Women, Race & Class*, published in 1981.[6] But the term, definitely coined by Kimberlé Crenshaw in 1991,[7] is not used by Audre Lorde, obviously. Still during her talk, she pointed out the patent racism of white feminists and the "academic arrogance" that lead to ignore the differences of situations between American women regarding their race, sexuality, class, ability, and age. Looking at the program, she demonstrated that the absence of black women in the others' panels was based on the assumption that female minorities—lesbians, the poor, blacks—had nothing to say about existentialism, heterosexuality, and power, or were unable to develop a consistent feminist theory, while too constrained within the exclusive limits of their own communitarian struggles. "Difference is that raw and powerful connection from which our personal power is forged," she wrote.⁸ She aims to make common cause with all these differences, to face oppressions instead of reproduce it. "Without community, there is no liberation," she wrote, without it, only a "temporary armistice between an individual and her oppression is possible."⁹ Therefore, she invites one to face up to the context of this conference: it is reproducing inside the feminist community oppressions from the outside, imposed by patriarchy.

This sentence, "The master's tools will never dismantle the master's house," has been quoted abundantly lately, in the context of discussing the contemporary uses of new technologies: at the 2018 Transmediale festival (Berlin),¹⁰ an annual event that aims at facilitating critical reflection on postdigital cultural transformation, also at the Centre Pompidou (Paris) in October 2017,¹¹ in order to highlight and discuss minoritarian forms of design, at La Gaité Lyrique (Paris) in spring 2018 during the Afrocyberfeminism conferences,¹² to name a few occurrences. These European recontextualizations of Lorde's thought-provoking statement invite us to ask: how to use new technologies against dominant power? Is insurrection rumbling through hashtags or are we delusional toward the fact that we've become merrily dependent on the society of control?

During the 1990s, cyberfeminism proposed to reconceptualize technology: instead of embodying white male capitalism, it could be an accomplice for minorities' emancipation. In her famous paper "Situated Knowledges: The Science Question in Feminism and the Privilege of Partial Perspective," Donna Haraway,¹³ who Judy Wajcman says has qualified science as a culture in an unprecedented sense,¹⁴ exposed and described the "god trick": the dominant representation of science as a rational, universal, objective, nontropic system of knowledge—the opposite of intersectionality. For some time then, the decentralized network of the internet appeared as a way to reach a nonhierarchical society. Nevertheless, cyberfeminism may have developed an excessive belief in the powers of new technologies as a set of tools for emancipation, and surprisingly forgot the social, economic, and political realities they were rooted in. As Rosi Braidotti pointed out in 1996, "new technologies will not be nearly as liberating as the cyber-artists and internet addicts would want us to believe."¹⁵ A statement reinforced by Edward Snowden's revelations in 2013: Deleuze's "societies of control"¹⁶ have haunted the network culture since the beginning. The very technologies that gave cyberfeminists reasons to dream of new forms of political empowerment had turned out to be repurposed as methods of surveillance and control over everyone.

We live in the era of simultaneity. We're no longer passing from one closed space to another, and as described by Giorgio Agamben,¹⁷ we are simultaneously the subjects of various apparatuses. As Deleuze said, "in the societies of control one is never finished with anything. [. . .] Control is short-term and of rapid rates of turnover, but also continuous and without limit, while discipline was of long duration, infinite and discontinuous."[18] By colonizing the imagination, contemporary subjectification process may direct our desires. Zeitgeist seems to engage ourselves in transformations that never end, that must never end. And if an ending happens or if the process stops, it wouldn't be noticed because our attention would be focused on the others' ongoing process, others' opportunities to engage. It is the area of "slasher": professional performance of multiple and simultaneous skills and professions. We can be a PhD candidate and a teacher and an artist and a waitress and a freelance junior graphic designer, all in the same period of time. During all these temporary contexts, we bend to a system where we are some "dividual" material to control. Each one is a *dividu*[19] who can be divided into several personalities: they are all true but different according to the context. It's up to us to deal with the simultaneity of the different systems we have to report to.

"The network and the networked individual, once the embodiments of new forms of resistance, now have become the basis for new forms of exploitation and oppression."[20] What are the forms of resistance on the contemporary networked society? Do they even exist? The hypothesis we propose is that there is an efficient subversive strategy in developing collective paradoxical "dividuation" processes through social networks. Therefore, we'll question their subversiveness and actual impact.

Magical Resistance on the Network

In the field of political activism, collective action is a strategy adopted to resist control mechanisms based on individualization. Such a strategy aims at thwarting the processes of subjectification by opposing them to ephemeral nebulae, for the duration of a demonstration, for instance. Here, the stakes of wearing a costume and, more specifically a mask, crystallize this issue. From a law enforcement perspective, the mask prevents identification, a process that has become particularly effective in the age of facial recognition algorithms. From the activist point of view, it summons powerful forces of imagination. Thus, this strategy is used by activists eager to mix spirituality and public protest, such as ecofeminists.

During the Trump campaign, the Republican candidate stigmatized Clinton's femininity calling her "Nasty woman," or a "Witch"—with an ambiguity between "Bitch" and "Witch." A few days after the November 2016 elections, several movements appeared in the streets and on the social networks. Some engaged a reversed stigmatization, bringing the WITCH movement back to life. The Women's International Terrorist Conspiracy from Hell (WITCH) was a feminist group active in the United States during the 1960s women's liberation movement. Dressed in black, carrying broomsticks, and wearing big pointed hats, they claimed equal rights for men and women, and their first action resulted in a march down Wall Street, to hex New York's financial district. WITCH's action would find an echo in the feminist-Marxist 1976 Italian slogan, "*Tremate, tremate, le streghe son tornate*" (Quake, quake, the witches are back!), and renew the forms of feminist activism, coloring it with humor and joy. Adopting modalities of burlesque hybridization, from formulae to exquisite corpses, the WITCH's collective actions look at the witchcraft register in order to find a lever to build an alternative, so as not to be swallowed up in the intentionality of the capitalist world.

The anonymous collective reformed itself in the wake of Donald Trump's election, first in Portland and then in many other American cities. The 2016 WITCH explicitly refers to their 1960s predecessors by quoting them on their Instagram. Yes, they use Instagram. And also, they have a YouTube channel—sharing only one video—and a website, which are their public tools where they proclaim their program: dismantle patriarchy and fight for justice: "You don't have to call yourself a witch to be a WITCH." It is a public political statement more than a spiritual one. Simultaneously, on Instagram and Twitter, the hashtag #BindTrump popped up, tagged in more than a thousand posts from November 2016 to October 2018. It was followed three months later by the hashtags #magicresistance (660 tags from February 2017 to October 2018) and #magicalresistance (150 tags from February 2017 to October 2018).[21] The movement reached an even larger audience when on February 24, 2017, the pop singer Lana Del Rey published a picture of herself on Twitter striking a pose with a sophisticated hand gesture, with the mysterious caption: "At the stroke of midnight," without any hashtag or explanation.[22] Those who knew made the connection and rapidly retweeted it. The media talked about it.[23] The revival of WITCH in the social network era has mobilized supporters of both sexes on social platforms, with Instagram at the forefront, for physical presence at collective actions, at demonstrations in public spaces, but also for collective ritual rendezvous performed individually and remotely at each full moon. A cyber-magic resistance is being organized: photographs of banishment rituals targeting the American president are published under the hashtags #bindtrump and #magicalresistance. This magical activism isn't without echoes of the approach of the American Satanist Church, activist occultists who deploy a strategy of polymorphic political action.[24] Maintaining an ambiguity as to their intention literally by seeking magical effectiveness, or figuratively—if not ironically—by seeking political effectiveness while mobilizing the formal register of magic. Indeed, they use, as a lever, the superstitious fears still hidden in the dark corners of common rational culture, and always prone to disturb American bigotry.

In the United States, spiritual warfare is taken very seriously, both by experienced sorceresses who call for greater caution and warn of the consequences of these rituals conducted by novices that mobilize negative energies on a global scale, and by frightened Christians who call for prayer to counter these evil spells, such as Pro-Trump evangelical nationalists who gathered, through the hashtag #PrayerResistance. A cyber-spiritual war is ongoing, at the crossroad between politics, technology, and magic or spirituality. Occupying public mediatic space is the point.

Advocated by feminist movements, this is the second political age of the Western witch: a reappropriation, a reversal of a stigmatizing figure initially constructed to designate and circumscribe a counterpower in order to fight it. Until modern times in Europe, the clergy (both Catholic and Protestant) slowly constructed the witch as a "moral scarecrow," to which any proximity or similarity could be fatal. In the fourth century, this aimed at discrediting pagan practices by denying them: Those women who claimed to have supernatural practices were declared heretics. In the fifteenth century, and particularly on the basis of the theories of the inquisitor Nicholas Jacquier, the opposite became true. The people designated as heretics were those who did *not* believe in the reality of the witches' sabbath and other occult abominations that the Inquisition literature endeavored to identify in great detail. Over the centuries, the construction of the witch stereotype spread throughout Europe from one trial to the next.

In the second half of the twentieth century, as a part of a strategy of stigma reversal deployed by minorities against their oppression, feminists used and laid claim to the subversive power of the witch: the WITCH coalition previously discussed, but also, among others, the anticapitalist actions of the reclaiming tradition (and its prominent figure Starhawk). For the philosopher of science Isabelle Stengers,

What witches do is force us to think about the de-production of immanent and multiple forces in the population and therefore also to think about the interest of groups seeking where the power to resist concerning what matters to them will come from. [. . .] They do not tell us how to do it [but] force us to think about how, how to make what we need to resist happen, and [to think about] what we need which talks already today about what is possible for what we are resisting.[25]

Today, one might wonder whether we are not witnessing the shift toward the third political age of the Western witch: the age of her polishing and capitalist recuperation, turning her into a profitable exotic item like any other, another trend. Her subversive power seems to have dissolved in the market too soon. We claim—figuratively—to be a witch, that is, a feminist with an ecological conscience, who can occasionally consult the Tarot. The literal existence of the witch, who seeks magical effectiveness, is forgotten and remains unthought of within the bestsellers devoted to the subject. This place at the forefront of the mediatic scene has been acquired at the expense of a neutralization of esoteric beliefs, in order to escape the registers of folklore and carnival. By becoming visible under these conditions, the witch has become acceptable, even respectable. However, calling yourself a witch on social media seems to be the first step of a public statement of political consciousness.

Technology, Magic, and Politics

In 2017 in France, a group of people moved by the writings of Starhawk (especially *Dreaming the Dark*,[26] recently republished in French) gathered around the reclaiming tradition and ecofeminist thinking. Starhawk is a witch, or so she calls herself. She is a writer and ecofeminist activist, as well as an American neopagan. She used to be part of far-left activism and feminist activism. Then and until now, Starhawk's fight is part of the global environmental justice movement. She unifies spirituality and politics into ecofeminism. Ecofeminism is a militant movement born in the eighties in the United States against the threat of nuclear war, and questions the link between the destruction of nature and the oppression of women, two forms of domination that, in the ecofeminist framework, stem from the same mechanisms and should be fought together. This emergent Parisian group that gathers regularly in order to celebrate Gaia, is planning its meetings and rituals using a Facebook private group. The use of this platform doesn't question the implication of Facebook in the constant monitoring of the people's social activity online, which seems to be a strong limitation of their political conscience. There is still no critical use of technologies; their wish to create a community is naive yet sincere.

The relationships between new technology, magic, and politics have precedents. Why not use new technologies to connect to a cosmic holiness? In Brazil, the festival called Technoshamanism[27] took place in 2014 and 2016. It is rooted in the political context of Lula's presidency, when tropicalist star Gilbert Gil was minister of culture. Under benevolent Gil's term, Afro-Brazilian and indigenous traditions found an opportunity to encounter permaculture, DIY, hacker culture, and electro music. Inspired by Deleuzian thinking, the organizers conceptualized such notions as *ancestorfuturism*, *noisecracy*, and *hyperstition*, each of these notions being based on the hybridization of archetypal and contemporary developments, looking for conceptual ways to open the one to the other—and reciprocally.

Everywhere across Europe, technological emancipation camps are blooming.[28] People are using politics, spirituality, ecological awareness, and technological empowerment try to explore converging paths. The magical aspect, especially exhibited on public networks such as Instagram, highlights a paradox, already identified by Jeanne Favret-Saada during her field study of rural witchcraft.[29] The people then interviewed by Saada, were paradoxically questioning the rationality of their own behavior while subscribing to the particular regime of agency of witchcraft—addressing this dissonance with the stereotypical sentence: "I know that [it can't be real, it sounds crazy, etc.] but [this has been happening to me, I trust the *desorceleur* to help me, I have to wear this charm, etc.]" This rational ambiguity and paradoxical attitude regarding what is said and what is done is quite similar to the way we use our devices today, after Snowden's revelations, especially when a political resistance or claiming is at stake: "I know that using Instagram to share a picture of the ritual I did last full moon to bind Trump is exposing myself to surveillance, but I will do it anyway," or "I know that using Facebook to organize a witchy anticapitalistic meeting is exposing myself and the attendees to any kind of surveillance, but I will do it anyway." According to Faisal Devij, we may have reached a paradoxical moment of "the simultaneous desire for and disenchantment with a life on the surface, one that doesn't live up to its promise of freedom and is haunted by nostalgia for depth and meaning."[30] It may be the end of the fetishization of visibility.

It may be the time to stop playing with illusions. It may be the time to search and create powerful ways of meaning-making.

At the time of fake news, it might be powerful to initiate a different kind of trouble within meaning-making. Thus, there may be a momentous topicality of esotericism. In ritual, belief isn't a prerequisite. Only intention is. Ritual is performative. Political resistance seems to be inventing new ways to exist in our contemporary society of control, ruled by new technologies. But are we still living under the regime of governmental control?

Postscriptum

In a recent paper,[31] Yves Citton has identified a fourth governmentality regime that superimposes itself to the ones Foucault and Deleuze identified: sovereignty, discipline, and control. Disciplinary societies, societies of sovereignty, and societies of control are leading us to both individual collapse (burnout) and collective collapse (climate change, ravaged biodiversity). "We simply cannot survive—neither collectively nor individually—if the majority of us do not learn to develop the gestures characteristic of the practices of intellectual research and artistic creation." This is the hypothesis developed by Yves Citton following Erin Manning and Brian Massumi: individual and collective collapses foreshadow the societal and environmental challenges that humanity will have to face in the coming years. Citton adds that this will require something other than "docile subjects, blinkered civil servants and opportunistic entrepreneurs." Yves Citton predicates a new regime of governmentality to be superimposed on the previous ones: the research-creation regime.

The huge challenges we are facing, the state of permanent crisis we're living in, open a third way between my earlier binary question, that is to say: Is insurrection rumbling through hashtags or are we in denial regarding our dependency on the technical infrastructure of control? Going back to obscurantism if not *obscurity* may be a way to fight capitalist irrationality—this way being itself moved by the paradoxical belief identified earlier: "I know that [posting this picture on Instagram will not impeach the president] but [I'll do it anyway]." After all, one needs a powerful wizard to fight a powerful curse. The real theater of operation may be less the political battle than the capture of imagination. Collective action can summon egregores, that is to say a psychic force generated by the emotions of several people, which manifests itself as an entity—a little demon responding to a collective invocation. *Egregor* can be both a magical term or a literary term to name the atmosphere of a place (such as a café) occupied by a community. Some self-proclaimed witches express themselves in the media and place the individual figure of the sorceress before the coven. To these solitary and fashionable ones, other witches of Instagram oppose the power of the collective. During nights of the full moon, when hundreds of Instagram accounts simultaneously posted pictures presenting various interpretations of the same ritual, the individual aesthetic experience blends into a collective experience that cannot be circumscribed by the sum of its participants. Do such digital and diffuse ceremonies succeed or fail to produce the egregor? Their full effectiveness may be an indication of something that is rumbling and is never going to be entirely somewhere but never anywhere either. The convergence between politics, spirituality, ecological awareness, and technological empowerment is actually ongoing. So mote it be.

Notes

1. Gilles Deleuze et Félix Guattari, *Capitalisme et schizophrénie 2: Mille plateaux* (Paris: Les Éditions de Minuit, 1980); Félix Guattari, *Lignes de fuite: Pour un autre monde de possibles* (La Tour d'Aigues, France: Éditions de l'Aube, 2011).

2. Presented from July 2 to September 23, 2018, in Croisière Rencontres Photo, the exhibition *1968, quelle histoire* ! *Barricades, expression, repression* was curated by Bernadette Caille. It gathered documents from the archives of the Paris Police Prefecture, the archives of *Paris Match* and the archives of Gamma-Rapho-Keystone. It resulted in the publication of *Une révolution esthétique ? Mai 68, des affiches "au service du peuple"* by Bernadette Caille, Michel Dixmier, and Sam Stourdzé (Arles, France: Actes Sud, 2018).

3. See, for example, Sherry Turkle, *Life on the Screen: Identity in the Age of the Internet* (New York: Simon & Schuster, 1995); Fanny Georges, "Représentation de soi et identité numérique : Une approche sémiotique et quantitative de l'emprise culturelle du web 2.0," *Réseaux* 154, no. 2 (2009): 165–93; Thierry Belleguic, Jérôme Coutard, and Milad Doueihi, "Les enjeux de la réputation à l'ère du numérique," *Sécurité et stratégie* 6, no. 2 (2011): 22–27.

4. Audre Lorde, "The Master's Tools Will Never Dismantle the Master's House," in *This Bridge Called My Back: Writings by Radical Women of Color*, eds. Cherrie Moraga and Gloria Anzaldùa (New York: Kitchen Table Press, 1983), 98–101.

5. Simone De Beauvoir, *Le deuxième sexe* (Paris: Gallimard, 1949).

6. Angela Davis, *Women, Race & Class* (New York: Random House, 1981).

7. Kimberlé Crenshaw, "Mapping the Margins: Intersectionality, Identity Politics, and Violence against Women of Color," *Stanford Law Review* 43, no. 6 (1991): 1241–99, www.jstor.org/stable/1229039.

8. Lorde, "The Master's Tools," 99.

9. Lorde, "The Master's Tools," 99.

10. See https://transmediale.de/archive/history/festival/2018.

11. Tiphaine Kazi-Tani, *Design et activisme : "chercher une arme,"* on October 5, 2017, at Centre Pompidou, Paris, with David Enon, Garnet Hertz, the collective Just for the Record (represented by Loraine Furter and Sarah Magnan), and Hélène Mourrier. Moderator: Romain Lacroix. The video of the round-table meeting is available online (in French): https://www.centrepompidou.fr/cpv/ressource.action?param.id=FR_R-8c76c1f73596cbf1b7e5a01e97612e3b&param.idSource=FR_E-8c76c1f73596cbf1b7e5a01e97612e3b.

12. See https://gaite-lyrique.net/cycle/afrocyberfeminismes and http://www.afrocyberfeminismes.org/.

13. "The detached eye of objective science is an ideological fiction, and a powerful one." Donna Haraway, *Primate Visions: Gender, Race and Nature in the World of Modern Science* (New York: Routledge, 1989), 13. The expression "god trick" appears in: Donna Haraway, "Situated Knowledges: The Science Question in Feminism and the Privilege of Partial Perspective," *Feminist Studies* 14, no. 3 (1988): 575–99.

14. Judy Wajcman, *TechnoFeminism* (Oxford, UK: Polity, 2004), 83.

15. Rosi Braidotti, "Cyberfeminism with a Difference," in *New Formations* 29 (Summer 1996).

16. Gilles Deleuze, "Postscript on the Societies of Control," *October* 59 (1992): 3–7.

17. See Giorgio Agamben, "Théorie des dispositifs," in *Poè&sie* 115, no. 1 (2006): 25–33, available online: https://doi.org/10.3917/poesi.115.0025; and Giorgio Agamben, *Qu'est-ce qu'un dispositif?* (Paris: Rivages, 2014).

18. Deleuze, "Postscript," 5–6.

19. See Gilles Deleuze, "Michel Tournier et le monde sans autrui," in *Logique du sens* (Paris: Minuit, 1969); Gilles Deleuze et Félix Guattari, *Mille plateaux. Capitalisme et schizophrénie II* (Paris: Minuit, 1980). Raphaël Josset, "De l'individu au dividu" in *L'homme postmoderne*, eds. M. Maffesoli and B. Perrier (Paris: Éditions François Bourrin, 2012); Keiichiro Hirano, *Compléter les blancs* [空白を満たしなさい] (Arles: Actes Sud, 2017).

20. Cornelia Sollfrank, "Revisiting the Future," *transmediale/art & digitalculture* (November 2017), https://transmediale.de/content/revisiting-the-future.

21. The scale of these hashtags is very smaller than #metoo which counted 1,520,000 posts on Instagram at the same period (October 2018).

22. pic.twitter.com/PsjNpIODZE.

23. Dominique Sisley, "Lana Del Rey 'to cast ritual binding spell on Donald Trump,'" *Dazed*, February 24, 2017, https://www.dazeddigital.com/music/article/

34876/1/lana-del-rey-to-cast-ritual-binding-spell-on-donald-trump; Daniel Kreps, "Lana Del Rey Joins Effort to Defeat Trump with Witchcraft," *Rolling Stone*, February 25, 2017, https://www.rollingstone.com/music/music-news/lana-del-rey-joins-effort-to-defeat-trump-with-witchcraft-127444/; Manon Michel, "Le jour où Lana del Rey est devenue une sorcière anti-Trump," *Les Inrockuptibles*, February 27, 2017. Online: https://www.lesinrocks.com/2017/02/27/musique/musique/jour-lana-del-rey-devenue-sorciere-anti-trump/.

24. See the documentary *Hail Satan?*, directed by Penny Lane (US: Gabriel Sedgwick Producer, 2019).

25. Isabelle Stengers about her reception of Starhawk's book *Dreaming the Dark*; interview broadcast on the France Culture radio station on September 15, 2019 (first broadcast in 2003), https://www.franceculture.fr/emissions/les-nuits-de-france-culture/les-vivants-et-les-dieux-symboles-et-religions-les-nouvelles-sorcieres-americaines-le-mouvement.

26. Starhawk, *Dreaming the Dark: Magic, Sex, and Politics* (Boston: Beacon Press, 1989).

27. See the blog of the organizers: https://tecnoxamanismo.wordpress.com.

28. See, for example, Kunlabora, *Ephemeral* Projects Cooperative in 2018 and "Hack the Earth" each year since 2016, both in Calafou, Spain; "Trans Hackmeeting" in 2018 at Le Goutailloux, in Tarnac, France; "Open Source Body" in 2017 at La Paillasse in Paris, France.

29. Jeanne Favre Saada, *Deadly Words: Witchcraft in the Bocage* (Cambridge, UK: Cambridge University Press, 2010). *Les mots, la mort, les sorts: La sorcellerie dans le Bocage*, 1st ed. (Paris: Gallimard, 1979).

30. Faisal Devji, "Life on the Surface," *Transmediale/ art & digitalculture* 1, *Face Value* (2018), https://transmediale.de/content/life-on-the-surface.

31. Yves Citton, "Post-scriptum sur les sociétés de recherche-création," in *Pensée en acte. Vingt propositions sur la recherche-création*, eds. Erin Manning and Brian Massumi (Dijon, France: Presses du réel, 2018). Another version of this text is published on AOC média (2018), https://aoc.media/analyse/2018/09/14/post-scriptum-societes-de-recherche-creation/.

Return to Form?

Expanded Formalism and the Idea of Literature

ALISON JAMES

Literary form has proven to be an elusive object of inquiry, even as its definition and significance are at the heart of debates over the objects and stakes of humanistic study. Admittedly, it has now been a few decades since Roland Barthes described a linguistically based literary science that would be "a science of the *conditions* of content, that is to say of forms" (une science des *conditions* du contenu, c'est-à-dire des formes)—in other words, a strict structuralism distinct from the literary *criticism* that deals in the meaning of these forms.[1] If we have since emerged from under the spell of language (or the "mirage linguistique," to borrow Thomas Pavel's term),[2] the twenty-first century has nevertheless seen a revival of debates around literary form on both sides of the Atlantic. The motivation behind this renewal ranges from an impatience with the limitations of earlier formalist/textualist methods (especially in France) to a frustration (especially in the US) with cultural-studies approaches that sometimes overlook questions of literary and artistic form.

This paper attempts to take stock of this recent return to form as well as to further the transatlantic conversation between recent reformulations (so to speak) of form as a guiding concept in literary studies. Without attempting to be exhaustive, I zoom in on two exemplary approaches: one that locates literary form at the nexus of a vast network of institutional and linguistic patterns (Caroline Levine) and another that identifies style as a point of mediation between a singular expression and its possible generalization (Marielle Macé). Located within different intellectual arenas, these approaches respond to different aspects of the complex and contradictory legacy of structuralist and poststructuralist theory. Defined differently in France and in the US, that body of theory had grounded (via structuralism) earlier formalist approaches to the literary text, but had also inspired (especially via Foucault) the new-historicist/cultural-studies turn in literary scholarship.[3] Responding to these theoretical traditions, contemporary formalisms develop a capacious understanding of the concepts of form or style, one that extends beyond the literary work to social life—and indeed to all life, in the case of Macé's "stylistics of existence." From this perspective, if the literary work contains form—since forms and styles are everywhere—it is not set apart as a formal shaping of language. Nevertheless, as I will suggest in my concluding section, the question of literary language as formal meaning persists for writers, less as the defining feature of the literary work than as the utopian horizon of creation.

New Formalism in the Twenty-first Century

In the Anglo-American context—or to be more precise, primarily in North American English departments—debates on form and formalism are bound up in the fraught legacy of New Criticism, which counted among its articles of faith the axiom that "Form is meaning." That is, to take up Cleanth Brooks's persuasive elaboration from 1951: the attempt to account for the work itself, as differentiated from other forms of cultural expression, necessitates a description of the work's specific structures, detached from concerns with biographical or historical externals, or from speculations on authorial intention.[4] The new historicism of the 1980s, by contrast, questions this separation of the literary work from other forms of discourse, and it turns to Foucault, in particular, to theorize the relationship of knowledge and power within discourse.[5]

The turn of the twentieth and twenty-first centuries brings another twist in the story: the emergence of a new formalism that, as Susan Wolfson wryly notes, reacts against new historicism, which had itself rebelled against new criticism, "which itself emerged in revolt against another moribund critical institution, old historicism."[6] A landmark publication is Wolfson and Marshall Brown's special issue of *Modern Language Quarterly* in 2000, later expanded and published as the volume *Reading for Form* in 2006.[7] Both formalism and "new formalism" have become useful umbrella terms, despite the former's having become what Richard Strier calls a "dirty word";[8] despite too, its association with what Wolfson calls "that 1980s Reagan-era school of American poetry called 'New Formalism,' a throwback to the new formalism of the 1950s, and, like it, invested in a reactionary poetics and politics."[9] As Wolfson's rejection of "reactionary" poetics, indicates, critical New Formalism is not simply a symptomatic swing of the pendulum back to an ideology of formal closure. On the contrary, it integrates the insights of new historicism by aiming to reconcile formal concerns with social and political questions and commitments. A case in point is Heather Dubrow's 2000 essay on the "country-house poem" (her influential contribution to the "Reading for Form" special issue). Dubrow argues that formal features such as prosodic technique function as tropes for certain patterns of thought and social organization—specifically, in the genre she analyzes, for the architectural containment and social order of the house—enacting a politics of "regulated hospitality."[10] However, a study of formal and rhetorical strategies also reveals discordant elements—whether at the level of genre, narrative structure, syntax, or meter—that are so many cracks in the "well-wrought urn" of poetic form.[11] According to Dubrow, this emphasis on rupture, discord, and contradiction brings the study of literary form into line with "poststructuralist paradigms."[12]

New formalism, then, is not antihistoricist, or apolitical; nor does it focus narrowly on the literary work, but on the contrary is often engaged with interdisciplinary fields, such as gender studies or postcolonial studies (for instance, W. J. T. Mitchell cites the exemplary formalist *and* committed work of Edward Said).[13] The theoretical affiliations of new formalist approaches lie, on the one hand, with Adorno (in Mitchell's case), and on the other, with the influential figures of "French Theory" notably de Man, the Barthes of the 1970s, and Derrida. Verena Theile and Linda Tredennick's edited volume, *New Formalisms and Literary Theory* thus aims to situate new formalism within the larger field of critical theory.[14] Nevertheless, to some extent this poststructuralist version of formalism ends up bracketing the previous structuralist moment, which in any case was more solidly established in France.[15] Admittedly, Wolfson cites a phrase from Roland Barthes's *Mythologies* (1957): "a little formalism turns one away from history, but a lot brings one back to it."[16] But rather than looking forward to the structuralist Barthes of *Critique et verité* (1966), the desire to reconcile formalism and history harks back to a moment before *Mythologies*: to the Barthes of *Le Degré zéro de l'écriture* (1953), with his focus on the historicity of literary forms.

First published in *PMLA* in 2007, Marjorie Levinson's wide-ranging review essay, "What Is New Formalism?" focuses on English-language scholarship published between 2000 and 2007. It offers a useful distinction between "activist" and "normative" new formalism: the former, continuous with new historicism, wants "to restore to today's reductive reinscription of historical reading its original focus on form"; the latter, part of a backlash against new historicism, "campaign[s] to bring back a sharp demarcation between history and art, discourse and literature, with form (regarded as the condition of aesthetic experience as traced to Kant—i.e., disinterested, autotelic, playful, pleasurable, consensus-generating, and therefore both individually liberating and conducive to affective social cohesion) the prerogative of art."[17] But we might ask what is really *new* in both cases; even "activist" new formalism can simply entail a mode of what Richard Strier calls "uninhibited close reading," that is, a mobilization of the traditional methods of textual analysis outside of any commitment to the closure of the work, and drawing on whatever is necessary for our interpretation.[18] This is what Strier had earlier called an "aesthetic formalism," as opposed to an "indexical" formalism that treats questions of style as "indices to large questions."[19] But these are orientations, toward the work or toward its context. As for Levinson's "backlash new formalism," with its normative emphasis on aesthetic closure, it seems to occupy a minority position.

Form, Foucault, Affordance

One of Levinson's most striking and undeniable points, from the vantage point of 2007, is her observation that new formalism lacks a concept of form: "Because new formalism's argument is with prestige and praxis, not grounding principles, one finds in the literature no efforts to retheorize art, culture, knowledge, value, or even—and this *is* a surprise—form."[20] Also published in 2007, Angela Leighton's *On Form: Poetry, Aestheticism, and the Legacy of a Word* explores the concept of form but is interested precisely in the multiple significations, innumerable associations, and contradictions of the word.[21] A notable attempt to rethink form appears in 2015: Caroline Levine's *Forms: Whole, Rhythm, Hierarchy, Network*. Opening with an account of the disciplinary order of Lowood School in *Jane Eyre*, the book argues, first of all, for extending the concept of form to "patterns of sociopolitical experience" in general. This approach entails a rejection of the gap between form, content, and context: "Formalist analysis turns out to be as valuable to understanding sociopolitical institutions as it is to reading literature. Forms are at work everywhere."[22] The notion of form can then encompass: "all shapes and configurations, all ordering principles, all patterns of repetition and difference."[23] Although we recognize a Deleuzian formulation here, Levine's major theoretical influences mainly lie elsewhere. They include Jacques Rancière's insistence on distributions and arrangements, and Bruno Latour's notion of networks as dynamic assemblages—conceptual configurations that are central to the ongoing reception of "French Theory" in the US.

However, the major theoretical reference point for Levine—and this is where her work aligns with new historicism—is the work of Michel Foucault. Even if Levine takes issue with Foucault's account of, in her words, "massive regimes of coordinated power,"[24] Foucault remains the master theorist of social forms and discourses. Yet Levine argues in her chapter on rhythms that institutional patterns more often than not "work across and athwart one another, generating a landscape of power that is nothing if not messy and uncoordinated."[25] The main question here is how forms operate together, neither in an organic whole nor exactly as what Foucault calls the *dispositif*, the set of mechanisms and systems that maintain power (although the term *dispositif* does not appear in Levine's book, she does refer to Judith Butler's account of gender as an "apparatus").[26] With Foucault, Levine conceives of ensembles of forms as composed of heterogeneous elements; against Foucault, she focuses on how these ensembles do not work together—on how forms, paradoxically, disorganize.

Undeniably compelling, this approach to form can nevertheless have odd results when it comes to poetic form. For instance, in her analysis of Elizabeth Barrett Browning's poem about Queen Victoria's accession to the throne, "The Young Queen" (1837), Levine argues that the poem's metrical form does not map in any meaningful way onto its subject matter. Neither experimental nor wholly conventional, the poem's "odd pattern" of lines of six, six, and fourteen syllables[27] does not evoke any of the specific temporal rhythms described in the poem—the time of mourning, the time of maturation, the time of royal succession. Meter simply adds yet another rhythm to the poem's "piling up of multiple institutional tempos," revealing that the poem's prosody is "incommensurable with the forms of the social world."[28] That is, the poem's (apparent?) aesthetic failure makes it an exemplary enactment of the disharmony of forms, since "it is precisely in this failure that the poem points the way to a new set of protocols for reading the relations between the time of poetry and the time of institutions."[29] In this analysis, the new-critical ideal of formal balance and harmony seems to have given way to a postmodern emphasis on disruption and tension.

The clash of forms, however, does not always produce this kind of disharmonious "piling up." Rather, Levine emphasizes the possibilities of "strategic formalism"; Michel de Certeau might say *tactical* formalism, since it is a way of working within existing forms, redeploying them rather than dismantling them, and seizing the occasion produced by the frictions and interferences of overlapping patterns.[30] This is the kind of strategic move depicted, according to Levine, in *Jane Eyre*, where a "clandestine network of women" operates as a social form that resists the patriarchal hierarchy at Lowood school.[31] Or, on a biographical level, Emily Dickinson's strategic retreat into the "bounded enclosure" of the home offers both relief from social responsibilities and participation in "a transnational literary community."[32] Thus, it seems then that the value of forms, whether literary or social, lies above all in their potential for political disruption or individual resistance. With the examples above, however, we see that literary forms can sometimes disappear from view behind forms of life.

The major contribution of Levine's book to the idea of form lies in its borrowing of the term *affordance* from design theory;[33] in the latter context it describes "the potential uses or actions latent in materials and designs"—for instance, "a fork affords stabbing and scooping."[34] In using this notion to define the operations of both social and literary forms, Levine unites constraint and capability, the particularity of forms and their mobility, materiality and the shapes imposed on matter, intended and unexpected uses of forms.

> What is a walled enclosure or a rhyming couplet capable of doing? Each shape or pattern, social or literary, lays claim to a limited range of potentialities. Enclosures afford containment and security, inclusion as well as exclusion. Rhyme affords repetition, anticipation, and memorization. Networks afford connection and circulation, and narratives afford the connection of events over time. The sonnet, brief and condensed, best affords a single idea or experience, "a moment's monument," while the triple-decker novel affords elaborate processes of character development in multiplot social contexts.[35]

The notion of affordance helps explain how forms constrain, differ, overlap, intersect, travel, and "do political work in particular historical contexts."[36] It accounts for both the specificity and the iterability of forms.

Styles, or Minding Our Manners

Whereas the New Criticism of the mid-twentieth century had justified its formalism in terms of attention to the specificity of the literary object, Levine's new formalism treats literary form simply as one more form among others, without posing the question of literariness or of the artwork as such. Hence the objections from critics who remain committed to the autonomy of the aesthetic. For instance, Robert Lehman, who makes the case for a Kantian approach to form, argues that "the new formalism has done nothing to answer the question: *what is literature?*"[37]; Josh Robinson, in his book on Adorno, asserts that an overly capacious understanding of form "loses sight of the specifically poetic aspects of form—its character as the mark of artistic making or technique."[38] But Levine is not concerned with the ontology of art. Along with other new formalists, she arguably engages in a formalist practice while breaking with the value commitments of what Richard Strier calls "formalist ideology"—thus tending to give up "both the question of value and the conception of 'the literary.' "[39]

But perhaps the question, "what is literature?" has simply become irrelevant in the twenty-first century. On the French side of the debate, the sense of literature's loss of autonomy and authority has become especially salient. In Dominique Maingueneau's book *Contre Saint Proust, ou la fin de la Littérature* (2006), for instance, "Proust" stands for a certain obsolete conception of the literary work and creative subjectivity, as well as for a certain manner of studying works, derived from Romanticism. The end of "Literature" (with a capital *L*) means, according to Maingueneau, that we must abandon the outdated idea of literary intransitivity and analyze, instead, a plural, disseminated literary activity as a type of communication among others—adopting, in short, Maingueneau's own linguistically based mode of discourse analysis.[40]

Yet, even as some (and Maingueneau is not alone),[41] toll the bell for the "age of style," others insist on the notion of style as *singularity*—thus reviving and rethinking both the Proustian notion of style as individual vision,[42] and Roland Barthes's account of style as deeply (and indeed irredeemably) personal ("the product of a drive, not an intention"/"le produit d'une poussée, non d'une intention").[43] The singularity in question, however, is no longer that of the literary work as such, but rather characterizes all living things considered in a broad ecological perspective. It is this project of constructing a "stylistics of existence" (a term borrowed from Foucault) that Marielle Macé announces in a 2010 special issue of *Critique* and develops in *Styles: critique de nos formes de vie* (2016).[44] While the book's title and subtitle already enact a shift between styles and forms—specifically forms of life, a notion with Wittgensteinian overtones—Macé's opening pages add other terms to the mix.

> I think that a life is actually inseparable from its forms, modalities, regimes, gestures, ways, gaits ... which are already *ideas*. That, from an ethical point of view, every being is a way of being. And that the world, such as we share it and give it meaning, can be divided not only into individuals, classes, or groups, but also into "styles," which are as many phrasings of living.
>
> Je crois qu'une vie est en effet inséparable de ses formes, de ses modalités, de ses régimes, de ses gestes, de ses façons, de ses allures ... qui sont déjà des *idées*. Que pour un regard éthique, tout être est manière d'être. Et que le monde, tel que nous le partageons et lui donnons sens, ne se découpe pas seulement en individus, en classes ou en groupes, mais aussi en "styles," qui sont autant de phrasés du vivre.[45]

In this slippage between "formes," "modalités," "régimes," "gestes," "façons," and "allures," Macé relates shapes and patterns to kinds of motion, and leads us to the "ideas" that are already present in forms. Style, as she theorizes it, is a singularity grasped in its movement toward stabilization and generalization: "identifying a style does not mean only taking note of an aspect, a phenomenality; it means perceiving within a singularity a movement of generalization, a capacity to take hold, repeat, stretch out."[46] In other words, style mediates between the particular and the general, the concrete and the abstract, spontaneous movement and regulated habit; it is "this intermediate order between singularities and the ideas they institute."[47]

Macé emphasizes the plurality and dynamism of "styles," their conceptual potential as well as their affective dimension. Forms, in this account, are always invested with values; they are "forms that count" (des formes qui comptent).[48] While she sometimes seems to use the terms *form* and *style* interchangeably, the reference to style privileges the possibilities of a literary method—stylistics—but extends it to existence as a whole, to the "phrasing of life" or the "phrasing of existence" (le phrasé du vivre, le phrasé de l'existence).[49] This move is in some respects similar to Levine's extension of the notion of form. But where Levine's forms are preexisting social or literary patterns whose affordances are mobilized in specific ways, Macé's styles emerge at another level, from the rhythms of life itself, before they move toward stabilization as a "regime." While Levine's forms are not necessarily aesthetic (they are often disciplinary forms, in the Foucauldian sense), Macé's ambition is to recuperate the aesthetic implications of style while also investing them with an ethical dimension. In this, she aims to look beyond the capitalist appropriation of "lifestyle," which is a "commercial confiscation" (*confiscation marchande*) of the notion of style.[50] But she also inflects the Nietzschean and Foucauldian ideas of an "aesthetics of existence"—away from the notion of a construction of the self, or of a self-stylization that is a version of dandyism. The aim is not to give oneself a style, but to imagine a self that can cope with the plurality of singular possibilities.[51] It is this attention to the plurality and singularity of ways of existing, and to their ethical potential, that gives literature its privileged place in Macé's project.

> Literature (especially modern literature) seems to me to be the main place where this attention to the stylistic character of life itself, to the plurality of styles of being, has been honed; attention to the fact that being indeed contains styles, ways of inhabiting forms and giving them meaning. Literature, in all its contradictions and uncertainties, takes on this task of elucidating values, since literary texts, in their very variety and singularity, constitute the primary place where the meaning of the "how" is contemplated without becoming fixed.[52]

Examples of this attention are Francis Ponge's evocation of the obstinate ways in which water flows or vegetation grows, and James Agee's description of the rhythms and "phrasing" of urban life in his *Brooklyn Is* (1939).[53] Both modernist reflexivity and documentary recording are recast here as meditations on styles of being, while style in literature merely intensifies the stylistic dimension already present in life.

Macé does not try to analyze literary texts as historically embedded cultural objects, or even (as Levine does) to examine the interaction and interferences of social and literary forms; rather, she theorizes style by thinking *with* literature: Baudelaire, Balzac, Michaux, Ponge, Kafka, Agee (and to a lesser extent with film, especially Pasolini). The literary text is taken less as an object of stylistic analysis than as an elucidation of style itself as a feature of existence—even as style retains its aesthetic implications. Macé's work thus takes on an anthropological dimension, following on from her previous book that emphasized the continuity between ways of reading and manners of being.[54]

This theorization of styles and manners breaks radically with an earlier mode of formalism in French literary studies, which separated textuality from social reality. If we cross the Atlantic once more, Macé's approach serves as one of the inspirations for Rita Felski's argument for "postcritical reading." In *The Limits of Critique* (2015), Felski cites Macé, along with Yves Citton, as exemplary of the "hermeneutic revival" now occurring in France, and that emphasizes "the text's entanglement with its readers."[55] She observes that Macé, by connecting literature to daily experience, reveals that "literature's singularity and its sociability are intertwined rather than opposed."[56]

Oulipotentiality, or the Utopia of Form

The expanded formalisms surveyed here all offer a dynamic account of forms and their interactions, moving beyond the bounded forms of New Criticism, the overly static systems of structuralism, or the notion of *écriture* as a "self-referential web of linguistic signs."[57] Still, while form and force are no longer in opposition (to cite Derrida's objection to structuralism in 1963),[58] the notion of form hovers ambiguously between process and result. As Angela Leighton points out, "form can signify both the finished object, the art form in its completion, or the parts that make up its technical apparatus. It can signify a visionary apparition in the mind, or the real, physical properties of a work. In addition, it can suggest the force that drives to completion: a resource, a goad, a ghost, an intention, a struggle, a desire."[59]

Here I will very briefly propose a test case for thinking form as both a resource and a final shape, as well as for reflecting more generally on literary formalism and its discontents: the experiments of the Ouvroir de littérature potentielle (Oulipo). The Oulipo's initial project, inaugurated in 1960, was set under the sign of "potentiality": its members aimed to rediscover or invent structures and procedures to be placed at the disposal of writers. The group has since come to be associated primarily with the notion of constraint-based writing.[60] Levine's analysis of forms might help us resolve the apparent ambiguity between constraint and potentiality: a form's *affordances*, its range of possibilities, go hand-in-hand with constraints, which limit the alternatives. The Oulipo also relies on the fact that forms are "portable" and can migrate across contexts—another point that is central to Levine's formalism.[61]

The externality of forms, also present in Levine's approach, is taken to an extreme by the Oulipo: on one level the group construes form as nonorganic, constructed, and freely chosen, far from Aristotelian or Romantic ideas of organic form. Oulipians thus conceive of form at a level of abstraction that has provoked strong denunciations.[62] Yet Oulipo writers also recognize that forms carry a history, and they use this historical embeddedness as an affordance. We might think here of Jacques Roubaud's reworkings of the sonnet,[63] or Jacques Jouet's deployment of various poetic fixed forms in *L'Histoire poèmes* (2000)—a collection that deals with precise historical events, and in which a sonnet or a ballad can reanimate the history of these poetic forms while highlighting their mobility and their potentiality in the present.[64] Or, like the lipogrammatic constraint of Georges Perec's *La Disparition* (1969), written without using the letter *e*, Oulipian constraints investigate the affordances of language itself (the lipogram itself being not a closed form but rather a generative constraint).

I will conclude with two points, the first being that the Oulipo's project, which is formalist not in a critical but in a creative sense, leads the group to confront problems that are sometimes elided by contemporary formalist criticism. These are, as we have seen, the question of the definition of literature and that of aesthetic judgment. In the Oulipo's early meetings in 1961, for instance, members of the group appeal to aesthetic pleasure as the criterion for validating the potentiality of a given form—that is, of the initial form as a guiding principle that is actualized in the final form of the work. There is a sense in which Oulipian "potential literature" is at once *always already* and *not yet* literature; in 1961, Noël Arnaud worries that the group is still producing only "Pre-potential Literature";[65] the phrase conveys the paradoxical idea of a potential potentiality. Returning to Levine's terms, this is perhaps what happens when affordance itself becomes the object of design. There is something of this same recursive logic at work when Marielle Macé treats literature as a mode of attention to styles rather than as an instantiation of style.

My second concluding point is that Oulipians are also concerned with the old problem of the relation of form and meaning. In his 1993 essay "L'impotentiel," Jacques Jouet argues that the Oulipo's work uses constraints to confront the task of literature itself, which is for Jouet a passage through nonmeaning to the production of meaning. The process is exemplified by Mallarmé's use of the invented word *ptyx*, a negative object that is itself negated by the poem ("no ptyx"/"nul ptyx"), thus producing something, or at least *not no-thing*.[66] The best-known Oulipian case is Georges Perec's conjoining of a fundamental absence and novelistic plenitude in *La Disparition* (*A Void*):

> *A Void* stands out through this formal metaphor of the lipogram, which has at once a negating and multiplying effect. The constraint both is and is not productive, is and is not reassuring. In other words, there is a real potential/impotential pairing in the Oulipo [. . .]. One cannot understand anything about Oulipian activity (*one* being many people) if one cannot see that it is simultaneously extremely conceptual and extremely artisanal, extremely production-driven and extremely negating.[67]

This "potential-impotential" dialectic enacts what Jouet calls "the utopia of form" (l'utopie de la forme):[68] the almost impossible convergence of a meaning with a way of meaning. It is a kind of cratylism that encounters the risk, in the process, of producing no meaning at all (since the perfect convergence of sign and meaning abolishes reference, as with Mallarmé's *ptyx*). In Oulipian work, according to Jouet, form and matter converge as the poem transforms its formal "scaffolding" into "the very matter" of the work—all the while revealing the presence of the formless at the heart of form.[69]

What resurfaces here is the idea of a formal adequacy and completion attained by a singular mode of expression. The Oulipian conception of form appears somewhat paradoxical, but is also totalizing: on the one hand, form (as constraint) is contingent, constructed, and "portable"; on the other, form becomes, in the completion of the work (that is produced *through* constraint), the locus of meaning. In other words, form as affordance meets style as singularity. Yet formal meaning (as Jouet describes it) does not define literature's essence, but rather serves as its necessary horizon: as a utopian closure that the literary text tends toward. It remains to be seen whether the Oulipian project is the last gasp of the age of Literature, or testifies on the contrary to writers' enduring attachment to literary form.

Notes

1. Roland Barthes, *Critique et vérité* (1966), bk. 2, *Œuvres complètes*, ed. Éric Marty (Paris: Seuil, 2002), 788, 792. All translations are my own unless otherwise indicated.

2. Thomas Pavel, *Le Mirage linguistique: essai sur la modernisation* (Paris: Éditions de Minuit, 1988).

3. On the construction and transformation of "French Theory" in the United States, see François Cusset, *French Theory: Foucault, Derrida, Deleuze & Cie et les mutations de la vie intellectuelle aux États-Unis* (Paris: La Découverte, 2003).

4. Cleanth Brooks, "The Formalist Critics," *The Kenyon Review* 13, no. 1 (Winter 1951), accessed April 10, 2019, https://www.kenyonreview.org/kr-online-issue/kenyon-review-credos/selections/cleanth-brooks-656342/https://www.kenyonreview.org/kr-online-issue/kenyon-review-credos/selections/cleanth-brooks-656342/.

5. On Foucault's influence see for instance Stephen Greenblatt's preface to the 2005 re-edition of *Renaissance Self-Fashioning* (Chicago: University of Chicago Press, 1980, 2005), xiv–xv.

6. Susan J. Wolfson, "Introduction," eds. Susan J. Wolfson and Marshall Brown, *Reading for Form* (Seattle and London: University of Washington Press, 2006), 8.

7. Susan J. Wolfson, "Reading for Form," special issue of *Modern Language Quarterly* vol. 61, no. 1 (March 2000); Wolfson and Brown, *Reading for Form*, op. cit.

8. Richard Strier, "Afterword: How Formalism Became a Dirty Word, and Why We Can't Do Without It," in *Renaissance Literature and Its Formal Engagements*, ed. Mark David Rasmussen (New York: Palgrave, 2002), 207–15.

9. Wolfson, "Introduction," 4.

10. Heather Dubrow, "Guess Who's Coming to Dinner? Reinterpreting Formalism and the Country House Poem," in *Modern Language Quarterly* 61, no. 1 (March 1, 2000): 62.

11. Heather Dubrow, "Guess Who's Coming to Dinner?," 72.

12. Heather Dubrow, "Guess Who's Coming to Dinner?," 96.

13. W. J. T. Mitchell, "The Commitment to Form; Or, Still Crazy after All These Years," in *PMLA* 118, no. 2 (2003): 321–25.

14. Verena Theile and Linda Tredennick, eds. *New Formalisms and Literary Theory* (New York: Palgrave Macmillan, 2013).

15. Cusset, *French Theory*, 40.

16. Quoted in Wolfson, "Introduction," 12.

17. Marjorie Levinson, "What Is New Formalism?," in *PMLA* 122, no. 2 (March 1, 2007): 558–69; reprinted in Levinson, *Thinking through Poetry: Field Reports on Romantic Lyric* (Oxford, UK: Oxford University Press, 2018), 142.

18. Richard Strier, "New Historicism, New Formalism, and Thy Darling in an Urn," in *A Companion to Renaissance Poetry*, ed. Catherine Bates (Hoboken, NJ: Wiley-Blackwell, 2018), 584.

19. Strier, "How Formalism Became a Dirty Word," 211.

20. Levinson, *Thinking through Poetry*, 146.

21. Angela Leighton, *On Form: Poetry, Aestheticism, and the Legacy of a Word* (Oxford, UK: Oxford University Press, 2007), 2.

22. Caroline Levine, *Forms: Whole, Rhythm, Hierarchy, Network* (Princeton, NJ: Princeton University Press, 2015), 2.
23. Levine, *Forms*, 3.
24. Levine, *Forms*, xiii.
25. Levine, *Forms*, 65.
26. Levine, *Forms*, 94.
27. Levine, *Forms*, 78.
28. Levine, *Forms*, 79.
29. Levine, *Forms*, 74–75.
30. On strategy versus tactics see Michel de Certeau, *L'Invention du quotidien 1: Arts de faire*, ed. Luce Giard (Paris: Gallimard, 1990), xlvi–lvii.
31. Levine, *Forms*, 2.
32. Levine, *Forms*, 119.
33. See Donald Norman, *The Design of Everyday Things* (New York: Doubleday, 1990).
34. Levine, *Forms*, 6.
35. Levine, *Forms*, 6.
36. Levine, *Forms*, 3–5.
37. Robert S. Lehman, "Formalism, Mere Form, and Judgment," in *New Literary History* 48, no. 2 (July 5, 2017): 246. Lehman finds in Kant's *Critique of Judgment* an account of the "impossibility of deriving a theory of the art object from a reflection on that object's formal properties." He distinguishes phenomenal form from "mere form"; the latter being "(merely) the subjective representation of an object insofar as it is constructed through a judgment of taste, constructed as the sort of singular representation that one cannot exchange for its concept, or its use, or another of its type" (252).
38. Josh Robinson, *Adorno's Poetics of Form* (New York: State University of New York Press, 2018), 217.
39. Strier, "How Formalism Became a Dirty Word," 209.
40. Dominique Maingueneau, *Contre Saint Proust ou la fin de la littérature* (Paris: Belin, 2006), 148.
41. See, for example, William Marx, *L'Adieu à la littérature. Histoire d'une dévalorisation, XVIIIe–XXe siècles* (Paris: Minuit, 2005); or, more recently, Alexandre Gefen, *L'Idée de littérature: De l'art pour l'art aux écritures d'intervention* (Paris: Corti, 2021).
42. Marcel Proust, *Le Temps retrouvé*, bk. 4, *À La recherche du temps perdu*, ed. Jean-Yves Tadié (Paris: Gallimard, 1989), 474.
43. Roland Barthes, *Le Degré zéro de l'écriture* (1953), bk.1, *Œuvres complètes*, 178.
44. Marielle Macé, ed., "Du style!," in *Critique* (Special Issue 2010): 752–53; and Macé, *Styles. Critique de nos formes de vie* (Paris: Gallimard, coll. "NRF Essais," 2016), 12–13.

45. Macé, *Styles*, 11.
46. Macé, *Styles*, 59, "identifier un style, ce n'est pas seulement prendre acte d'un aspect, d'une phénoménalité, c'est percevoir dans une singularité un mouvement de généralisation, une puissance de maintien, de répétition, d'élongation."
47. Macé, *Styles*, 31, "cet ordre intermédiaire entre les singularités et les idées qu'elles instituent."
48. Macé, *Styles*, 11.
49. Macé, *Styles*, 11, 28, 63, 113.
50. Macé, *Styles*, 161.
51. Macé, *Styles*, 226.
52. Macé, *Styles*, 48, "La littérature (en particulier la moderne) m'apparaît comme le lieu principal où s'est affûtée cette attention au caractère stylistique de la vie elle-même, au pluriel des styles de l'être, au fait qu'il y ait effectivement là des styles, des façons d'habiter les formes et de leur donner sens. La littérature assume cette tâche d'explicitation de valeurs jusque dans ses contradictions et ses incertitudes, les textes littéraires, dans leur variété et leur singularité même, constituant le lieu par excellence où se médite sans se fixer le sens du 'comment.' "
53. Macé, *Styles*, 243–47.
54. Macé, *Façons de lire, manières d'être* (Paris: Gallimard, 2011).
55. Rita Felski, *The Limits of Critique* (Chicago, IL: University of Chicago Press, 2015), 175.
56. Felski, *The Limits of Critique*, 176.
57. Felski, *The Limits of Critique*, 175.
58. "La forme fascine quand on n'a plus la force de comprendre la force en son dedans." Jacques Derrida, "Force et signification," in *L'Écriture et la différence* (Paris: Seuil, 1967), 10.
59. Leighton, *On Form*, 3.
60. On constraint versus potentiality see Jean-Jacques Poucel, "Oulipo: Explore, Expose, X-po," in *Drunken Boat* 8 (2006), accessed April 30, 2019, www.drunkenboat.com/db8/index.html.
61. Levine, *Forms*, 6.
62. Henri Meschonnic, *Politique du rythme, politique du sujet* (Paris: Verdier, 1995), 179–80.
63. See Jacques Roubaud, ∈ (Paris: Gallimard, 1967); *Churchill 40* (Paris: Gallimard, 2004).
64. Jacques Jouet, *L'Histoire poèmes* (Paris: P.O.L., 2010).
65. Jacques Bens, *Genèse de l'Oulipo: 1960–1963*, ed. Jacques Duchateau (Bordeaux: Le Castor astral, 2005), 108.
66. Jacques Jouet, "L'impotentiel," in *Quai Voltaire* no. 7 (1993): 46.
67. Jouet, "L'impotentiel," 50, "*La disparition* brille par cette métaphore formelle du lipogramme, qui a un effet à la fois négateur et multiplicateur. La contrainte est et n'est pas productive, est et n'est pas rassurante. Autant dire qu'il y

a un véritable binôme potentiel / impotentiel dans l'Oulipo [. . .]. On ne comprend rien à l'activité oulipienne (*on* est légion) si l'on n'aperçoit pas qu'elle est à la fois extrêmement conceptuelle et extrêmement artisanale, extrêmement productiviste et extrêmement négatrice."

68. Jouet, "L'impotentiel," 50.

69. Jouet, "L'impotentiel," 50.

Not Reading Blanchot
Theory and Practice

ÉMILE LÉVESQUE-JALBERT

> In some ways, I've always had a certain political passion. Public things often provoke me. And political thought is possibly always still to be discovered.[1]
>
> —Letter of Maurice Blanchot to Roger Laporte from December 24, 1984

In a gesture borrowed from the bipartition of Blanchot's book *La Communauté inavouable*,[2] this paper is split into two dissymmetrical parts. In the first part, I follow the theme of community through two important readings of Blanchot's work, that is, Jean-Luc Nancy's *La Communauté désavouée*[3] and Jacques Derrida's *Politiques de l'amitié*.[4] In that regard, I am engaging more with readings of Blanchot than with Blanchot's own text. In the second part, I suggest that reading might not be the appropriate response to Blanchot's question.

We Are Together, Aren't We?

Maurice Blanchot's book *La Communauté inavouable* published in 1983, is a "response" to Jean-Luc Nancy's article of the same year "La Communauté désœuvrée," which then appears in the book of the same title.⁵ After *La Communauté désœuvrée*, Nancy wrote three books more or less related to Blanchot's response: *La Communauté Affronté* (2001), *Maurice Blanchot: Passion politique* (2011), and *La Communauté désavouée* (2014).⁶ Only the last one engages directly with Blanchot's text and argument. Nancy's reading of Blanchot is characterized by three elements: (1) Nancy's own difficulty to respond to Blanchot, (2) his critique of Blanchot's obscure writing style, and (3) his critique of Blanchot's anti-ontological standpoint. If the three points are related and feed into each other, the principal one would be Blanchot's anti-ontology. To schematize this move, I would say that Blanchot is opposing Levinas to Hegel and Heidegger, which means that he proposes alterity as irreducible to totality and Being ("Sein"), alterity as nontotalizable and indifferent to Being.⁷ This priority of alterity poses ethics as more profound than ontology and dialectic, before and in excess to it. The most compact, dense expression of this displacement does not appear in *La Communauté inavouable*, but rather in the chapter "The Most Profound Question" of *L'Entretien infini*.

> In this sense, the dialectic, ontology, and the critique of ontology have the same postulate: all three deliver themselves over to the One: be it that the One accomplishes itself as everything, be it that it understands being as gathering, light, and unity of being, or be it that, above and beyond being, it affirms itself as the Absolute. With regard to such affirmations, must we not say: "the most profound question" is the question that escapes reference to the One? It is the other question, the question of the Other, but also a question that is always other.⁸

As we can see this refusal is not, per se, a refusal of dialectic and ontology, Blanchot's thinking seeks the unworking of the two. This unworking, that he calls *le désœuvrement* corresponds to a form of negativity that depends on a certain work (*travail*), but one that does not have any directionality, any *telos*. Suspending directionality, this unworking opens a space of questioning, or more precisely an encounter with what puts being into question. In the discussion on the community, this takes the shape of contestation.

> A being does not want to be recognized, it wants to be contested: in order to exist it goes towards the other, which contests and at times negates it, so as to start being only in that privation

that makes it conscious (here lies the origin of its consciousness) of the impossibility of being itself, of subsisting as its *ipse* or, if you will, as itself as a separate individual.[9]

The encounter with the other is not a struggle for recognition, but a contestation. Consciousness itself would arise from this contestation by the other and self-consciousness depends on this relation. That contestation names a form of negative recognition, one that happens from outside the self, constitutes the self as a fragment. Nancy notes the following on non-Hegelian dialectic:

> Although for Hegel the passage from one into another produces a third term, and although for Bataille the impossibility of the passage opens as the night into which one must enter, Blanchot desires that the passage itself passes and takes place only in its effacement. He desires to pass beyond suture and tearing apart, beyond identity and difference, without ending up either with identity or with the difference between the two. Why this desire? We must return to this question, without perhaps knowing how to respond.[10]

We now see how with Blanchot the ground for human relation, or intersubjective relation, is without a ground. "Fond sans fond," the *Urgrund* is an *Ungrund*. Community is grounded in discontinuity. Nancy is not satisfied with this non-*lieu* of the relation and proposes that connection happens and is realized in and through the body.

> But this is the point of the disagreement [*différend*] with Blanchot: Either the instant is identified with its own disappearance and so never takes place, or it takes place as the infinitesimal suspension of time where gazes—voices, silence—are exchanged and bodies touch. In this suspension, something appears—one might say, a world—and doesn't disappear.[11]

Then, to the Blanchotian model of impossible communication (which is a spatio-literary one), Nancy opposes a temporal model: contemporaneity. What we share and, consequently, what gives rise to the community is time, the instantaneity of time, as felt by the body. This suggests a form of immanence on which we will come back. But before doing so, I would like to bring into play the work of Derrida, *Politiques de l'amitié*, in order to see another aspect of the Blanchotian model of communication and antimodel of community.

(In the first part, we encounter Blanchot's ex-centric model of philosophy, which places ethics before, as more essential than, philosophy and ontology. Before asking "what is X" or asking for the meaning of the Being of "is," there is the Other. The relation with the self is one of contestation, a negative form of recognition that unbinds the self and his or her consciousness. In that, Blanchot's community corresponds to boundless friends of solitude, a negative community, a community of those without a community. Nancy challenges Blanchot by proposing that the contemporaneity felt through the body is the binding force of community, its being-together. Derrida, on that point, stays close to Blanchot's notion of community, albeit without fully adhering to it. Through Derrida, we will see how the nonlinguistic [temporal] model of Nancy does not have a future.[12])

Derrida, in *Politiques de l'amitié*, deconstructs friendship as the fundamental homogenous, autochthonous, and genealogical ground for togetherness. He does so by showing how friendship shaped philosophy, theology, and politics. In those three fields, the friend is the metaphor for unity at the basis of their discourse. Friends are one soul in two bodies, but one belongs to a group as a brother, hence the group is *like* a family, that is, a fratrocentric family. Derrida's inquiry underlines the exclusions generative of friendship: women, enemies, and insulars are nonbrothers, they are the Other of fraternity. Historically, as Derrida plainly showed, friendship implied brotherhood.

Then, distinguishing between the friend and the enemy seems to be the original and primordial gesture of politics. Unification is based on exclusion. Derrida's reading of Carl Schmitt is particularly salient on that point: "Here is the Schmittian axiom in its most elementary form: the political itself, the being-political of the political, arises in its possibility with the figure of the enemy."[13] This suggests that our societies need the enemy; to lose the enemy would be to lose politics. It would mean a depoliticization of politics. But instead of despair and pessimism, Derrida invites us to "mourn politics." He does so "to think and live a politics, a friendship, a justice which *begin* by breaking with their naturalness or their 'original' homogeneity . . . that has already come and that alone can come, in the future, to open them up. If only unto themselves."[14]

Here, in that gesture, Derrida tries to open a space for "another Democracy," where friendship instead of being the primitive element of community, would rather be "incommensurable," "sans commune mesure."

> We would not be together in a sort of minimal community—but also incommensurable to all others—speaking the same language or praying for translation against the horizon of a same language, if only to manifest disagreement, if a *sort of friendship* had not already been sealed, before all contracts; if it had not been avowed as the impossible that resists even the avowal, but avowed still, avowed as the unavowable of the 'unavowable community': a friendship prior to friendships, an ineffaceable friendship, fundamental and groundless, one that breathes in a shared language (past or to come) and in the being-together that all allocution supposes, up to and including the declaration of war.[15]

The deconstruction of friendship does not propose, like what we saw in Nancy, a "minimal community," one rooted in shared experience and shared presence. This quote shows at least three things: (1) how Derrida proposes for community a linguistic model (perhaps I should say poetic model) based in responsibility where responsibility is asymmetrical both means being responsible and allowing a response. (2) This community, since it is nonassertive and always in a preliminary state, is oriented toward an undetermined future. It plays on the deferral of the limitation of community in the expectation of something to come. (3) We also see that the entire enterprise of reading the history of the Western notion of friendship is a sort of detour to read Blanchot. Derrida concludes his essay by situating himself in relation to Blanchot. At this point, his reflection takes a turn. He is talking to a friend, more so than he is talking about friendship or about a friend.[16] After the deconstruction of friendship, the address remains. Even though Derrida does not thematize this substrate, it seems to bring him back to Blanchot.

> Now here we have what is happening to us today with the ruin which affects us and which we have adopted as our theme: this collapse of the friendship concept will perhaps be a chance, but, along with Friendship, the collapse carries of the Friend too, and there is nothing fortuitous in the fact that the sudden burst of this chance at the heart of ruin is still linked, in what is in our time is mostly untimely, to literature, to the 'literary community,' of which *The Unavowable Community* also speaks.[17]

Through the deconstruction of friendship, are we then losing the friend? Is the "we," allowed by friendship, impossible then? This comment corresponds to the larger critic of Blanchot by Derrida. He finds traces of the tradition of friendship in Blanchot's language, traces of *philía*, religious fraternity, and a sort of residual phallocentrism. This leads to a confession in which Derrida declares his reticence regarding the word *community* even the inoperative, unavowable community of Blanchot. Derrida's reticence indicates a certain attachment on his part to the word "democracy." In that, Derrida suggests that Blanchot's community does not correspond exactly to what Derrida names "the democracy to come," as if it were the very word "community" that would still remain linked to fraternity. Through his discourse on community, Blanchot appears somehow before the law of democracy. It is why Derrida can claim to have said nothing against "fraternity" per se: "No protest, no contestation."[18] As we have mentioned, deconstruction aims at opening a space. But Derrida's abstentionist conclusion, one that refuses to contest seems to challenge Blanchot and his insistence on community as nonnegative space for alterity. But we might have to read this "no contestation" as also related to the structure of Otherness, since as we have seen earlier, Blanchot poses contestation as the primordial scene of consciousness. Derrida's democracy, perhaps, opens the future of a nonexclusive and open "we," where Blanchot insists on the community of a refusal of community. For Blanchot, the literary community would be an exception: an archipelago of friends through an impossible solitude.

There Is Hope, but Not for Us

How might we read Blanchot then, and especially Blanchot on community? As Leslie Hill[19] puts it, Nancy's dismissive reading of *La Communauté inavouable* results in a devaluation of Blanchot based on his past.[20] Hence, Nancy's reading or failure to read tells more about himself and his regrounding of politics in an ontology of the common than about Blanchot. Derrida's deconstruction of the community as inherently phallocentric invites us to dismiss the notion in order to embrace the democracy to come. In that sense, both readings appear dismissive, turning Blanchot against himself and engaging with his thought while staying outside.

How then to read Blanchot? Perhaps not by reading him, not framing him in a reading (negating, grasping, conceptualizing his writing into a reading). Perhaps, the best way would be to repeat him, to repeat the very question that animates his writing. To repeat it not as an instrument or as a prayer, but rather as a ghost, a haunting presence. Blanchot insistence on the deepest question, "how is community possible?" demands of us to be heirs of a problem rather than a text. The demand of such a question is less an answer to it than to let it accompany us. Only the repetition of a question without having any answer might offer "la question toujours autre" or the always other question, that could build this obscure and wild community, addressed to the unrepresentable Other, through a language that stages this impossibility. "To *name* the possible, to *respond* to the impossible."[21] Perhaps it is the unity of the "we" that does not have a future, perhaps we do not have a future, but perhaps there is a future. The writer would be the witness to this impossible relation, this relation without relation. Let it come to us without us, unexpected. If Derrida invited us to mourn politics—and despite Nancy's ontology of togetherness—for Blanchot politics was, and maybe should remain, an unavoidable and unavowable "passion."[22]

Notes

1. "En quelque sorte, j'ai toujours eu une certaine passion politique. La chose publique me provoque souvent. Et la pensée politique est peut-être toujours encore à découvrir," in Jean-Luc Nancy, *Maurice Blanchot: Passion politique* (Paris: Galilée, 2011).

2. Maurice Blanchot, *La Communauté inavouable* (Paris: Seuil, 1983). Translations will be from Maurice Blanchot, *The Unavowable Community*, trans. Pierre Joris (Barrytown, NY: Station Hill Press, 1988).

3. Jean-Luc Nancy, *La Communauté désavouée* (Paris: Galilée, 2014). Translations will be from Jean-Luc Nancy, *The Disavowed Community*, trans. Philip Armstrong (New York: Fordham University Press, 2016).

4. Jacques Derrida, *Politiques de l'amitié* (Paris: Galilée, 1994). Translations will be from Jacques Derrida, *The Politics of Friendship*, trans. George Collins (London, New York: Verso, 1997).

5. Jean-Luc Nancy, *La Communauté désœuvrée* (Paris: Christian Bourgois, 1986).

6. Jean-Luc Nancy, *La Communauté affrontée* (Paris: Galilée, 2001); *Maurice Blanchot: Passion politique* (Paris: Galilée, 2011).

7. On Nancy's understanding of the Blanchotian dialectic, see *La Communauté désavouée*, 84–85.

8. Maurice Blanchot, *The Infinite Conversation*, trans. and ed. Susan Hanson (Minneapolis and London: University of Minnesota Press, 1993), 440. "En ce sens, la dialectique, l'ontologie et la critique de l'ontologie ont le même postulat, toutes trois s'en remettent à l'Un, soit que l'Un s'accomplisse comme tout, soit qu'il entende l'être comme rassemblement, lumière et unité de l'être, soit que, par-delà

et au-dessus de l'être, il s'affirme comme l'Absolu. Au regard de telles affirmations, ne faudrait-il pas dire: 'la question la plus profonde' est la question qui échappe à la référence de l'Un? C'est l'autre question, question de l'Autre, mais aussi question toujours autre," *L'Entretien infini* (Paris: Gallimard, 1969), 34n.

9. Blanchot, *The Unavowable Community*, 6. "L'être cherche, non pas à être reconnu, mais à être contesté: il va, pour exister, vers l'autre qui le conteste et parfois le nie, afin qu'il ne commence d'être que dans cette privation qui le rend conscient (c'est là l'origine de sa conscience) de l'impossibilité d'être lui-même, d'insister comme *ipse* ou, si l'on veut, comme individu séparé," *La Communauté inavouable*, 15. As Christophe Halsberghe points out, Blanchot here argues not only against Hegel, but even more so against Alexandre Kojève. Christophe Halsberghe, "Au Prix de la béance," in *Maurice Blanchot: Récits critiques* (Tours: Farrago, 2003), 340.

10. Nancy, *The Disavowed Community*, 36. "Alors que pour Hegel le passage de l'un en l'autre produit un troisième terme et que, pour Bataille, l'impossibilité du passage s'ouvre comme la nuit dans laquelle il faut entrer, Blanchot désire que le passage lui-même passe et n'ait lieu que dans son effacement. Il désire passer outre la suture et la déchirure, outre l'identité et la différence, sans aboutir ni à l'identité ni à la différence entre les deux. L'infime suspens du temps, son battement, n'est-il pas le temps lui-même? son coeur et sa loi?" *La Communauté désavouée*, 85.

11. Nancy, *The Disavowed Community*, 71–72. "Mais c'est le point du différend: ou bien l'instant s'identifie avec sa propre disparition, et en somme n'a jamais lieu, ou bien il a lieu en tant que l'infime suspens du temps où s'échangent des regards, se touchent des corps, des voix et des silences. Dans ce suspens, quelque chose apparaît—un monde, si on veut—et ne disparaît pas," *La Communauté désavouée*, 153.

12. The debate between Nancy and Derrida as it appears in *Politics of Friendship* might be seen as an extension of Derrida's opposition to Nancy's thought. See Jacques Derrida, *Voyous* (Paris: Galilée, 2003), 88–89.

13. Derrida, *The Politics of Friendship*, 84. "Que le politique lui-même, que l'être-politique surgisse, dans sa possibilité, avec la figure de l'ennemi, voilà l'axiome Schmittien sous sa forme la plus élémentaire." *Politiques de l'amitié*, 103.

14. Derrida, *The Politics of Friendship*, 105. "pour penser et vivre une politique, une amitié, une justice qui *commencent* par rompre avec leur naturalité ou leur homogénéité "originaire" qui est déjà venue et qui peut seule venir, à l'avenir, les ouvrir. Fût-ce à elles-mêmes." *Politiques de l'amitié*, 128.

15. Derrida, *The Politics of Friendship*, 236. "Nous ne serions pas ensemble dans une sorte de communauté minimale—mais aussi incommensurable à toute autre—parlant la même langue ou priant pour la traduction dans l'horizon d'une même langue, fût-ce pour y manifester un désaccord, si une sorte d'amitié n'avait pas été scellée, avant tout autre contrat, si elle n'avait pas été avouée, avouée comme l'impossible qui résiste même à l'aveu, mais avouée encore, avouée comme l'inavouable de la "communauté inavouable": une amitié d'avant les amitiés, une amitié ineffaçable, fondamentale et sans fond, celle qui respire dans le partage de

la langue (passée ou à venir) et dans l'être-ensemble que suppose toute allocution jusque dans la déclaration de guerre." *Politiques de l'amitié*, 264.

16. In the book he sent to Blanchot, Derrida wrote an inscription that shows all the complexity of their relation. "Pour Maurice Blanchot, à qui ce livre est en premier lieu—secrètement mais aussi de toute publique évidence—dédié, adressé, dévouée jusque dans les questions les plus indirectes, avec mon admiration, ma gratitude et à jamais ma fidélité, Jacques Derrida, le 17 novembre 1994" (Blanchot Papers, Houghton Library). It is worth noting that Derrida presents Blanchot in this inscription as the secret but publicly evident addressee of his book. In that sense, Derrida makes explicit that his own intervention contains an implicit reference to Blanchot. The implicit, hence quasi-absence, of Blanchot's work in *Politiques de l'amitié* is also apparent in the choice of the epigraphs. Derrida wrote by hand in Blanchot's copy, in addition to two others epigraphs, a quote from *L'instant de ma mort*: "Désormais il fut lié à la mort par une amitié subreptice" (Blanchot Papers, Houghton Library). The "amitié subreptice" here, as a form of private joke, is at the same time reverent and irreverent. While Derrida avows his debt to Blanchot by this handwritten private epigraph, the "surreptitious friendship" it contains might as well refer to Derrida's criticism of Blanchot's notion of friendship, which is deemed by Derrida as fratro- and phallocentric. Surreptitious indeed.

17. Derrida, *The Politics of Friendship*, 302. "Or voici ce qui arrive aujourd'hui avec la ruine qui nous affecte et dont nous faisons ici notre thème: cet effondrement du concept d'amitié sera peut-être une chance mais outre l'Amitié il emporte aussi l'Ami; et il n'y a rien de fortuit à ce que le sursaut de cette chance au cœur de la ruine soit encore lié, dans le plus intempestif de notre temps, à la littérature, à la « communauté littéraire » dont parle aussi La Communauté inavouable." *Politiques de l'amitié*, 335.

18. Derrida, *The Politics of Friendship*, 305. "Aucune protestation, nulle contestation." *Politiques de l'amitié*, 338.

19. Leslie Hill, *Nancy, Blanchot: A Serious Controversy* (London: Rowman & Littlefields, 2018).

20. Leslie Hill shows accurately the dismissive aspect of Nancy's reading. Nancy suggests that Blanchot's notion of the "unavowable" is a form of repentant attachment to his Christian and nationalist position of the 1930s. The unavowable itself would be this resilience in Blanchot's thinking to abandon the religious aspect of community hence if anything, turning his work into an "ultrathéologie," *La Communauté désavouée*, 93. On the accusation of Christology, see Leslie Hill, 204, 242.

21. Blanchot, *The Infinite Conversation*, 65. "Nommer le possible, répondre à l'impossible." *L'Entretien infini*, 92.

22. Maurice Blanchot, *Lettre de Maurice Blanchot à Roger Laporte du 24 décembre 1984*, in Nancy, *Maurice Blanchot: Passion Politique*, 62.

Politics and Life Are Not Coextensive

Nancy, Badiou, Balibar, and General Equivalence

ALBERTO MOREIRAS

Catastrophic Calculation

One of the most interesting, and at the same time most widely disregarded, aspects of the legacy of May 1968 is the perhaps inconspicuous and nevertheless effective sundering of any possible identification between life and politics. This might be counterintuitive. The notorious slogan "The personal is political" implied the obvious acknowledgment that a politicization of life was needed, because it was lacking, but the intent of the explicit politicization of life was not the turning of life into the instrument or even the consequence of politics. On the contrary, the intent was that of a liberation of life, whatever that may have meant in concrete terms for the different constituencies that have not stopped using the slogan. So many years later, the capture of life by politics is undeniable—biopolitics has indeed made the personal political, perhaps even terminally, and not always in precisely liberatory ways. My contention is that a reversal of the slogan—not "The personal is political" but "Let infrapolitics be"—remains within the legacy of May '68, even if it obviously means taking a step back from the political sphere.

I think Alain Badiou is right when, in his short essay on May 1968, *On a raison de se révolter* (*There Is a Reason to Revolt*), he says: "what is primarily decisive is to maintain the historical hypothesis of a world delivered from the law of profit and of private interest."[1] But can we have a world beyond profit, private interest, calculation, general equivalence? And then, is the destruction of the structure of general equivalence preliminary to any possible "liberation of life" from capture by the law of profit today? In *After Fukushima: The Equivalence of Catastrophes*, Jean-Luc Nancy discusses how the Marxian notion of "general equivalence," applied of course to money as the general equivalent, has come to absorb "all the spheres of existence of humans, and along with them all things that exist."[2] This is a fundamental phenomenon of our age, of course, tendentially present since the beginnings of modernity but now endowed with a new intensity. If general equivalence today is the totalizing principle for the administration of life, the very region of politics, then a subtraction from it destroys the totality; no totality will subsist if exceptions multiply that undo its all-encompassing character. Hence the importance of its thematization, that is, the thematization of the possibility of a radical existential subtraction from general equivalence, even if it is just, or primarily, a conceptual and not a practical thematization. But all conceptuality is practical, too.

Nancy wants to situate equivalence today within a catastrophic horizon. Or rather, as he says, "it is . . . equivalence that is catastrophic."[3] Not all catastrophes are the same, and we cannot compare Auschwitz to Fukushima, or global climate change to the 2008 financial crisis. However, there is a comparison to be made, since equivalence itself is the catastrophe. General equivalence, in fact, preempts the possibility of noncomparison; and this is, in a marked sense, because general equivalence ciphers the general ontological horizon of our time. It is the last doctrine of being, the last metaphysical ontology. Nancy's thoughts on general equivalence are powerfully premised on the later Martin Heidegger's critique of the technological gigantic.[4] The gigantic, which takes globality as inception, is total interconnectedness. But it is the interconnectedness of that which has crossed a limit, and has reached the unlimited. I think it is important to understand properly what Nancy is proposing here. He says the following:

> What is common to both these names, Auschwitz and Hiroshima, is a crossing of limits—not the limits of morality, or of politics, or of humanity in the sense of a feeling for human dignity, but the limits of existence and of a world where humanity exists, that is, where it can risk sketching out, giving shape to meaning. The significance of these enterprises that overflow from war and crime is in fact every time a significance wholly included within

a sphere independent of the existence of the world: the sphere of a projection of possibilities at once fantastical and technological that have their own ends, or more precisely whose ends are openly for their own proliferation, in the exponential growth of figures and powers that have value for and by themselves, indifferent to the existence of the world and of all its beings.[5]

What holds for Auschwitz and Hiroshima holds also for many other events of technological gigantism, including the development of surveillance society, of the society of exposure, down to the not-so-banal everyday extreme, in the workplace for instance, of any technical system regulating compensation, for instance, or travel expenses, or labor time, always looking for its own relentless completion, for the execution of consistency, no matter how lunatic, and regardless of external damage. Whether it is fifty million Facebook users, or eighty-seven million, or even two hundred million instrumentalized by Cambridge Analytica in the most recent US elections, with a lot of subsidiary complicities, to undermine or destroy the very essence of the democratic system of rule, the indifference across the limit marks a threshold. The indifference across the limit unleashes the unlimited, and first organizes an absolute illimitation that is radically metaphysical in nature, gigantic indeed, and from which equivalence ensues as a paradoxical way of warding off madness, of indexing the continuum, of mapping the grid. Within the catastrophic gigantic, names do not pass beyond but rather "fall below all signification. They signify an annihilation of meaning" that equivalence must both signal and make up for.[6] Not all catastrophes are the same, but the inevitability of catastrophic comparison based on equivalence turns the principle of equivalence into the principle of the annihilation of meaning. Within the principle of general equivalence, all words and all bodies fall below signification. Calculability fights the incommensurable, which alone grants meaning. Nancy establishes the very narrative of why an unlimited principle of equivalence is the very interruption of relational rapport between nonequivalents; but this means that, in the gigantic unleashing of productive forces, something inconspicuous takes place, which is the loss of every possibility of relation. From now on, there is only measurement in a continuum—the personal, indeed, has become political. A certain modern apocalypse has already taken place. This is Nancy:

> Forces fight each other and compensate for each other, substitute for each other. Once we have replaced the given, non-produced

forces (the ones we used to call "natural," like wind and muscle) with produced forces (steam, electricity, the atom), we have entered into a general configuration where the forces of production of other forces and the other forces of production or action share a close symbiosis, a generalized interconnection that seems to make inevitable an unlimited development of all forces and all their interactions, retroactions, excitations, attractions, and repulsions that, finally, act as incessant recursions of the same to the same. From action to reaction, there is no rapport or relation: There is connection, concord and discord, going and coming, but no relation if what we call "relation" always involves the incommensurable, that which makes one in the relationship absolutely not equivalent to the other.[7]

Not just Auschwitz and Hiroshima calculate, not just Fukushima and the 2008 financial crisis are the results of catastrophic calculation. We live our entire lives, increasingly, with diminishing margins, within a horizon of exhaustive calculability. In political terms, even hegemony theory, which is the last political doctrine of the left, based as it is on the formation of chains of equivalences, is little more than a methodology for political calculability at the service of an effective alternative administration of the body politic.[8] Research today, at the university, is nothing but accumulation and quantification. Our Facebook posts are produced, or not, according to the number of projected "likes." Soon our life expectancy will hinge on our ability to pay deductibles for "extraordinary" (that is, more expensive) medical treatment.[9]

For Marx, the pure technology of calculation is money. In Nancy's words, "by designating money as general equivalence, Marx uttered more than the principle of mercantile exchange: He uttered the principle of a general reabsorption of all possible values into this value that defines equivalence, exchangeability, or convertibility of all products and all forces of production."[10] We calculate the incalculable even when we refer to the incalculable as incalculable, or precisely by doing so. If my post has fewer "likes" than yours, we calculate respective values on the basis of the principle of equivalence. If your book sells better than mine, I calculate as well, and my resentment—even when, or precisely because, I know that my book is better than yours—is based on a calculus that throws a deficit that happens to be mine. "The incalculable is calculated as general equivalence. This also means that the incalculable is the calculation itself, that of money and at the same time, by a profound solidarity, that of ends and means, that of ends without end, that of producers and products, that of technologies and profits, that of profits and creations, and so on."[11] The extension of general equivalence as the incalculable itself posits general equivalence as the latest, if not the last, name of being, and as the ultimate metaphoric background and purveyor of metaphors that equivalence itself reduces to nothing: all metaphors under the principle of equivalence are, after all, dead metaphors.

But—and this marks Nancy's difference from Marx and any Marxism—breaking away from general equivalence means abandoning the calculations of production. There was no production at the beginning, and there can be no production at the end. There can be no demystification of production for the sake of a proper communist production—production is always necessarily its own mystification. The real movement of things may be a movement of production, yet that is the movement that infrapolitics at the same time identifies and then brackets and refuses. About communism as production, Nancy says: "The possibility of representing a 'total' human, free from alienation, emancipated from all natural, economic, and ideological subjection, has faded away in the very progress of general equivalence becoming the equivalence and interconnection of all goals and possibilities."[12] This amounts to nothing other than the collapse, not of politics, but of any possibility of a new (human) subject of the political, perhaps even the end of the possibility of any political anthropology. Still for Nancy: "This condition imposed on our thinking surpasses greatly what we sometimes call 'a crisis of civilization.' This is not a crisis we can cure by means of this same civilization. This condition also goes beyond what is sometimes called a 'change of civilization': We do not decide on such a change; we cannot aim for it since we cannot outline the goal to be reached."[13] The end of political anthropology is also the end of any possible philosophical anthropology—something else is called for.

So, what is to be done? Short of giving ourselves over to thoroughly accomplished general equivalence, since there does not seem to be any other thing to do? What is there to do in order to suspend the sway of general equivalence, in order to subtract from the totalizing principle of civilizational life? Nancy says: "no option will make us emerge from the endless equivalence of ends and means if we do not emerge from finality itself—from aiming, from planning, and projecting a future in general."[14] But, with this, the difference between general equivalence and its critique emerges as the very difference between politics and infrapolitics. Infrapolitics would then be "the care for the approach of singular presence."[15] Nancy refers to persons and moments, places, gestures, times, words, clouds, plants. When they come, they come incommensurably. Nancy's "communism of nonequivalence" is my infrapolitics, where "democracy should be thought of starting only from the equality of incommensurables: absolute and irreducible singulars that are not individuals or social groups but sudden appearances, arrivals and departures, voices, tones—here and now, every instant."[16] The proposal here is for the recognition of an equality not premised on equivalence but rather on radical singularity—there can be no value calculation, no comparison, hence no hierarchy between incommensurable singularities. As we say in Spanish, *Nadie es más que nadie*. We could add, a bit gnomically, *Nada es más que nada*.

It Is Now Too Late

As we saw, for Badiou the refusal of general equivalence in the abandonment of the law of profit is essential. He states that a "fidelity" to May 1968 hinges on that very issue. It is well known that he will call his "historical hypothesis" the "communist hypothesis,"[17] which is the hypothesis of a social world delivered from the law of profit, but we should recognize that the "communist hypothesis," in that determination, remains a merely negative one: yes, we may want to elude capture by the commodity and by the common equivalent, money. How communist is that? For Badiou an "idea" is necessary today for the reformulation of the communist hypothesis and to escape "corruption."[18] For Badiou—and he does claim in his little pamphlet that May '68, "*c'est moi*"; he claims to be, "with some others," the embodiment of its survival—the communist idea is the embrace of what he terms a "true politics" and a "true life."[19] True politics leads to a true life in the same way a false life is possible through bad politics. Communism can fix both, it is said.

In spite of Badiou, I believe the notion of a "true politics" and the notion of a "true life" do not necessarily imply each other. Politics and life are not coextensive. To think that politics and life are in fact coextensive—a common conceit today in our academic world even if nowhere else—implies life's sacrifice and it is a likely reactive position itself thoroughly dependent on capitalist discourse and its principle of general equivalence. There will be no sundering from the law of profit and of private interest, no exit from capitalist discourse, if we persist in the deluded presumption—even if everything seems to point at it—that politics and life are coextensive. The true legacy of May 1968 might in fact be the dissolution—the cutting—of the link between the notion of politics and the notion of life in favor of a reformulation of the notion of existence. We know this much: May '68 was the declarative end of the old politics in favor of a new existential experience, itself not deemed antipolitical. But this became forgotten.

Heidegger mentions in his seminar on Heraclitus, from 1943 to 1944, an old word of the Ephesian thinker. In R. D. Hicks's translation, Diogenes Laertius's paragraph reads: "But he [Heraclitus] would retire to the temple of Artemis and play at knuckle-bones with the boys; and when the Ephesians stood around him and looked on, 'Why, you rascals,' he said, 'are you astonished?' Is it not better to do this than to take part in your civil life?"[20] *Touto poiein*, to play knuckle-bones with the kids, to do just that is better than *politeuesthai*, to take care of the *polis*. *Politeuma*, the substantive, refers to the business of government, to administrative issues, and *politeuo*, the verb, goes from meaning "to live like a citizen, *politēs*" to "getting involved in politics," or to "concerning oneself with the business of city management." Heraclitus says, according to Diogenes Laertius, that playing with the kids in the temple of Artemis is better, *kreitton*, that is, "stronger" and "more powerful," than devoting oneself to politics, and assuming the conditions of the citizen. There is a nontrivial context for this, which according to Diogenes has to do with the banishment from the city of Heraclitus's old friend Hermodorus. Heraclitus thought his city, Ephesus, was badly run, there was no proper *politeuma* there. He had no respect for the politicians, for those near him who filled their mouths with political talk. "The Ephesians," Heraclitus said, "would do well to end their lives, every grown man of them, and leave the city to beardless boys."[21] So, he preferred to play with the kids.

We will never know, and can only imagine, what old Heraclitus thought of the *kakoi*, the rascals and scoundrels that stood around him and pretended to be surprised that such a great and lofty man, a philosopher, would waste his time that way rather than joining them to do administrative business. But something translates. I am not interested—I could not do it—in re-creating the Heraclitean moment, but only in what perhaps banally translates into our own time—when the shrinking of experience has reached such proportions that many among us, even, would think that nobody should or ultimately could talk of anything but politics, nobody should do anything but politics, because everything, alas, is political. Politicize, always politicize! And yet is it still possible to hear Heraclitus say that sometimes it is better to play knuckle-bones than politicize? Even for the sake of a better politics? Can we take it seriously? Perhaps against Badiou, although things are not so simple, but certainly not against the spirit of May '68.[22]

Jacques Lacan gave a lecture at the University of Milan, in Italy, in May 1972, where he claimed he was rescuing notes from three years earlier,[23] thereby putting his lecture materials chronologically very close to 1968. It is an enigmatic lecture, but some things in it are clearly comprehensible. He says at one point: "The crisis, not of the master's discourse, but of capitalist discourse, which is its substitute, is open."[24] In the previous page, and talking to students at Milan, Lacan retakes his old 1968 lines. He says: "To make revolution . . . you should have understood that that means . . . to return to the point of departure"; and "there is no master's discourse as severe as the one that obtains where revolution is made."[25] But what is more seriously striking in this lecture, titled "On Psychoanalytic Discourse," is the assertion that "it is now too late."[26] Too late for what?

There is a capitalist discourse that has left the master's discourse behind, that has substituted for it, that promises to "march on like a roulette, could not march any better, but precisely it marches too fast, it consummates itself, it consummates itself to such an extent that it consumes itself."[27] This does not mean, as I understand, that it will come to an end—rather that it has left all limits behind—and what may be paired to it is perhaps no longer an oppositional analytic discourse, as the case may have been a few years earlier, when it would have been possible to oppose a master's discourse to it, but rather some other "pestiferous" discourse, Lacan says, "at the service of capitalist discourse."[28] This is what makes it already too late politically speaking. It is up to us to determine what kind of discourses can be classified as "pestiferous"—what the range is. Let me limit the reach of the adjective a bit: a "pestiferous" discourse is a discourse that serves capitalist discourse in the sense that it will not move toward an exit from it. Another way of putting it could be to say that capitalist discourse implies the capture and cancelation of the absolute difference between life and politics ("too late" begins there, in that capture), which ("pestiferously") undermines the position of every other discourse, now only possible in reference to capitalist discourse. No doubt we can be certain that some discourses are pestiferous precisely in that regard, but we may not be able to be so certain about others. What about, for instance, Etienne Balibar's recent insistence on the renovation of a philosophical anthropology? Is philosophical anthropology a discourse at the service of an exit from capitalist discourse? Or does it serve it, no matter how equivocally or counterintentionally? Balibar's position—from the old hermeneutical rule that we must critique every position at its strongest not weakest point—will stand here for a host of other positions that are quite common in US university discourse. Is philosophical anthropology not an attempt to suture life to politics, an attempt not to permit an outside to politics that cannot be discursively controlled? Are there discourses, on the other hand, that could be said to subtract themselves from this Lacanian pest?

Balibar's mantra is: "the becoming-citizen of the subject and the becoming-subject of the citizen."[29] There is a silent articulation here of a total historical project based on a philosophy of history, even if it is more tenuous than Hegelian phenomenology. Balibar invokes an "anthropological difference" that becomes foundational for the question of philosophical anthropology, hence, from the Balibarian perspective, it is itself the very name of a new politics. Balibar is not seeking to establish philosophical anthropology as a regional ontology, his attempt has little to do with responding to the old Kantian question "What is man?" through a series of precise theoretical determinations that would allow for the establishment of a disciplinary object among others. The attempt is, however, still perhaps essentially Kantian in a specific, transcendental way: to place the anthropological question at the very center of philosophical reflection in the present, that is, to turn the question into the object itself of philosophical reflection. This is not trivial. It calls for a suture of life and politics, of the real and of reflection on the real, of being and thinking—and it is a suture that, lamentably enough, is not generally recognized as a choking ideologeme, but rather saluted as a somehow liberatory truth.

This requires a radical torsion of the philosophical enterprise, which is perhaps no longer so Kantian. Balibar posits a necessary supplementation of philosophy that dislocates the latter and makes it synonymous with thought in general. Balibar's "philosophical anthropology" emerges in that way as a theoretically totalizing attempt concerning philosophy (it does not much matter that the totalization may refer to an unfinishable task, a totalization of the *plus d'un* or of the *pas tout*). This is the sentence that gives Balibar away: "the adjective 'anthropological,' more than a given field or a regulative idea, designates a critical question apropos of the necessary but ambivalent relation that exists between philosophical or sociological concepts and modern politics."[30] As the context makes clear, Balibar is saying that the task of philosophical anthropology is the suturing of practico-theoretical reflection, that is, of modern theoretical practice, to politics. It announces that there is no thought outside politics and that there is no politics outside thought. And, to my mind, he is wrong on both counts (but the first count matters more). Is it a harmless mistake, or is it an error that makes

Balibar complicit with a reading of history that will end up strengthening the claim of capitalist discourse in its Lacanian characterization (which I have not yet properly discussed)?

"Modernity is the age or rather the 'moment' defined by the overlapping and contradictory processes of the becoming-citizen of the subject and the becoming-subject of the citizen," says Balibar.[31] He is moving toward a final formulation that will make things taut and clear and leave the tautology behind: "modernity is the 'moment' at which the human can only become coextensive with the political (which no society has ever known)."[32] This is the dead center of Balibar's project—to establish the nonsimple "coextensiveness" of humanity and politics, itself "overlapping and contradictory," never lineal, never merely progressive or merely reactionary, but at the end of the day normative for the Balibarian tenuous or dissembled version of a philosophy of history: Balibar is offering us in his book a phenomenology of the forms of consciousness (I would even say: a phenomenological teleology of forms of consciousness, a kind of fantasmatic summary of Hegel's *Phenomenology of Spirit*, no less) that may regulate the precise interpretation of the posited coextensiveness at every stretch of the way. Perhaps humanity and politics were not always coextensive, perhaps life and politics have never been the same thing, no previous society has ever known their identity, even if its latency was always there, but now, in modernity, in our times, well, now what was always necessary but concealed has become explicit. From there it is no longer possible and it will no longer be possible to affirm any *Kehre*, any turn, any radical exit from the historical continuum. Modernity continues its old itinerary through the present and there is no room in it to speak of any alternative beginning for thought.[33] The idea is here, then—is this consistent with Badiou's communist hypothesis or yet something else?; would Badiou's hypothesis also be at the service of the reproduction and advancement of capitalist discourse?—to continue the old, in a renewed and sufficiently complex way, and thus to revitalize a form of thinking whose ambition is to dissolve the frontier between political praxis and theory, making the two not just the same and more of the same, but subordinating both to an ontologico-historical sameness that no society has known until now, but that ours may indeed be starting to know: the identity between humanity and politics is of course the corollary to the deceitful alternative, "becoming-citizen of the subject/becoming-subject of the citizen." This is a grand, ambitious plan to restore and restitute metaphysical thought, without compunctions, in the modern tradition. It takes its point of departure from the identification of (human) life and politics, whose absolute difference modernity would have come to relativize, hence cancel out. But I think it is preferable to imagine an alternative.

The Lacanian discourse of the master is sometimes assimilated to Absolute Knowledge, that is, to philosophy in a Hegelian vein. The identification of life and politics has Hegelian and Hegelo-Marxian roots (even if Marxism could have followed a different route).[34] Balibar's discourse, by making philosophy coextensive with politics, indeed by making humanity, the subject of philosophy, coextensive with politics, removes a final barrier and makes philosophy circular—the citizen-subject is the subject-citizen is the citizen-subject, for ever more. There is no longer a limit. A revolution has been accomplished that may mean, however, that we are back where we started, at the point of departure, that is, no longer in the discourse of the master, but now in its substitute and successor, capitalist discourse. There is no exit, only a meek acceptance of a dialectic that triumphantly moves forward into total assimilation, which is also total transparency—assimilation into transparency, radical consummation of an accumulation without remainder, full-blown equivalence, total disposability, an unlimited continuum: life is politics is life is politics, thinking and being are the same. And what has been excluded is the possibility of taking a step back, looking for a sheltered place, to breathe freely, and to play knuckle-bones in open dismissal of the makers of politics, the business administrators, the Heraclitean rascals. Is there no longer a function for thought that may vindicate its own extreme politicity otherwise, namely, in its rejection of the pretension of a unity in the field of the real, now granted by a (quasi) totalizing philosophical anthropology? Our freedom does not depend on any "anthropological difference," but rather on an absolute difference that subtracts itself from the anthropological closure of the world (and refuses the discourse of transparency in favor of a phenomenology of the inapparent, but that is something else).[35]

I use "absolute difference," a Freudian expression, in the sense invoked by Jorge Alemán in a recent booklet titled *Lacan y el capitalismo*.[36] I confess I am not able to interpret the Lacanian algorithm for capitalist discourse, which of course depends on its difference from the algorithms for the other four discourses, namely, the discourse of the master, university discourse, the analyst's discourse, and the discourse of the hysteric.[37] So I trust Alemán to interpret for me. He notes that capitalist discourse thrives on the logic or the law of the superego—that is, it forces us to give up on our pleasure in order to feed the instance that takes pleasure in the renunciation itself. Or, in other words, it forces us to forfeit pleasure in order "to accumulate a satisfaction that nurtures itself from the satisfaction on which the subject gives up."[38] Is that not precisely the type of enjoyment affirmed by the partisans of the seamless identification of life and politics, the great revolutionists and/or the great bureaucrats that end up meeting there, in the superegoic *jouissance* of cumulative renunciation, the death drive? Alemán's "absolute difference"—ultimately the expression of an existential *jouissance* not controlled by the superego or the death drive—is the counterpart to the "absolute rationality" of capitalist discourse, which he assimilates to the Heideggerian notion of technology. Both capitalist discourse and the discourse of technology, which wish to bring to absolute fulfillment the illimitation of the continuum of humanity and politics—a politics now turned mere administration, are discourses of the unlimited, and discourses without a limit. But the absolute rationality of capitalist discourse—and its supplement: a philosophical anthropology that feeds the subject into politics with no way out, that feeds politics into the subject as its apotheosis and final consummation—is also the absolute rationality of an unhinged death drive that will "make the world uninhabitable."[39] Philosophical anthropology, in Balibarian terms, as the index of an exhaustive coextensiveness of humanity and politics, is also the emptying out and the nihilist leveling of existence. Should we not be looking away from philosophical anthropology into a possibility of thought that would allow us to look for an exit to the illimitation that links both life and politics to the death drive?

Absolute difference refers to whatever obtains in the constitution of a mortal, sexuated, and speaking existence that cannot be "absorbed by the circular and unlimited movement of Capital."[40] It is what remains, if it remains. Alemán calls this "the Common," and defines it brilliantly as "that of which no expert may talk."[41] Or any nonexpert, to be precise. Alemán is referring to a facticity of existence that will not be reached by any totalizing anthropology, and remains enigmatic. It does not have a name, in the sense that it cannot be reduced to a concept or essence—it is not a "thing," but the remainder of the thing, something that sub-ceeds or ex-ceeds, noncapturable insofar as one can only deal with it by suppressing it or letting it be, but never by taming it, never appropriating it. I call it the infrapolitical region, as a way of naming without naming—in that failure of nomination existential facticity perhaps emerges as a site for thought. The infrapolitical region is an exception to political existence—for instance, the region of the Ephesian temple to which Heraclitus could withdraw with the kids, under the protection of no lesser god than Artemis—that nevertheless holds the secret of a radical politicity (or ultrapoliticity, or perhaps impoliticity—since it is a form of nonpoliticity that becomes a condition of every politics and of every enjoyment of being).⁴² In that secret of which no one, no other, may speak—the secret that opens a caesura in every politicization of existence and that offers itself to it as its most intimate exception and its ultimate radical impossibility—what is common for another beginning of thought that will not end in Absolute Knowledge plays itself out. True, infrapolitics does not have Hegelian roots, and subtracts itself from any Hegelianism, from the moment when it departs from an absolute caesura between being and thinking (yes, which means the denial of the old Parmenidean word on the identity of the two).⁴³

True Life

In a book published a couple of years before *There Is a Reason to Revolt*, that is, *La vraie vie*, True Life (2016), Badiou sets forth his notion of a true life, which he thinks must arise in the context of a universal "egalitarian symbolization."⁴⁴ This egalitarian symbolization would be the region of absolute difference, of the rupture of the principle of equivalence, of the exit from the commodity and private interest: in other words, the (common) place of communism. It is interesting that also in Badiou there is a recourse to the kids, as in Heraclitus. The philosopher feels old and wants to talk to the young ones. Badiou speaks of two errancies. The first errancy is the errancy of those who have a confused destiny ahead, crossed by the death drive, inhabited only by a proliferation of empty *jouissance*, consumerist, senseless, "suspended in the immediacy of time"—the possible and dominant errancy of the young.⁴⁵ There is an alternative to this, of course, for a certain percentage of the population: "to find a good place within the existing social order."⁴⁶ But there is a second errancy, the errancy without errancy, the immobile errancy of the old ones without authority, condemned to await their second death (since their first death, the death of old age, has already happened) in medicalized living spaces (residences, hospices, sanatoriums). Badiou states that a conjunction of both errancies can produce "a militant idea," that is, an alliance, "against today's adults," in favor of the true life.⁴⁷ This would be a properly philosophical alliance, since "true life is philosophy, its theme."⁴⁸ The alliance would seek to secure a true life in the militant conjunction of the two errancies in favor of the communist idea, that is, in favor of universal egalitarian symbolization.

Young and old understand that today's crisis is not primarily a crisis of financial capitalism. It is rather the great symbolic crisis, in preparation since the Renaissance, which is now understood as the final accomplishment of modernity, and that consummates itself, through the power of money as *Grundwesen*, in the principle of general equivalence. For Badiou we are in the midst of "a gigantic crisis in the symbolic organization of humanity" for which there is no precedent ("it has no precedent"),[49] even if it is very precisely announced by Marx and Engels in *The Communist Manifesto*. Our world is factually the world of the icy waters of selfish calculation mentioned there, in the face of which there are three possible reactions: one is of course the "unlimited apology of capitalism";[50] the second one is the "reactive desire for a return to hierarchical, traditional symbolization"[51]—which is, of course, starting to wreak political havoc all across Europe, and it has only just started. Those two are no good, according to Badiou; but there is a third one: "communist desire," which posits the invention of a new "egalitarian symbolization."[52]

These three options present any number of false confrontations among them, from the secondary contradictions between capitalist enthusiasts and Arcadian reactionaries to the mere competition between political options within a liberal democracy itself overwhelmed by the death of symbolization. But the real conflict, according to Badiou, is the conflict between the "communist desire," which is the new egalitarian symbolization (no further precisions or determinations are given), and the forcefully "a-symbolic vision of Western capitalism" that today cannot but create "monstruous inequality and pathogenous errancies."[53] For the old philosopher, there, in the invention of what one can or could do, which is always necessarily the construction of "a new idea of collective life," there arises "true life, situated beyond mercantile neutrality and beyond old hierarchical moons."[54] But also, we should add, beyond the line of encounter of those who have nothing to lose, because they have already lost their time, and those who have everything to lose, since they still have time. Communism, in Badiou's terms, is egalitarian symbolization—of universal humanity. He claims that only egalitarian symbolization can offer a positive exit from the planetary nihilism that results from money and its extrapolation into the principle of general equivalence as the new name of Being and the only universal referent. But this is of course a *desideratum* more than a *demonstratio*. As a *desideratum*, however, is it not necessarily conditioned by an overwhelming finality? We must remember here Nancy's abjuration of finality.

The question is, how do we go about egalitarian symbolization? From where can we even start thinking about a situation that, from our present, cannot find more than a hypothetical trace of itself, not even a concept, not even the beginnings of an articulation? Surprisingly, Badiou says, without quite saying it, by just omitting the political dimension of it, hence bracketing for a moment the question of finality, that it is not primarily a question of politics. It is necessary, first, to conceive of a "true life," which cannot be done in any old way. In fact, it requires at least two constructions, two positions, "according to whatever a girl or a boy are."[55] Boys will get the short shrift. Boys, destined in traditional society to be men through the fulfillment of a number of initiation rituals that would culminate (or not) in the incorporation of the Name of the Father, on the structure explicated by Freud in *Totem and Taboo* and *Moses and Monotheism*, are ill-starred today. They have been badly affected by the fact that the death of traditional symbolization, that is, the death of the order of the Law, means "a thought of truth despoiled of transcendence. God is really dead. And since God is dead, the absolute One of masculine closure can no longer rule over the total organization of symbolic and philosophical thought."[56] At best we are left with a sort of

> Christianity without God: Christianity, since it is the son that is promoted as a new hero of an adventure that, in mercantile modernity, is nothing but fashion, consumption, and representation, all of them attributes of youth; but without God, which means without an access to a true symbolic order, because, if the sons rule, it is only over appearances.[57]

The Freudian myth is now liquidated in a scansion without foundation, "doomed to repetition, hence governed by the death drive."[58] In other words, according to Badiou, there is no longer the rise of the son, only the fall of the father, which dooms the masculine position to ruin.

Within that context, the initiation of the boy is only an initiation into the market, "into the circulation of objects and the vain communications of signs and images."[59] It is an initiation without initiation, an empty initiation that will not carry the boy into manhood but that will reduce him to perpetual adolescence. Within this perpetual adolescence that defines masculine possibilities today, Badiou finds three distinct options that are in fact, come to think of it, a sort of philosophical anthropology, except that they do bring it to an end in philosophical terms: they are what Badiou calls the "perverted body," which is a body without a subject, a body sustained in inert repetition, a body without an idea; the "sacrificed body," which is the body that desperately seeks a return to tradition, that seeks to get rid of the perverted body through the lethal embrace of the Law and that finds its impossible subjectivation in martyrdom; and the "deserving body," the average body of he who has some merit or makes merits, the body that embraces general equivalence as the only possible law, selling himself in the market at the proper, that is, properly equivalent price.[60] Unless you are too old or too young you will have to recognize yourself, impossibly, in one of those figures that mark what Badiou calls the destiny and the mystery of the "de-initiated son."[61] Are you not an uninitiated son, if you are male, given over to general equivalence as a meritorious idiot, gainfully employed, or a pervert, with drunkenness and other addictions defining your everydayness, or a sorry-ass sacrificial victim working in heroic soldiering? If not, what are you? Is there a fourth position? Do you claim it?

Badiou's philosophy is generally speaking optimistic, so he does point out that there is a way for the terminally de-initiated boy to come close to a new practice of truth: the perverted body could find rescue and redemption in love; the meritorious body could transcend himself in intellectual invention, be it science or art; and the sacrificed body could opt for a politics of nonpower, a communist politics maybe. But we just do not know how. Or do we? Does Badiou? We want to believe it, or we believe it to be possible to exactly the extent that philosophy has as its only function to aid life, which means "to help so that the question of the son, now subtracted from the typology of the three bodies, can be given back to the order of truths."[62] In other words, philosophy can help rescue the otherwise doomed body. It does not seem to me a particularly promising state of affairs, to have to trust the finality of philosophy, which now substitutes ambiguously for political finality—and the alternative is of course resignation to the fact that the boys can in the future do nothing but occupy themselves with the "servicing of the goods," to use the Lacanian expression, unable to access any possible subjectivation (since subjectivation for Badiou amounts to subjectivation to truth). But there will be no truth for the de-initiated boy.

Girls seem to have a better shot at things, but not without a price to pay. If for the boys the end of initiation implied the fixity of infinite adolescence, for the girls "the absence of separation—a separation that was in the past structurally provided by masculine mediation through marriage—between daughter and mother, between the young daughter and the adult woman as mother, implies the immanent construction of a femininity we will call premature," Badiou says.[63] A girl is today always already a woman, prematurely. Let us remember that the end of symbolization doomed life to being a life without an idea, so that the categorical imperative of contemporary capitalism is "Live without an idea!"[64] The young males are given over to stupid life, which could be ciphered in an "eternally competitive and consumerist adolescence."[65] For women—for girls, that is—adolescence arrives otherwise, "through the impossibility of being girls, of living in the glory of being girls, through the premature woman-becoming that orients the cynicism of becoming social."[66] Under those circumstances we need to forgive Badiou a tendency to exaggerate a little and present the world as a "troop of stupid adolescents led by skilled careerist women."[67] But things of course do not end there in Badiou's analysis.

There is extraordinary pressure on contemporary women: "Contemporary capitalism demands, and it will end up requiring, that women take upon themselves the new form of the One that capitalism itself seeks to replace the One of symbolic power, to replace the religious and legitimate power of the Name of the Father."[68] That new One is the one of consumerist and competitive capitalism, to which the men-boys, that is, the boys-men, can only offer a playful but precarious longing. The demand to women is that they offer, that they take it upon themselves to offer, "a hard, mature, serious, legal, and punitive version" of such a new One. Badiou says: "this is why a bourgeois and dominating feminism exists" whose project is not to build a new world but rather "to release the world such as it is to the power of women."[69] Badiou is serious and provocative both, when he says that, in that precise sense, women are today "the reserve army of triumphant capitalism."[70]

Under those circumstances, with women whose One is increasingly more solid than the One of the men, why should we not start foreseeing the disappearance of the masculine genre? What would be the latter's function, other than perhaps rather uninspiring entertainment, in a world where technology can compensate a hundredfold for the absence of the reproductive drone? Badiou also thinks, however, as it was the case for men, and with equal optimism, that, for women, we can also postulate the destruction of their traditional role and function without having to endorse their dubious function as the new reserve army of capital.[71] We can also here, in the case of women, imagine a new interruption of the death drive that would necessarily consist in linking woman to a philosophical gesture, since it could be neither a biological, nor a social or a juridical one.[72] Women, Badiou trusts (he says he "gives them his trust, absolutely"), will "become the new woman" able to give herself over, in her embrace of the four types of truth (namely, amorous, political, scientific, artistic), to a new symbolic production, a "new universal symbolization" that would have to be communist—women are, therefore, the only possible future of communism as egalitarian symbolization.[73]

In the first essay of the book, Badiou proposes a militant commitment to the idea of a new symbolization that receives no specification; in the second essay, he proposes a destruction of traditional sexual difference that continues in the third, where it resolves into a question of optimistic faith in the capacity of every youngster, whatever their sex, to embrace a new dispensation of truth. We can only imagine that such a dispensation, regulated as it would be by a non- or even antitraditional perspective, could only be radically egalitarian. But it has not been decided, or at least it has not been demonstrated—I think it has perhaps been hinted at, insinuated, suggested, but never stated—that such universal symbolization would be something other than the mere inversion of the general principle of equivalence as money into a general principle of equivalence as truth or militant faith. Badiou's communism, based on the production of an idea, may still be or sounds very much like a communism of equivalence, based on political finality, and its egalitarian symbolization, pending new theoretical developments, reduces difference, starting with sexual difference, to its dissolution into a certain idea of the common that may not go far enough, may not be useful enough. The common, Badiou seems to offer, is a potency: it is the common subjectivation to truth.

For Badiou philosophy is, or it seeks, true life. I cannot avoid thinking of the definition a young Heidegger would have proposed of philosophy in his 1922 essay on Aristotle. There Heidegger states that philosophy is "fundamentally atheistic" to the precise extent it occupies itself with factical life, seeking its destruction in favor of a concept of existence, or proper existence.[74] Factical life against existence, this is Heidegger, but he does not seem so far from Badiou's claim regarding the possibility of a true life that can be acquired in a commitment to a type of truth after the destruction of patriarchal and capitalist symbolization. Philosophy is, Heidegger says, "simply the explicit interpretation of factical life,"[75] but it is of course an oriented interpretation, and it is an oriented interpretation that goes through destruction: "Existence becomes understandable in itself only through the making questionable of facticity, that is, in the concrete destruction of facticity with respect to its motives for movement, with respect to its directions, and with respect to its deliberate availabilities."[76] In reaching for existence Heidegger is looking at philosophy as "true life," as an initiation into true life. The concrete destruction of facticity in the relentless attempt to analyze, in every case, the concrete conditions of everyone's time, of the historical time of everyone, can only be done from the singular existent, since factical life is in every case the factical life of the individual. Heidegger's philosophical hermeneutics, like Badiou's, in fact, takes its distance from God and abandons the Name of the Father as *archontic* or principial being, as guarantor of the symbolic edifice. And, like Badiou, he also fundamentally sends us back to history and to the history of the present as the only possible way of entry into another history. Heidegger says: "The very idea of facticity implies that only authentic [*eigentlich*] facticity—understood in the literal sense of the word: one's own [eigen] facticity—that is, the facticity of one's own time and generation, is the genuine object of research."[77] Heidegger goes on to say that "the hermeneutic carries out its task only on the path of destruction."[78] This destruction, to conclude with a question—how does it compare to the Badiouan one, and to Badiou's own path?

Heidegger's facticity is always in every case one's own. This seems to imply—we already saw it in Nancy—that a radical nonequivalential egalitarianism obtains—the symbolization of the world that starts in facticity, in fact, in the destruction of facticity, is an egalitarian symbolization that does not rely on equivalence. Badiou supplements it with the possibility of access to the types of truth. From there, is it really possible to name this new egalitarian symbolization communism prior to having submitted communism to its necessary destruction? If one cannot have true life—or *Existenz*—without an infrapolitical destruction of factical life, would it not be necessary to add that no infrapolitical destruction is possible from the overwhelming postulation of a communism of equivalence? And isn't Badiou's communism of the idea always a communism of equivalence? Although, if we call communism the mere new egalitarian symbolization, against the exhaustion of the traditional world in the exit from modernity, against the technical closure of the world, then perhaps communism, infrapolitics, and existential hermeneutics come to the same thing. This can in fact only be worked out in concrete historical analysis. Badiou's communism, based on the production of an idea that would replace the equivalence of bodies by a common militant faith, may still be or sound very much like a communism of equivalence in the reduction of absolute difference based on political finality, on the joint commitment to a militant fidelity. We can talk about that, and every expert will in fact never cease chattering about it—Badiou's common subjectivation to truth, standard in the left, standard for every affirmation of hegemony as an instrument of politics, may after all be not very far from the unlimitedness of the superegoic law of capitalist discourse. It might be a bad exit, a distraction.

But we might be able to use the two errancies not in order to request from them the construction of an idea, which would be just more errancy, and errancy of errancy, but rather to move toward an explicitation of their truths in a common infrapolitical destruction. Is this not a condition—the very condition—of a clearing in which all politics must test itself? The recuperation of the instance of existence—and we all have it, so far, insofar as you are or could be reading this—as the knuckle-bone game, as the enigmatic region of thought, against both politics and life, against their coextensiveness, is no refuge from politics—it is rather an act of extreme politicity without which all politics will end up where they started. That is, badly, as Lacan suggested. There is too much to lose.

Notes

1. Alain Badiou, *On a raison de se révolter: L'actualité de Mai 68* (Paris: Fayard, 2018), 51.

2. Jean-Luc Nancy, *After Fukushima: The Equivalence of Catastrophes*, trans. Charlotte Mandell (Stanford: Stanford University Press, 2014), 5.

3. Nancy, *After Fukushima*, 6.

4. See Martin Heidegger, *Contributions to Philosophy (Of the Event)*, trans. Richard Rojcewicz and Daniela Vallega-Neu (Bloomington: Indiana University Press, 2012), 106–109 and 348–49 for an early conceptualization; see also his "Age of the World Picture," in *The Question Concerning Technology and Other Essays*, trans. William Lovitt (New York: Harper Torchbooks, 1977), 115–54.

5. Nancy, *After Fukushima*, 12.

6. Nancy, *After Fukushima*, 13.

7. Nancy, *After Fukushima*, 26.

8. On hegemony theory, let me make the following remarks. Toward the end of *En la frontera: Sujeto y capitalismo. Conversaciones con María Victoria Gimbel* (Barcelona: Gedisa, 2014), Jorge Alemán offers an abbreviated description of his intellectual and existential project: "analytic discourse can contribute to highlighting what structural aspects in the constitution of a mortal, sexuated, and speaking existence are not available, for ontological reasons, for absorption by the circular and unlimited movement of Capital," 124–25. Alemán's wager for analytic discourse against capitalist discourse is understood by him as a wager at the limit, and it is a wager for another beginning. Alemán rereads Marxian surplus value from the Lacanian plus-de-jouir and the Freudian unconscious from the subversion of the subject in Heidegger and Lacan. His explicitly political wager is to suspend the principle of equivalence from which capital produces subjectivity, hence predicting an exit, which is both an exit from capitalism and an exit from metaphysics. The exit, Alemán says, would have to be understood as "another discourse of the master," 121, where the master is either the unconscious or philosophy itself, now fully homologous. Who

anchors this new discourse of the master? Alemán says: hegemony, in the Laclauian version, or rather, in Alemán's version of the Laclauian version. Hegemony stands in, in Alemán, as the aporetic or impossible configuration of a solitude and a commonality that, upon articulation, subvert the subject of will to power, the modern subject, the Cartesian-Hegelian subject that sits at the center of capitalist discourse or is capitalist discourse as such. Alemán says: "the discourse of the master can be interpreted as the concept of hegemony in Laclau. And this is because if . . . no collective will exists a priori, if there is no people that is already constituted in its field and its being, then only hegemony, when it appears, permits the retroactive translation into a collective will," 121. In other words, only hegemony, as precarious and even contingent articulation of a set of singular demands that comes together in an equivalential chain, has a political chance. Only hegemony—hegemony theory—is left standing from the collapse of modern categories, or the categories of political modernity. Hegemony counters domination precisely because hegemony articulates multiple singularities in their demands against domination, and because the articulation of singularities is ceaseless and never reaches the point of identification with a leader—it always transcends it. This is, of course, Alemán's version of a new egalitarian symbolization, which only the left can accomplish, he claims, in its material search for an exit from capitalist discourse against every "conservative and nostalgic dream of a return to the symbolic Father," 107. But here is the problem. The fact that political praxis can or may open the possibility of a new social bond does not necessarily mean that political praxis will do so. Yes, hegemony theory, in Laclau's theorization, does affirm that every hegemonic articulation is always already punctual and contingent, finite, never given beforehand, never eternal, radically open, and only sustained and sustainable in and through its very cathexis, which depends on the articulation of social singularities. The result is that the social bond is precarious and always partial. But this is no guarantee that the very hegemonic process does not, therefore, and in virtue of its very precariousness, articulate a conversion that will suture singularity into equivalence every time. The articulation of equivalential chains is no defense against a radical reassertion of the principle of general equivalence in hegemony theory—on the contrary, I would say: it sets its very ground, its very plausibility.

    9. Could we change our lives in favor of the incommensurable? For Nancy, "[the incommensurable] opens onto the absolute distance and difference of what is other—not only the other human person but also what is other than human: animal, vegetable, mineral, divine," *After Fukushima*, 27. And yet it is perhaps not necessary to bring these reflections into the sphere of the thought of the totally other, of the other of the other, or of otherness in general. Whatever is incommensurable is also nonappropriable, it resists capture, and it embodies a remainder of signification that we probably should not push into any radical beyond, where, by definition, it would remain out of reach, hence also out of any possible relationality.

    10. *After Fukushima*, 31.

11. Nancy, *After Fukushima*, 32.
12. Nancy, *After Fukushima*, 33.
13. Nancy, *After Fukushima*, 35.
14. Nancy, *After Fukushima*, 37.
15. Nancy, *After Fukushima*, 40.
16. Nancy, *After Fukushima*, 41.
17. Badiou, *On a raison*, 51.
18. Badiou, *On a raison*, 55.
19. Badiou, *On a raison*, 35 and 56.
20. Diogenes Laertius, *Lives of Eminent Philosophers*, vol. 2, trans. R. D. Hicks (Loeb Classical Library, Cambridge: Harvard University Press, 1995), 9.3.
21. Laertius, *Lives of Eminent Philosophers*, 9.2.
22. See for all of this Martin Heidegger, *Heraclitus: The Inception of Occidental Thinking and Logic: Heraclitus's Doctrine of the Logos*, trans. Julia Goesser Assalante and Shane Montgomery Ewegen (London: Bloomsbury, 2018), 10, passim. The first part of the seminar is an extended commentary on the knuckle-bones fragment. Let me add that I do not refer to this seminar casually—a lot of what goes on in it is consistent with what I will later thematize as infrapolitics. Following it up in the Heideggerian text will have to wait for another occasion.
23. Jacques Lacan, "Du discours psychanalytique" (lecture, University of Milan, Milan, Italy, May 12, 1972) http://ecole-lacanienne.net/wp-content/uploads/2016/04/1972-05-12.pdf, 1.
24. Lacan, "Du discours psychanalytique," 10.
25. Lacan, "Du discours psychanalytique," 9.
26. Lacan, "Du discours psychanalytique," 10.
27. Lacan, "Du discours psychanalytique," 10.
28. Lacan, "Du discours psychanalytique," 10.
29. Étienne Balibar, *Citizen Subject: Foundations for Philosophical Anthropology* (New York: Fordham University Press, 2017), 17.
30. Balibar, *Citizen Subject*, 17.
31. Balibar, *Citizen Subject*, 17.
32. Balibar, *Citizen Subject*, 17.
33. Up until the late 1930s Heidegger had only spoken about a "destructive repetition" of the history of thought understood as the history of metaphysics. The series of notebooks started in 1936 that would later form *Contributions* and other volumes and would only end in the 1940s, and insist forcefully on the notion of "another beginning" of thought, another "inception," but this is a history whose reach remains opaque and radically enigmatic. It is interesting that Friedrich Nietzsche also announced, toward the end of his life, a splitting of history into two, and the necessity of a new beginning for thinking. The point I wish to make here, anticipating developments in the main text, is that Heidegger's "other beginning" has a lot to do with his attempts to leave behind the residues of "transcendental anthropology" that

still clung to *Being and Time*'s Dasein: entirely to leave behind an understanding of the human as animal rationale and to proceed, through transitional thinking, to the production of a notion of Da-sein would mean to leave metaphysics behind. For people like Jorge Alemán, leaving metaphysics behind is a necessary condition of finding an exit to capitalist discourse. See Heidegger, *Contributions*, 139–47.

34. Possible alternative routes for Marxism could be glimpsed in Sergio Villalobos's "La desarticulación: Epocalidad hegemonía e historicidad" (unpublished manuscript) and Gareth Williams's "Infrapolitical Passages: Decontainment, Narco-Accumulation, and Populism" (unpublished manuscript, 2008). Like the previous two books, Jacques Lezra's *On the Nature of Marx's Things: Translation as Necrophilology* (New York: Fordham University Press, 2018), renews the materialist tradition and opens theoretico-critical pathways. See also Carlos Casanova, *Estética y producción en Karl Marx* (Santiago de Chile: Metales pesados, 2016).

35. At the end of the seminars conducted in Le Thor and Zähringen in the 1960s and 1970s, the editors note that Heidegger referred, in relationship to certain Parmenidean fragments, and especially fragment 1, verse 28—"it is necessary to experiment, to make the experience (pithesthai) of all things"—to a "tautological thought" that would be the "primordial sense of phenomenology." This is the movement that Heidegger describes: "phenomenology is a path that leads away to come before . . . , and it lets that before which it is led show itself," *Four Seminars*, trans Andrew Mitchell and François Raffoul (Bloomington: Indiana University Press, 2003), 80. That tautology of the inapparent is the decisive infrapolitical experience that makes it distinct from any form of "inner experience." Infrapolitics is very much an attempt at letting things be in their unconcealed concealment.

36. Jorge Alemán, *Lacan y el capitalismo* (Granada, Spain: Universidad de Granada, 2018), 56.

37. See on this Jacques Lacan, *The Seminar of Jacques Lacan, Vol. 17: The Other Side of Psychoanalysis*, trans Russell Griggs (New York: W. W. Norton, 2007).

38. Alemán, *Lacan*, 22.

39. Alemán, *Lacan*, 28.

40. Alemán, *En la frontera*, 124–25.

41. Alemán, Lacan, 60.

42. An example of infrapolitics would be the one associated with Antigone, a crucial figure of the Western tradition whose infrapolitical drift, a condition of its tragicity, has been denied and disavowed over and over again. For an infrapolitical Antigone, see Moreiras, "Infrapolítica marrana: Cercanía contra comunidad: La errancia y el ojo demás," *Pléyade* 19 (2017): 113–43. But a wider consideration would have to take on several recent texts, particularly feminist readings of *Antigone*, from Luce Irigaray to Judith Butler, from Adriana Cavarero to Moira Fradinger, from Bonnie Honig to Fanny Söderback. See particularly Butler's *Antigone's Claim: Kinship Between Life and Death* (New York: Columbia University Press, 2000), Honig's *Antigone, Interrupted* (New York: Cambridge University Press, 2013), and

Söderback ed., *Feminist Readings of Antigone* (Albany: State University of New York Press, 2010). See also Philippe Lacoue-Labarthe's "De l'ethique: A propos d'Antigone," in *Lacan avec les philosophes* (Paris: Albin Michel, 1990), 19–37.

43. There are many places in Heidegger's work that mention the Parmenidean identification of being and thinking (*einai-noein*). See, for instance, *Identidad y diferencia/Identität und Differenz*, ed. Arturo Leyte, trans. Helena Cortés and Arturo Leyte (Barcelona, Spain: Anthropos, 1988), 68–69, passim. But see Daniel Dahlstrom, "Heidegger's Initial Interpretation of Parmenides: An Excursus in the 1922 Lectures on Aristotelian Texts," *Review of Metaphysics* 70 (2017): 507–27, which is a tracing, starting in the seminar on Aristotle from 1922, of how Heidegger read Parmenides's Fragment 3 both positively and also from the point of view of its "recuperative destruction." Dahlstrom shows how the fragment begins to figure, in Heidegger's reading, as one of the decisive deviations in metaphysics toward the interpretation of Being as mere presence. To break the metaphysical identification of being and thinking implies the opening of the temporal-historical horizon in infrapolitical experience.

44. Alain Badiou, *La vraie vie* (Paris: Fayard, 2016), 54.
45. Badiou, *La vraie vie*, 16.
46. Badiou, *La vraie vie*, 17.
47. Badiou, La vraie vie, 34.
48. Badiou, *La vraie vie*, 14.
49. Badiou, *La vraie vie*, 43.
50. Badiou, *La vraie vie*, 45.
51. Badiou, *La vraie vie*, 46.
52. Badiou, *La vraie vie*, 48.
53. Badiou, *La vraie vie*, 47.
54. Badiou, *La vraie vie*, 51 and 52.
55. Badiou, *La vraie vie*, 117.
56. Badiou, *La vraie vie*, 114.
57. Badiou, *La vraie vie*, 64.
58. Badiou, *La vraie vie*, 66.
59. Badiou, *La vraie vie*, 68.
60. Badiou, *La vraie vie*, 69–71.
61. Badiou, *La vraie vie*, 73.
62. Badiou, *La vraie vie*, 80–81.
63. Badiou, *La vraie vie*, 90.
64. Badiou, *La vraie vie*, 90.
65. Badiou, *La vraie vie*, 94.
66. Badiou, *La vraie vie*, 94–95.
67. Badiou, *La vraie vie*, 96.
68. Badiou, *La vraie vie*, 107.
69. Badiou, *La vraie vie*, 107.

70. Badiou, *La vraie vie*, 108.
71. Badiou, *La vraie vie*, 112.
72. Badiou, *La vraie vie*, 113.
73. Badiou, *La vraie vie*, 115. The extraordinary link that Badiou posits between feminism (if that is the word) and communism in this text is consistent with the Lacanian determination of female enunciation and the Not-All. Infrapolitics endorses it. Gabriela Méndez Cota, in "Feminismo, infrapolítica, extinción," *Pensamiento al margen*, Special issue on Infrapolítica y democracia (2018), has begun to study it in reference to the work of Claire Colebrook. See Colebrook, *Death of the Posthuman: Essays on Extinction*, vol. 1 (Ann Arbor, MI: Open Humanities Press, 2014) and *Sex after Life: Essays on Extinction*, vol. 2 (Ann Arbor, MI: Open Humanities Press, 2014).
74. Martin Heidegger, "Phenomenological Interpretations with Respect to Aristotle: Indication of the Hermeneutic Situation by Martin Heidegger," trans. Michael Baur, *Man and World* 25 (1992): 355–93, 367.
75. Heidegger, "Phenomenological Interpretations," 369.
76. Heidegger, "Phenomenological Interpretations," 366.
77. "Phenomenological Interpretations," 369.
78. "Phenomenological Interpretations," 371.

Is Love Revolutionary?

Lacan and Duras after '68

FERNANDA NEGRETE

"Destruction and Language" is a 1969 *Cahiers du cinéma* interview with Marguerite Duras, Jacques Rivette, and Jean Narboni, published as an appendix to *Destroy, She Said*, the English translation of her novel *Détruire dit-elle*, also published in '69. A shift in Duras's mode of work is taking place at the time, from writing novels to making films, which become her focus for the next decade.[1] She states, "I can't read novels at all anymore. Because of the sentences."[2] It seems that writing them is also coming to a point of exhaustion for her. The interview suggests profound disappointment experienced by French-language writers after May '68, which seems to provoke an exhausted, ateleological style that Blanchot discusses in *L'entretien infini*, from '69 again, featuring a discussion of Duras's work, among others. For many, it is a way of making writing recoil from the given social order. While Duras was thus deeply immersed in this resistant and avant-garde endeavor—placing its "destruction" aspect in a prominent role—she was also consistently, from the beginning of her writing trajectory in the late 1940s all the way to the final texts from the 1990s, invested in the problem of love. Love, of course, was a key slogan of the May '68 movement in Paris, but it is also evidently far from an unaddressed literary theme across the ages, and, considered from a revolutionary perspective, one could find it even traditional, if not commonplace. So why did Duras insist on love, even as she broke out of language that merely reproduced the values and ideals of her culture, which is what her revolt against novels is all about? We can start by noting that the injunction proffered by a feminine subject, "*détruire, dit-elle,*" seems strictly contrary to that slogan's ("*Faites l'amour pas la guerre,*" "Make love not war"). It raises the questions, too, of who "*elle*" "she" could be, why her word is "*détruire*" "to destroy," and *what* should be destroyed.

Though *love* is an old word, '68 and the sexual revolution, in particular, certainly had in mind something different from the bourgeois model of the monogamous couple and the family. But not that different, after all. The problem with both this monogamous domestic scenario and with the promotion of "free love" pitted against war is the illusion that fulfillment lies somewhere in reality, in an object to make one's own, or a social contract to implement, as if these could effectively eradicate lack, which would then have been merely accidental. It is well known that Lacan was highly critical of the '68 movement, skeptical of its actual transformative potential, and also that he turned to love in his seminar of 1972–1973 titled *Encore,* where he discussed the problematic wishes of forming the One, but also outlined another mode of exploring love that would not be caught in the illusion of wholeness. Both Lacan and Duras interrogated love's potential—not to form "the uppercase One," but instead to open up a space for the transformation of and the encounter of (two) subjects, beyond the order of self- and group-identities.[3] In both accounts, such a space would embrace the disruptive force of the unconscious, and, in particular, a dimension of the letter, located beyond the purview of the signifier.[4] Their invitation to different spaces, clinical and literary, I find, aims nonetheless at enabling subjects to make a more radical intervention in the space of coexistence. So, let us enter clinical and literary space with them to highlight a certain convergence around love and letters.

In a session of Seminar XX called "L'amour et le significant," "Love and the Signifier," Lacan famously stated that love "makes up for the sexual relation insofar as the latter is inexistent."[5] As others have already explained,[6] what Lacan means by "no sexual relation" is not that sexual intercourse does not exist, but rather that an absolute correspondence of bodies, or of the two sexes, for instance, is impossible. How does love make up for the impossible sexual relation, then? The myth of love's origin evoked by Aristophanes in Plato's *Symposium,* and recalled by both Freud and Lacan,[7] posits a previous state of things in which humans had spherical bodies with two heads and two sets of limbs (although already sexed male, female, or androgynous). Since the gods found them threatening, these spherical creatures were cut in half and left longing for their other half, with their bodies marked by this wound at the navel and genitals. Like all myths, this one is a construction, and in Plato's works, especially, myths show their supplementary function, there where *logos* and memory reach their limit,[8] while an urge to speak truly endures. That supplementary function brings myth and love structurally close together. So, while the Platonic myth of love has, to this day, nurtured the fantasy of restoring a lost state of wholeness, the truth of the myth lies elsewhere, as psychoanalysis emphasizes. The displacement that the myth allows, from the fantasy of the whole to the construction around a navel, or hole (whose lack—say, of a *w*—has introduced the need for some kind of knot to hold things together), opens up a very different perspective on how and where love may move us.

Unsayable

It's well-known that love was a lifelong investigation in Duras's writing. From her first widely read novel from 1950, *Un barrage contre le Pacifique*, to the late *L'Amant de la Chine du Nord* in 1991, the work of writing—the same event from her adolescence in the previous two examples, in fact—is not about autobiography or memory, but instead about *an unsayable*, whose force the event of love makes present for those enduring it, and this includes Duras's readers. After returning to the novel genre, and to the same event as the aforementioned novels in *L'Amant* in 1984, Duras tried to collaborate on an adaptation of the film directed by Jean-Jacques Annaud and produced by Claude Berri, but she ended up rejecting this project.[9] The problem with this film's approach to a text by Duras is that it misses the crucial point of the unsayable. The certainty that "that's not it" pushes Duras, who by that time had directed several films herself, to rewrite the novel and publish *L'Amant de la Chine du Nord* (with guidelines for its execution as a film or play at the end). It is noteworthy that to Lacan's ear it is exactly a *"ce n'est pas ça,"* "that's not it" that formulates "the cry through which the obtained jouissance is distinguished from the one awaited. It is where what can be said in language becomes specified. Negation by all appearances comes from there. But nothing more."[10] These sentences insist on a location ("where," "*où*") that cannot be fully inhabited by language, a breaking point that prompts the final "but nothing more." As Duras writes on, her orientation is closely related to Lacan's concern for negation and for revealing and upholding the precise location of a gap that Annaud instead misses, seeming to want to cover it up. The crucial moment in *L'Amant* is thus the lovers' mutual confession, once they are together in his bedroom, of a fundamental, unassailable loneliness: "He says he is alone, atrociously alone with this love he has for her. She says she also is alone. She does not say with what."[11]

What is most interesting about Duras's insistence on writing love, lies in its very effects on her writing style, and on the act of reading for which it makes a space. Continuing to write, she reduces the number of words, the phrases' length, the details of the plot and characters, as though clearing the text to allow the essential elements of love's specificity to emerge. One can describe the transformation across, for instance, the three previously mentioned novels dealing with the same story, and, more broadly, across more than four decades of writing in terms of a reduction of narrative and content to a minimum, to give full force, instead, to the precise setting, gestures, and utterances related to the love event. The transformation I see in Duras's writing style through unique procedures of evacuation aims at nothing less than giving access to a nonspecular experience of love, whereas Annaud's film aims, in his own words, at the spectator's "identifying with the characters" and building excitement about what he calls "*la prise de plaisir*," "the taking of pleasure," that is, the sex scenes, so that pleasure can be shown in the erotic encounters between the story's two lovers.[12]

As the idiomatic phrase puts it (at least in English and French), love is something one *makes*—at once due to, and out of the impossibility of sexual relation, or the fundamental solitude of speaking beings. If, as Lacan's statements indicate, love is a matter of *making*, insofar as the sexual relation fails, it logically follows that any preestablished idea, image, and word of love is inadequate to the task. Duras's entire oeuvre develops from her own discovery of this very position. Like Aristophanes' myth and the other speeches about *Eros* in the *Symposium*, the world's concurrent abundance of platitudes and excellent poetry about love only confirms language's inadequacy to it. Words are never enough, never just right. Why not? To begin, because, when one is moved to speak, words are already there, ready-made, exchangeable for each other, so they fail to capture love's singularity. The language of speaking beings is necessarily the Other's language, as Lacan insisted, and as Duras is highly aware. So how can writing love be something other than an ideal of civilization that therefore merely contributes to the repression of unconscious desire?

Duras investigates love as an effect of literature situated *beyond* the realm of feelings, or in Freudian terms, beyond pleasure. Hence the injunction, "*détruire, dit-elle*," where the death drive resonates. "Making love, as the locution indicates, is poetry,"[13] Lacan states, through this definition, (making) love is removed from the register of pleasure to become a rare, challenging task of creating something with the constraints of language.[14] It is crucial to take into account that this "act of love" involves very different things in a man and a woman, as two positions for speaking subjects, which are *not* equivalent to gender identities or biological sex.[15] This fundamental difference appears in the previously cited passage from *L'Amant*, where he, the man the title refers to (the lover), is alone "with his love," whereas she, the narrator reconstructing from her memories, "does not say what she is also alone with."[16] He is alone with his object, she is alone with an unsayable. In Seminar XX Lacan is curious about a love, *amour*, that would be something different from the approach of an object-cause-of-desire (in a woman), or *objet a* as narcissistic support (for a man), for which he proposes the spelling *amur*—a love where "*a-wall*" of language as phallic law, is in play. This other, feminine *amour*, with its hollow letter *o* restored at the center, *as something real* that resists the signifier—perhaps ravages it, like the Pacific Ocean that destroys the sea wall built by the mother to protect the rice fields in *Un barrage contre le Pacifique*—is what concerns Duras's writing. This is where the perspectival shift to the unique mark of a "navel" becomes crucial, so let us now attempt an approach of such a navel.

The Hole

A "navel" (*nabel*) and a "hole" (*trou*) are key figures in Freud's *Interpretation of Dreams* and Duras's *Le ravissement de Lol V. Stein*, respectively. In both cases, the figure of the navel emerges when a male subject (Jacques Hold and the dreaming Doctor Freud) asks the question "what might have happened?" (*que se serait-il passé?*), considering the speech and silence of a woman (Duras's Lol, and Freud's hysteric patient Irma). The "navel of the dream" first appears in a footnote to Freud's analysis of a part of his own dream of examining Irma's throat, where he recognizes his frustration with the patient and his wish that she "would have *opened her mouth properly*, and have told [him] more."[17] In the footnote to this phrase, Freud, considering that his analysis of this part of the dream remains incomplete, makes the following decisive statement for the practice of psychoanalysis: "There is at least one spot in every dream at which it is unplumbable—a navel, as it were, that is its point of contact with the unknown."[18]

I'll come back to Freud's words. Let us contrast them with the other navel or *trou*. In Duras's *Le ravissement de Lol V. Stein*, from 1964, Jacques

Hold, the narrator who becomes Lol's lover, gives the following hypothetical account of the traumatic scene that would have marked Lol and by which *he* is moved to write the following:

> Lol does not go far in the unknown this instant opens onto. She does not have any memory available, not even imaginary, she has no idea about this unknown. But what she believes, is that she had to penetrate it, that was what she had to do, it would have been forever, for her mind and body, the greatest pain and the greatest joy confounded to their very definition, turned unique but unnamable for lack of a word. I love to believe, like I love her, that if Lol is silent in life it's that she believed, in the space of a lightning bolt, that this word could exist. For lack of its existence, she is silent. It would have been an absence-word, a hole-word, pierced at its center by a hole, of this hole where all the other words would have been buried. It wouldn't have been possible to say it, but it would have been made to resonate. Immense, without end, an empty gong.[19,20]

The "hole-word" in Duras's novel emerges as its narrator, the man whose words on an event he never witnessed are all that's available to read, tries to approach an experience of Lol V. Stein, the protagonist who had witnessed a "ravishing" love scene that disrupted her life profoundly, and ten years later has disruptive consequences in others too. But what *is* this scene? Truth is deliberately destabilized to an extreme, on every level of the text—from the event's nature (love itself?) to the man taking on the role of witness (who was not there), to the account's place (within a novel authored by Duras). "This instant" indicated at the beginning of the passage is not something Jacques Hold merely missed, but assumes or knows Lol saw; rather, it is a later instant, unseen by Lol, between the lovers Anne Marie Stretter and Michael Richardson, whom she has watched dancing the night away, after which they leave Lol behind.[21] She has no memory available for that instant out of time, so exemplary of the primal scene; Duras's point is that no one does, and yet, it is concerned with "the greatest pain and the greatest joy confounded to their very definition." Above all, this impossible instant that escapes any conventional means of verification, has consequences for others too.

Freud's text may, at first, seem very different in its position with regard to truth. The idea of a "navel of every dream" emerges in the context of Freud's efforts to demonstrate the technique of dream interpretation, and of his wish to establish the validity of psychoanalysis in the medical field at the time of Irma's treatment, which the dream of finding something in her throat reveals. Yet Freud is dealing with dreams, in other words, with accounts of events that only "happen" to the dreamer, or the most personal and least empirically verifiable of stories. Just as Jacques Hold is only trying to approach something unknown but distinctly present in Lol, Freud does not know what makes Irma suffer,[22] as he can acknowledge when analyzing his own dream in his book, that is, after the treatment, which, he admits, occurred at a time when he was worried about his reputation. As both men, moved by a desire to know about a woman's unconscious desire, interrogate the cause of a rebellious jouissance in these women's bodies, they approach a mysterious, hollow unknown, a cavity that transforms their own search and even, one might say, their own being. Freud leaves the position of wanting success and his peer's recognition to embrace his commitment to the unconscious, which is indifferent to ideals of success. For his part, Hold—where Lol and the English "hole" resonate—follows Lol back to the stage and staging of this love event with the status of a primal scene, losing any sense of mastery along the way.[23]

Since "it wouldn't have been possible to say" this "hole-word," and, for its part, the "spot" discerned by Freud in every dream is "unplumbable" or uninterpretable, "hole" and "navel"[24] indicate the necessity of a different speech. A human navel may be hollow or protuberant, yet in both cases it indicates an interruption in the continuity of a skin surface, and, it is also certainly the interruption of prenatal connection to a maternal womb. In the context of Freud's first introduction of the navel of the dream, and in the context of the parallel I wish to draw between it and Jacques Hold's words on the hole-word, I tend to consider the navel as hollow. Furthermore, there is something not only hollow and mysterious, but also endless about these hollow figures, since, "pierced at its center by a hole," the "hole-word" discloses a mise-en-abyme (its gonglike resonance would be "immense, without end"), and since the open mouth revealing a "throat" that leads to a "navel" opens onto "the unknown." The navel or hole-word thus shows and exceeds the limits of the signifier, there where the drives attest to the Other, nonphallic jouissance Lacan discusses in the seminar for whose title he chose a word to convey exactly this infinite excess beyond meaning (*Encore*: "still," "again," "more").

The Letter's Resonance

Lacan's concept of "the letter" is highly relevant to discern the operations of the different speech required by the perspective of the navel or hole, in relation to literature as much as to feminine jouissance. In his 1965 "Hommage fait à Marguerite Duras, du ravissement de Lol V. Stein," a year after the novel's publication, Lacan writes that in paying homage to Duras he is bearing witness to the fact that "the practice of the letter converges with the use of the unconscious."[25] He also recalls Freud's claim that the artist *precedes* the psychoanalyst and paves the way for the latter.[26] This important point emphasizes the dimension of writing, reading, and the letter that Lacan works to foreground at the beginning of his homage, for instance, by interrogating the relationships, not only between characters in the novel, but also between the author and her readers. He explicitly takes the position of reader when he proposes that Duras ravishes "us" with her text.[27] A question his proposition raises, is, what, indeed, are the effects of Duras's ravishing on Lacan's work on the letter? One might say an effect appears as the homage itself. In light of this question, one should also bear in mind that writing and the letter logically imply a temporal lag, between the time of the inscription and the time of reading, and that what becomes inscribed can remain dormant for a long time. The specific effects on Lacan of the hole-word in *Le ravissement de Lol V. Stein* are, I find, confirmed almost ten years later, in the striking resonance between the cited passage from Duras's 1964 novel, where "for lack of [this word's] existence, [Lol] is silent" and Lacan's stress, in 1973, on "mot" "word" as the negation of words, "*motus*" "not a word," that is to say, on word as silence, or uncanny word that names its absence: hole-word. Furthermore, this aspect of "mot" comes up in the seminar when Lacan speaks of feminine *jouissance*, about which, to the psychoanalyst's frustration (as featured in Freud's dream of Irma's throat), women who may experience it remain silent: "not a word! We've never been able to get anything out of them."[28] The subsequent seminar session in *Encore* specifies the place of this "no answer, not a word" as marking the limit and failure of meaning. Lacan says he adopts this phrase from literature ("*pas de réponse, mot*, dit quelque part La Fontaine").[29] It is also remarkably close to the "empty gong" Jacques Hold (Jacques Lacan's uncanny namesake[30]) proposes to think the hole-word.

While the letter brings Lacan close to literature, it also plays a crucial role in the clinical context itself, where the analysand's speech, rather than written text, is the sole resource.[31] The approach to love that literature facilitates for Lacan reveals the central role of letters and reading in analytic work. The analysand's demand to the analyst as "subject supposed to know," combined with the analyst's desire, which supposes a *savoir* to the analysand's unconscious, is the condition to initiate an analysis and what sustains its work of deciphering and construction. Lacan even makes an equation between "transference" and love.[32] This enables the analyst to slip out of the position of frustration at the lack of a word from the hysteric's mouth, interpreted as *resistance*, in order to embrace the emergence of the uninterpretable hole-word.[33] Love, understood as the address of something unsayable to someone supposed to know what this Thing is about, along with the analyst's love of the unsayable Thing, can then be a cornerstone of the analytic experience. This configuration approaches what Duras sets up in *Le ravissement*, insofar as the core of Lol's experience resides in this unknown Thing that is not the scene per se of Richardson stripping Anne Marie Stretter's dress off, but rather what this scene opens onto, as well as what it opens up, both for the man who insists on approaching this Thing in Lol, and, crucially, for the reader. Lacan indicates that this is about removing "the dress" of the narcissistic image.[34] Love would then emerge in this work *of letters*, between two, of releasing the subject's unsayable Thing from its signifiers, so that its unique resonance could be felt. And this is certainly a revolutionary act whose effects cannot be calculated in advance.

Notes

An extended version of this essay's main arguments, beyond the context of May '68, and examining additional works by Duras, is included in chapter 5 of my book, *The Aesthetic Clinic: Feminine Sublimation in Contemporary Writing, Psychoanalysis, and Art* (Albany: State University of New York Press, 2020), and in *S: Journal of the Circle for Lacanian Ideology Critique* 12 (2019) under the title "Acts of Love and Unconscious Savoir in Marguerite Duras' Writing."

    1. I engage with a short film from this period of her work in Fernanda Negrete, "Duras' *Césarée* and the Subject of Love," *CR: New Centennial Review* 15, no. 3 (2015): 167–99, and more broadly in a chapter devoted to Duras's work in my forthcoming book.

    2. *Cahiers du Cinéma* 45 (November 1969); "An interview with Marguerite Duras, Jacques Rivette, and Jean Narboni," in *Destroy, She Said* (New York: Grove Press, 1994): 91.

    3. Alain Badiou, Lorenzo Chiesa, and Alenka Zupančič have all developed the question of love, sexual division, and "the two." Badiou, "What Is Love?," *UMBR(a): One*, no. 1 (1996): 37–53; Chiesa, *The Not-Two: Logic and God in Lacan* (Cambridge, MA and London: MIT Press, 2016); and Zupančič, *What IS Sex?* (Cambridge, MA & London: MIT Press, 2017).

    4. There are different accounts of this problem among Lacanian thinkers. Lucie Cantin, for instance, investigates writing where it "is disanchored from the

signifier and cannot be told, constitute the object of a narrative, or recuperated in a history," "Practices of the Letter: Writing a Space for the Real" *UMBR(a)* (2010): 12; whereas Zupančič recently put it in terms of something of the signifier that is more than itself and skews it, preventing it from ever being a smooth system of correspondences with things. Alenka Zupančič, *What IS Sex?*, 40.

    5. Jacques Lacan, "L'amour et le significant," in *Encore: Le séminaire, livre XX*, ed. Jacques-Alain Miller (Paris: Seuil, 1999), 59. All translations are my own, unless otherwise indicated: "Ce qui supplée au rapport sexuel en tant qu'inexistant . . . Ce qui supplée au rapport sexuel, c'est précisément l'amour."

    6. See, for instance, Bruce Fink, "Knowledge and Jouissance," in *Reading Seminar XX: Lacan's Major Work on Love, Jouissance, and Feminine Sexuality*, eds. Bruce Fink and Suzanne Barnard (Albany: State University of New York Press, 2002); and more recently Alenka Zupančič, *What IS Sex?*, and Alain Badiou "Love Must Be Reinvented," trans. Duane Rouselle *Theory & Event* 22, no. 1 (January 2019): 6–17.

    7. See Freud's *Delusions and Dreams in Jensen's* Gradiva. *The Standard Edition of the Complete Psychological Works of Sigmund Freud*, ed. James Strachey, vol. 11, *Five Lectures on Psycho-analysis, Leonardo and Other Works* (London: Vintage, 2001 [1910]). See also Jacques Lacan "Position of the Unconscious" in *Ecrits II* (Paris: Seuil, 1999); and "Lituraterre" in *Autres Écrits* (Paris: Seuil, 2001).

    8. Jacques Derrida's "La Pharmacie de Platon," in *La Dissémination* (Paris: Seuil, 1972), remains an important analysis of this complex problem in Plato's philosophy. For an account of the role of myths in Plato in relation to previous uses in Greek texts, see Caitlin Partenie's introduction to *Plato's Myths*, ed. Caitlin Partenie (Cambridge, UK: Cambridge University Press, 2009).

    9. See https://www.marguerite-duras.com/L-amant.php.

    10. Lacan, *Encore*, 142. "Le cri par où se distingue la jouissance obtenue, de celle attendue. C'est où se spécifie ce qui peut se dire dans le langage. La négation a toute semblance de venir de là. Mais rien de plus."

    11. Marguerite Duras, *L'Amant* (Paris: Éditions de minuit, 1996), 48. "Il dit qu'il est seul, atrocement seul avec cet amour qu'il a pour elle. Elle lui dit qu'elle aussi elle est seule. Elle ne dit pas avec quoi."

    12. *Jean-Jacques Annaud Tourne L'Amant*. Renn Productions. Available at https://www.dailymotion.com/video/xiuvoq.

    13. Lacan, *Encore*, 93. "Faire l'amour, comme le nom l'indique, c'est de la poésie."

    14. On "enabling constraints" in literature see Tracy McNulty, *Wrestling with the Angel: Experiments in Symbolic Life* (New York: Columbia University Press, 2014).

    15. In spite of the well-known feminist and queer criticism against sexuation, Lacan's statements are very nuanced in this seminar, where the formulas of sexuation are introduced; he repeats that "man" and "woman" are signifiers and positions in which subjects situate themselves. He considers, for instance, the mystic Saint John of the Cross on the feminine side of his formulas of sexuation. Other commentators of Lacan have addressed this issue. See, for instance, Bruce Fink, *Reading Seminar*

XX and Joan Copjec, *Read My Desire: Lacan against the Historicists* (Cambridge, MA: MIT Press, 1994).

16. Duras returns to this difference and split in various works. Kristyn Gorton's commentary on a similar passage from the 1982 piece *La Maladie de la mort* highlights the interesting tension of roles in which the woman appears caught, between her ordinary position and the mystic, unconscious knowledge she has access to. See Kristyn Gorton, "Critical Scenes of Desire: Marguerite Duras's *Le Ravissement de Lol V Stein* and *Moderato Cantabile*," *Dalhousie French Studies* 63 (Summer 2003): 100–19.

17. Freud, *Standard Edition*, 4: 111, emphasis in the original text.

18. Freud, *Standard Edition*, 4:111.

19. Marguerite Duras, *Le ravissement de Lol. V. Stein* (Paris: Gallimard, 1964), 47–48. "Lol ne va pas loin dans l'inconnu sur lequel s'ouvre cet instant. Elle ne dispose d'aucun souvenir même imaginaire, elle n'a aucune idée sur cet inconnu. Mais ce qu'elle croit, c'est qu'elle devait y pénétrer, que c'était ce qu'il lui fallait faire, que ç'aurait été pour toujours, pour sa tête et pour son corps, leur plus grande douleur et leur plus grande joie confondues jusque dans leur définition devenue unique mais innommable faute d'un mot. J'aime à croire, comme je l'aime, que si Lol est silencieuse dans la vie c'est qu'elle a cru, l'espace d'un éclair, que ce mot pouvait exister. Faute de son existence, elle se tait. Ç'aurait été un mot-absence, un mot-trou, creusé en son centre d'un trou où tous les autres mots auraient été enterrés. On n'aurait pas pu le dire mais on aurait pu le faire résonner. Immense, sans fin, un gong vide."

20. Serge André quotes this Durasian concept from her novel to explain feminine castration in psychoanalysis. See his *Que veut-une femme?* (Paris: Navarin, 1986), 186–87.

21. Catherine Millot has developed a reading of this instant as primal scene. She states that this passage where the "hole-word" appears "calls to mind a sort of primary repression" (69), and she considers Lol's engagement with it as "equivalent to the construction of the fantasy in the psychoanalytic cure" (72), "Why Writers?" in *UMBR(a): Writing* (2010): 65–75.

22. Irma's being a young widow plays an important part in this, which, to Freud, does not explain the specificity of her problem away.

23. In his reading of *Le ravissement de Lol V. Stein*, Dominiek Hoens convincingly proposes the novel as tragic, and wonders whether its tragic figure is Hold, rather than Lol. "When Love Is the Law: On *The Ravishing of Lol V. Stein*," *UMBR(a)* (2005): 105–16, 106.

24. The "navel of the dream" remains the crucial element of the clinic of the dream in the teaching of *GIFRIC* (*Groupe interdisciplinaire freudien de recherches et d'interventions cliniques et culturelles*) in Quebec.

25. Lacan, *Autres Ecrits*, 193. The letter in Lacan's writing and teaching repeatedly features a link of the unconscious to literary productions. for example, Poe, Provençal courtly poetry, Duras, Joyce, and Beckett.

26. Freud makes this claim in *Delusions and Dreams in Jensen's* Gradiva.

27. Lacan, *Autres Ecrits*, 191. Millot in "Why Writers?" explores the ternary structures at work in Lacan's homage to Duras.

28. Lacan, *Encore*, 96. ". . . eh bien, motus! On n'a jamais rien pu en tirer."

29. Lacan, *Encore*, 100.

30. Lacan draws attention to proper names as a writing of the subject's destiny where the real can come forth. In his paper, "L'instance de la lettre dans l'inconscient," he states that the subject "if he can seem to be a servant to language, is more so the servant of a discourse, in whose universal moment his place is already inscribed at birth, if only under the form of his proper name." *Ecrits I* (Paris: Seuil, 1999), 492. Lacan developed wordplay on his own name, exploring the unconscious work of these meanings on his life. Dany Nobus in a lecture on psychoanalysis as poetry remarks on a poem by Lacan where the signature "Lacan" becomes "là . . . quand?" "there . . . when?" and observes that "meaning is balanced against a hole/gap," in "The Poetic Wisdom of Psychoanalysis: On the Trail of Lacan's New Signifier" (lecture, for the Center for the Study of Psychoanalysis and Culture, State University of New York at Buffalo, Amherst, NY, March 1, 2017). In her article, Millot suggests that one of the text's ternaries is "composed of Jacques Lacan (provoked, in a way, by the Jacques of Jacques Hold)," "Why Writers?," 70. In his analysis of Lacan's response to Duras's novel, Jean-Michel Rabaté highlights the name "Lol V. Stein" as a kind of "anagram of LOVe," "Ravishing Duras or the Gift of Love," in *Jacques Lacan: Psychoanalysis and the Subject of Literature* (New York: Palgrave, 2001), 134.

31. Colette Soler highlights the fact that psychoanalysis is "a practice that has no other instrument than speech," which forces her to interrogate Lacan's insistent statement that through "analytic saying, something writes itself." *Lacan: The Unconscious Reinvented*, trans. E. Faye and S. Schwartz (London, UK: Karnak, 2014), 19.

32. In *Encore*, Lacan states, "I believed I had to support the transference, insofar as it does not distinguish itself from love, with the formula *the subject supposed to know*" (87). In *Le transfert* (*The Transference*), he echoes Genesis (to distinguish its mode of beginning from that of psychoanalysis) in stating that "In the beginning of the psychoanalytic experience, let us remember it, there was love." *Le Transfert. Le Seminaire VIII (1960–1961)* (Paris: Seuil, 2001), 11.

33. Bracha L. Ettinger reads Hold's position as an ethical act of impossible witnessing with Lol. See "Fascinance and the Girl-to-m/Other Matrixial Feminine Difference," in *Psychoanalysis and the Image*, ed. Griselda Pollock (Oxford, UK: Blackwell, 2006), 60–92.

34. Psychoanalyst Catherine Millot considers it "a laying bare" of the subject (as *objet a*) in "Why Writers?" (2010): 71.

May '68 and *SubStance*

MICHEL PIERSSENS

May '68 had begun well before 1968, and, in a way, is still not complete. It was a particularly spectacular episode in the history of contemporary France, but this particular episode was far from being purely French in its origins and it was far from remaining so in its consequences. May '68 was a sudden crystallization in a brief moment of "waves" from far back in time, just as its extension, from the Parisian home, was indicative of a broadening network occupying fragmented spaces but, as seen retroactively, seem to have been connected through this very dense nexus of causes that, for a brief period of time, led to the political convulsion that paralyzed Paris and its surroundings and then the whole of France.

If I mention my own trajectory before and after this special collective moment, it is not to relish in a moment of creative autofiction but it is because I believe my personal itinerary is significant as it mirrors these complex interlacings of time and space marking May '68 that remain partly to be understood still today by those who have lived through it from near or far—very close and faraway.

I did not live in Paris during the actual events of May '68, or in the years before it, or those that followed. This lag in time and space seems significant to me because it is also the situation of the vast majority of direct or indirect actors of May '68. The few thousand students who demonstrated in the Latin Quarter are not necessarily the ones who gave the movement its strongest meaning. Thousands of others who were sometimes faraway seized on what they perceived and amplified it immensely by transforming it and rebroadcasting it in environments and territories that had nothing to do with the limited Left Bank of Paris. May '68 is also often used as the modern name of a form of viral misalignment with earlier similar events well known to historians, and conversely with later movements such as the weekly demonstration of the so-called yellow vests or even the public demonstrations under the label #MeToo. Actually, I believe and hope that my itinerary will confirm this view, that May '68 had no past and did not have any future.

First, as everyone who was there can remember, at that time the ever-present reference to Marx was used in almost every circumstance, in every meeting. In accordance with the tradition of that time, I would first reference him when he said that when we estimate that history keeps repeating itself, he was suggesting that what was first seen as a tragedy, when repeated, could be viewed as a farce.

This is interesting and particularly, when France is considered, since this country has a problem with historical repetition. This is true in matters of revolutionary movements. First, we mention this because, as you might remember, May '68 was first considered by its detractors as a remaking of a similar earlier revolutionary movement. This was nothing of that sort, but anytime that this type of movement happens, either political or social, it is immediately compared to earlier events, and indeed it happened in 1830, 1848, and 1871 when insurgents dreamed of replaying 1789. Every time there was a revolution it was recounted as earlier manifestations of the same type. So, May '68 was considered to be exactly the same.

But at the core of May '68 there was a strong basis for the idea of "rupture," for a break with what had happened in the past. And it is fascinating that May '68 itself is not part of a repetitive event. May '68 has not been repeated. This was the first time in French History that such a movement did not repeat itself. Fifty years later, we can assert that with a certain confidence. Usually the repetition happens every twenty or thirty years. So, what does it mean? We have to consider that certain components were very much present at that time and they have faded away as permanent elements of our everyday life. They have completely disappeared and have no way to reappear to reestablish the same type of movement as May '68.

The question then is what was replaced. What now exists in French society that is completely different? What enacted the rupture with what existed before? Of course, the difference is probably exaggerated, but since May '68 was not repeated, it is quite legitimate to list the components that have more or less totally disappeared from the French social, intellectual, and political scene. So, I would like to offer a long list (be reassured, I will be concise) of elements that have now disappeared since May '68. Basically, Marxism that was so prevalent has disappeared as a major component of the French intellectual life; yes, from time to time, there is a quote, here and there, as I have done earlier, but it is no longer a mandatory intellectual reference. The artistic reference to Surrealism, which was very present in arts, graphics, and slogans of May '68; many of the often-quoted phrases of May '68 directly came from the Surrealist movement. Maoism, which was a fantastic force at the time, has rapidly faded away. Psychoanalysis was dominant at the time, as well; it was impossible to offer a textual analysis without interjecting a few Freudian quotes, without glossing Lacan or his fantastic galaxy of disciples who were repeating each other on any intellectual topic. This has disappeared, and today in France, psychoanalysts complain that they have no more clients. Something that has also disappeared is anti-Americanism; an ideologic aspect of French opinion that was extremely important at the end of the 1960s. This has been mentioned a few times also in this colloquium; it was the end of the Vietnam War. Even in the US, as I discovered when I arrived in Madison, Wisconsin in 1970 (yes, Verena and Tom Conley were there too, and I am sorry to evoke such a distant past). Something that has disappeared too, now coming closer to the question of literature and *"sciences humaines,"* is the importance of the journal *Tel Quel* under the activist direction of Philippe Sollers and at the core of the intellectual "revolution" published by the Editions du Seuil under the leadership of François Wahl. At that time, it was inconceivable that any graduate student preparing for his or her thesis would discuss any topic without mentioning a recent book published by Le Seuil or an article published in *Tel Quel*. If you look at the bibliography of the theses published during that period, you will find a multitude of references to the Le Seuil publications. This has now disappeared. *Tel Quel* does not exist anymore, it has been reincarnated in *L'Infini*, now published by Gallimard, but I have never met anyone who has published or read an article in *L'Infini*. It is exactly like *La Nouvelle Revue Française*, no one ever reads *La Nouvelle Revue Française*.

All these overdetermining intellectual factors in the premise of May '68 are no longer present. So, it is like the song that was resonating in the streets of Paris in May '68, "Du passé faisons table rase" (Of the past let us make a clean slate), *The Internationale*, has been enacted. Tabula rasa!

I will then be forgiven, I hope, for not falling in line with this suggested collective amnesia and pursuing the description of my personal trajectory, as I believe that my personal history seems necessary to enlighten my understanding of what is represented in the popular and intellectual movement of May '68; with this approach, my assessment is not abstract or pseudodetached. My personal wanderings are also essential to explain the genesis at Madison of the intellectual journal *SubStance* in the late 1960s and early '70s, and how it contributed, I believe, in a central way to the general development of Continental Theory in the US.

Others than I had many more central experiences, but mine had the relative advantage of a certain marginality: I was in no way an "heir" or an institutional affiliate. Before going to breathe the last fumes of tear gas in Aix-en-Provence at the beginning of the 1968 academic year, I had spent the spring of 1968 in Mexico, which was excellent for learning Spanish, since it was by reading the remarkable *L'Excelsior* reports that I was able to follow the events day after day, in support of the images broadcast on television. I could recognize the wonderful bric-a-brac of references and slogans that had accumulated in previous years (from 1966 to 1968) I had spent in Montreal, with many excursions on the West Coast as on the East Coast, from New York to San Francisco, from the Village to the mythical City Lights or a Berkeley bookstore. My culture was both very literary and very philosophical, very obsolete and very modern, from Greek and Latin classics to the intellectual stars of the day—French (Lacan, Barthes, Foucault, Deleuze, Althusser) but not only (Marcuse, Gramsci, Freud, Nietzsche, etc.), as well as the theorists of Anglo-Saxon literature that were then ignored in France (I had even set out to translate Frye). All this seasoned with situationist or assimilated readings, not to mention sociologists of various traditions. I was not particularly politicized, even though I knew many Marxists, especially Althusserians but also Maoists and Trotskyists of all shades. After Montreal I had joined Aix to enroll in thesis preparation with Raymond Jean, who has been unjustly forgotten today but whose essays and articles on contemporary and modern poetry and novels I appreciated, though less his own novels.

A former medical student who converted to letters, a keen lover of the history of science and epistemology, I had disdained the prestigious fields that produced rebellious *normaliens*—but who would not remain so for long. Registered for the *Agrégation*, I had boycotted the contest, like many others in those years, which definitely closed the classical university path that I snubbed anyway. This did not prevent me from doing courses in Aix as a lecturer on highly sensitive subjects such as literature and Marxism or literature and linguistics—with all the representatives of the different militant factions on campus, from the worst "Stalinists" to the most picturesque "Mao-spontex." I have kept a very solid knowledge of the classics in both fields.

But it turns out that I had also been recruited by the program of the Junior Year Abroad of Michigan-Wisconsin, installed in Aix for a few years like many other American programs, where I found with pleasure the cultural background that had permeated me in previous years. My English was also quite good, acquired long before, at the very active American Cultural Center of Tours, where I had earned my bachelor's degree. Thus, equipped like many with a heterogeneous intellectual cocktail, but fortunately free of dogmatic servility and otherwise equipped with a certain familiarity with American culture and counterculture, I landed in the fall of 1970 in Madison, Wisconsin, as French lecturer for two years, under the virtual uniform of a military "coopérant" (because military service still existed).

The day before I arrived, a bomb killed a young mathematician who had lingered at night in his office. For many observers, this event was to mark a major inflection point in the movement against the war in Vietnam. Very quickly, I was able to measure the depth of the abyss that separated my cultural universe from that which formed the basis of the teachings offered by the Department of French and Italian. In poetry, it was only about Hugo, Musset, or Baudelaire. In the novel, it was to fill with modernity Malraux, Sartre, and Camus (of whom Germaine Brée was the high priestess). For me there was only Rimbaud, Lautréamont, Dada and the Surrealists, Sade, Artaud, Bataille, some new novelists, *Tel Quel*, and so on—and for the concepts all that would become the French Theory, whose premises had been laid during the famous and inaugural symposium in 1966. Madison was then a major magnet for many New Yorkers in love with counterculture and subversion of the American way of life, populating for many, the many communes of the surrounding area. Like all the great public universities then in full expansion, Madison recruited many young professors trained mostly—but not all—in good traditional departments (Yale, Harvard, Columbia) but eager to shake up the dust a little.

Among them, Sydney Lévy had just landed from Urbana-Champaign and Irvine with an unusual thesis on Max Jacob and the game, after an atypical itinerary that had begun in Cairo, like Eugenio Donato, Gerald Prince, or Josué Harari, whose influence on French studies is known in the United States. Immediately, we found ourselves on the same intellectually diverse wavelength.

I had experienced the intellectual turmoil in Montreal and Aix. I had practical experience in the technical aspects of journalism, acquired in the printing shop under the leadership of the CGT book workers, as editorial secretary in a daily newspaper. A whole tradition—from the small press of the nineteenth century to Situationism through Dadaist and surreal creativity in this field, inevitably led to the idea of creating a magazine that would be the emanation of a collective.

In a very short time, Sydney and I were able to develop the model that would give rise to the magazine that still exists today, fifty years later (now with Johns Hopkins University Press). This model had organizational, material and intellectual characteristics that bear the profound mark of the May '68 years, both French and American. Editorial collective, broad appeal to the network of authorities, recognized by the younger generation, crowd-funding, modest but modern technical tools (IBM Selectric, Offset, group manual collating, broaching). Faced with this movement of young people full of energy and conviction (I was twenty-five years old), the reaction of well-established colleagues was extraordinarily tolerant and friendly. If there was a conflict of representations and prodromes of future culture wars, there was no generational conflict, absolutely the opposite of what was being played out in France at the same time and the exact opposite of what these French journals were, not simply the echo of the movement, but their flag bearers. Other journals had been born elsewhere in the United States with sometimes similar perspectives (*Diacritics, New German Critique*); exchanges took place, but the relationship with Paris had to remain predominant, with the concern to never seek to align with a particular current or pledge allegiance to an exclusive master. The distance and eclecticism of our background allowed us total freedom of exploration and curiosity. *SubStance* was thus interested in the various psychoanalytic currents without becoming Lacanian, Derrida, and deconstruction without ever pouring into blind worship, in Deleuze, Michel Serres, Bourdieu, Rancière, Blanchot, Leiris, Perec, philosophy, epistemology, critical sociology, and so on. Typical evolution of those years and experiences, the initial collective inevitably dispersed quite quickly, leaving the two initiators at the helm of the magazine. Sydney Lévy was the organizer of the transition to an institutional form of publishing under the University of Wisconsin Press Pavilion and then Johns Hopkins Press—but the journal remains owned by a nonprofit corporation, completely independent, which ensures its sustainability. Also, on the editorial level, changes were made thanks to the recruitment of new partners who could bring, with friendship and dedication, new knowledge and perspectives. I met J.-J. Thomas when I left Madison for Ann Arbor, and later, those who now provide editorial direction for the magazine, recruited by Sydney, who remains the attentive manager of the company: David Bell, Paul Harris, Pierre Cassou-Noguès, or by me: Éric Méchoulan, my colleague in Montreal.

My role vis-à-vis the journal is now largely only symbolic, a link between moments now very distant from a history where May '68 was the crucible of a lasting upheaval of ideas and forms. But with the intensity of the past involvement in seeking articles by special contributors, the insistence on producing a special issue dedicated to an urgent topic or a fascinating new figure in the world of the "*sciences humaines*" or literature, I can better evaluate today what I had, what I left and what is still here in this moment of the journey.

When I left Madison to go to the University of Michigan at Ann Arbor in 1972, *SubStance* was considered an up-and-coming journal that was part of the general movement of continental invasion that was contaminating the university presses of Nebraska and Minnesota; and friends had created their own activist press, Coda Press, to fast and furiously publish French contemporary texts in translation so that they would satisfy the intellectual appetite of a new generation of graduate students eager to explore new domains of literature or new domains of historical studies in the line of the choices offered by this new Continental wave. This eagerness for a new mode of thinking, this lust for a level of "intellectual consciousness," was not separated from an acute political activism. The mix was exciting. And indeed, Ann Arbor was, of course, a great place for revolution; in particular, these were the last years of the Vietnam War; there was an extraordinary interest in the ideas of the international movements. The Michigan campus was an important base for the Students for a Democratic Society (SDS), a movement that was discussed briefly during one of the panels. Its members were very aware of what was going on in Europe at that time, and the ideas that were circulating there, not only about the political situation, but also about its intellectual connections to violence, repression, human rights, and so forth. This sense of wonder and this sense of eagerness toward foreign ideas is something that we should remember when we talk about the intellectual climate of that time in the US, and more particularly on US campuses.

This brief recollection, not because I think we should be dwelling unnecessarily in nostalgia and the things of the past, but because we should remember what made us eagerly jump out of bed each morning, fueled our intellectual curiosity, activated the frenzy of our IBM Selectrics and our young offset presses; we should remember how all of this was innovative and exciting.

So, as I have explained, if the many things that made May '68 have disappeared, since history dislikes the void, we should now turn to what has come to replace these lost elements. We should turn ourselves toward the positive side of history, and make an effort to list the innovations that should interest us now and should be able to generate the same excitement that we have lived through during the years after '68. This is a very effective domain of intellectual inquiry and what I would like to discuss, briefly, with you now.

From my point of view, I believe that innovation can be found today in different works that deserve our interest. There are names that I would mention since I did not hear them during the colloquium. This is the case, for example, for the work of a few historians. I believe that Ivan Jablonka, for one, has very interesting ideas, and he is a real innovator, both in the way he is writing history and the way he is transforming it; he is reevaluating Foucault, and he believes that history is the "véritable théorie littéraire" (true literary theory).[1] There are also great sociologists, who are also introducing interesting hypotheses about our society as they are breaking away from Bourdieu; this is the case of Nathalie Heinich, who was very close to Bourdieu and has now chosen to develop her own path. This is true also of a number of writers. First, I would mention Houellebecq, whose name I heard mentioned several times here; he is a very important writer. He has managed a veritable rupture in French letters, there is no doubt about that. Probably the most misanthropic literary figure of his generation, he has developed a cult for the nineteenth-century French writer Karl-Joris Huysmans and his fascination for a literature devoted to "soumission" (submission), which is also the title of one his most-read novels, published the very day of the *Charlie-Hebdo* terrorist attack in Paris and associated with it in the mind of many French readers because of its morose tone.[2] I could also quote the name of Camille de Toledo, a writer and visual artist who has gained fame with *Visiter le Flurkistan: Ou les illusions de la littérature-monde*,[3] a book that is free from many of the constraints of form or genre and actually plays the role of a philosophical reflection on the "literature-world," rather than limit itself to the usual format of a travel journal. De Toledo also offers an innovative view on how history influences literature; his view is that for a very long time we have focused on a negative view of history, while we should look at history in a positive way and consider what it tells us about the future; that is a completely different approach from what we are used to. I could also advance many other names such as Jérôme Ferrari or Aurélien Bellanger. They are very interesting because they are reconnecting literature with what has always been among the best partnerships: literature and the sciences. I am not going to develop that, but I believe that the past connection of literature and science was a very potent moment in our literary history.

With that subjective statement, I will now stop, but again, I would plead for us to look at writings that do not neglect the epistemological questions that shape our contemporaneity and how scientists create innovations that shape our imagination. So, May '68 is gone, we should look at the future and to these ideas that are out there, ready to be discovered. I think that they are very exciting. May '68 existed because it was thrilling, and today there are things that exist that are equally stimulating and we should continue our quest for what will help us happily get up each morning in the pursuit of innovations and wonders.

Notes

1. Ivan Jablonka, *L'histoire est une littérature contemporaine: manifeste pour les sciences sociales* (Paris: Seuil, 2004).
2. Michel Houellebecq, *Soumission* (Paris: Flammarion, January 7, 2015).
3. Camille de Toledo, *Visiter le Flurkistan: Ou les illusions de la littérature-monde* (Paris: Presses Universitaires de France, 2007).

May '68 and the Crisis of Philosophy of History

Georges Bataille, Furio Jesi, and Latin America

SERGIO VILLALOBOS-RUMINOTT

> In a revolt, a reality manifests itself that is also objective, collective, exhaustive, exclusive. Parties and unions are driven back by the revolt into the "before" and "after" of the revolt itself. Either they accept to temporally suspend their self-consciousness of their own value or they find themselves in open competition with the revolt. In the revolt, parties and unions do not exist anymore—only groups of contenders. The organizational structures of parties and unions can be used by those who prepare the revolt. But once the revolt begins they become simple instruments to guarantee the operative affirmation of values that are not the values of the party and the union but only the intrinsic value of the revolt.
>
> —Furio Jesi, *Spartakus*
> *The Symbology of the Revolt*

'68 and the Question of Radical Negativity

As Kristin Ross affirms in her timely book on May '68,[1] the debates about the consequences of these events are far from exhausted. The fact that we are still discussing them confirms precisely how alive those events are for us. But what is the nature of these events? In what sense do they, as a constellation, import a different understanding of historical time? Or, alternatively, up to what extent have the events related to May '68 precipitated a radical change not *in time* but *in our relation to* time and its representation? In what follows I will contend that, somehow, May '68 marked the exhaustion of the modern relationship between philosophy and politics and opened a process of disarticulation between theory and practice that almost all philosophical elaborations in the aftermath would have been trying to rearticulate or to *suture*. May '68, as the historical mark of a radical disarticulation, yields a break away from the modern philosophy of history and triggers an interrogation about the categorical order of modern thought.

It is from this interrogation of the link between ontology and politics that Bataille's questioning of Hegel's notion of negativity and Jesi's questioning of the temporality of the revolt become important, since these interrogations, among others, allow us to understand the general state of culture and politics of those years, not only in France but also in Latin America, without reducing it to a conventional narrative about historical progress, international politics, the Cold War context, or any other customary reference. This is also the reason why I have selected these two prominent names for my subtitle. In fact, Bataille's radical negativity is already a problematization of the archeo-teleological mechanism informing Hegel's philosophy of history as an autotelic evolving process, where the end is already set at the beginning. Whether we pay attention to the notion of expenditure or to the question of sacrifice, what matters for me here is Bataille's resistance to the Hegelian ruse of reason, that is to say, to the positivizing mechanism distinctive of Hegel's dialectics.[2]

In fact, "The Notion of Expenditure" and, up to a certain point, *Summa Atheologica* (of which the first part is *The Inner Experience*), are, in his own terms, an attempt to elaborate a critique of the "restricted economy" and the nonsovereign experience that supplement the metahistorical functionalization of negativity by attributing to it a final positive function in history.[3] For Bataille, sacrifice does not have a foundational character, as in the French tradition of partisan thought, it rather "performs" a deactivation of conventional politics in so far as politics should not be imagined as the result of an instrumental use of violence, in the form of sacrifice or expenditure—Bataille's unrestricted expenditure, his negativity *without reserve*, is not to be politically used as a means to something else. Here lies, certainly, his difference with Sorel and his "functionalist" version of the general strike, but here too the a-principial and amoral character of Bataille's elaborations becomes explicit, an a-principiality and an amorality that distinguishes him from the modern utilitarian and normative traditions of thought that most of the time are at the core of what we called partisan politics.[4] In fact, Bataille considers sacrifice in two different levels: first, as an exploration of the ontological status of experience, without subordinating it to any principle of reason, to any subjective account or recollection (as in the Hegelian *Erinnerung*); and it is this "sovereign inner experience" that differentiates him from Hegel and his "subsumption" of experience to the sovereignty of reason and its supplementary conception of the subject. Second, in so far as Bataille deepens his notion of "inner experience," the sacrifice becomes useless to ground any politics based on a teleological rationality, as in the secret kernel of normative (protestant) asceticism, as well as in the heroic self-sacrificial partisanship of the revolutionary left. In this sense, Bataille, as the anti-Durkheim and the anti-Weber, is also a radical detractor of official Marxism and its restitution of the "militants' sacrificial commitment" (in economy and politics). In other words, his critique of the "restricted economy" informing our political rationality is also a critique of the common ground to which capitalism and the so-called real socialism belong, in as much as they share the same onto-anthropological understanding of human beings as productive agents of history, but a history already subsumed to the form of an archeo-teleological disposition of temporality that characterizes Western metaphysics.[5]

Bataille's critique of Hegel's negativity is not, in other terms, a naive or hyper-Hegelian attempt to "overcome" it, it is rather a deactivation that "works" as an interrogation addressed to the dialectical mechanism that assigns to negativity a final positive function within the system (which already implies the subsumption of history to that system), a function that only the "sage" can properly perceive. Let me quote Derrida's clever formulation here.

> The Hegelian *Aufhebung* is produced entirely from within discourse, from within the system or the work of signification. A determination is negated and conserved in another determination which reveals the truth of the former. From infinite indetermination one passes to infinite determination, and this transition, produced by the anxiety of the infinite, continuously links meaning up to itself. The *Aufhebung* is included *within* the circle of absolute knowledge, never exceeds its closure, never suspends the totality of discourse, work, meaning, law, etc. Since it never dispels the veiling form of absolute knowledge, even by maintaining this form, the Hegelian *Aufhebung* in all its parts

belongs to what Bataille calls "the world of work," that is, the world of the prohibition not perceived as such, in its totality. [. . .] The Hegelian *Aufhebung* thus belongs to restricted economy, and is the form of the passage from one prohibition to another, the *circulation* of prohibitions, history as the truth of the prohibition.[6]

In this sense, Bataille is not just criticizing some aspect of Hegel's philosophy (like his particular reading of the conflict between the master and the slave, or his Pauline conception of universalism and history, to say, of universal history); on the contrary, he is deactivating the general dialectical operation, *suspending it*, in order to embrace the radical consequences of a negativity, of a sacrifice, that cannot be subsumed to any principle of reason, to any logic of the system.

The blind spot of Hegelianism, *around* which can be organized the representation of meaning, is the *point* at which destruction, suppression, death, and sacrifice constitute so irreversible an expenditure, so radical a negativity—here we would have to say an expenditure and a negativity *without reserve*—that they can no longer be determined as negativity in a process or a system.[7]

Of course, I am not suggesting that people involved in the '68 uprisings, in France and elsewhere, were fervent readers of the French writer; on the contrary, what I mean is that his problematization of Hegel's, and more directly, of Kojève's version of universal history, enables an interpretation of the May '68 riots and protests far from the conventional reading performed by sociologists and by the official Marxist intelligentsia for whom '68 is an event or a series of events that confirms the very logic of historical development. In other words, Bataille's emphasis on negativity without a synthetic recovery allows us to think the riots and revolts related to '68 beyond the demands for strategic rationality, tactical organization, and subjective command. If you like, the revolts of '68, as a series of unproductive expenditures, mark the exhaustion of politics as calculative thinking and positions the claims of the insurgents beyond the so-called fights for recognition.[8]

Yet, my whole argument here attempts to read these events as a radical disarticulation of ontology and politics, since the modern articulation of ontology and politics (the modern *ontopolitics*) would have achieved in Hegel its most radical and complex formulation. This is, certainly, what makes of

Hegel one of the most relevant thinkers of our time, since the ontopolitical articulation that characterizes our modern conception of history is already fully elaborated on his thought. In other words, I am not calling for a dismissal of Hegel, but for a meditative confrontation with his ontopolitical understanding of history, a confrontation that Bataille is not afraid of elaborating and whose consequences are far from being totally understood.

It is Bataille's notion of radical negativity that then interrupts and suspends the sequential logic of historical temporality understood already as an archeo-teleological disposition, something Benjamin anticipates allusively in his cryptic but interesting conception of capitalism as religion.[9] This suspension is what I am reading as a disarticulation of politics and ontology, choosing to dwell on it rather than attempting to produce a new suture, as in the general tendency of contemporary post-'68 thought, which in general could be regarded as a permanent reactivation of the ontological determination of history, despite the historical, fragmented, elastic, foaming, objective, and/or contingent condition of these new ontologies.

The Revolt as the Suspension of Historical Time

By the same token, I am referring to Furio Jesi's singular conception of the revolt. In fact, the recent attention the Italian thinker has received is due not only to his complex elaboration of the mythological machine (as emphasized by Giorgio Agamben[10]) or his disputes with the Hungarian philologist Károly Kerényi and other important mythologists of the twentieth century; it is also related to his singular understanding of the immanent character of the revolt, which is perfectly consistent with our main hypothesis. In fact, Jesi's reading of the Spartacist revolt in Germany (1919), could be taken as a model to read the singular character of many other revolts, including May '68, as he emphasizes how the nature of the revolt is the very suspension of historical time, that is to say, the suspension of the temporal structuration of history from a principle of reason that gives reason precisely to the revolt imposing on it a normative schema.[11] In fact, the revolt is without a reason and without a principle, or, as the mystical philosopher Meister Eckhart would have put it, the revolt is like a life that perseverates in living without a why.[12]

> I use the word *revolt* [says Jesi in his work on the Spartacist riots] to designate an insurrectional movement that differs from

revolution. The difference between revolt and revolution should not be sought in their respective aims; they can both have the same aim—to seize power. What principally distinguishes revolt from revolution is, instead, a different experience of time. If, following the ordinary meaning of the two words, a revolt is a sudden insurrectional explosion, which can be placed within a strategic horizon but which does not in itself imply a long-distance strategy, and revolution is a strategic complex of insurrectional movements, coordinated and oriented over the mid- to long term towards ultimate objectives, then we could say that revolt suspends historical time. It suddenly institutes a time in which everything that is done has a value in itself, independently of its consequences and or its relations with the transitory or perennial complex that constitutes history. Revolution would, instead, be wholly and deliberately immersed in historical time.[13]

The main consequence of Jesi's understanding of the revolt and its distance from the modern, conventional notion of revolution, including the official Marxist version of it, is that revolution seems to confirm, even if accelerating, the very logic of historical development, while the revolt is an interruption, not a confirmation, of this logic and cannot be subsumed to the notion of accident without subordinating it at the same time to the archeo-teleological disposition of temporality. Certainly, from the progressists' point of view, the revolt not only differs from the revolution and its systematic and strategic orientation toward a "revolutionary goal," it also might be conceived as a reaction in so far as it represents a deterrence and/or a delay from achieving this goal. Actually, it is not by chance that we tend to associate the revolt with irrational irruptions, nonstrategic riots, and liminal subjectivities, remainders of the past, not fully articulated as revolutionary subjects. The prestige of the revolt within revolutionary circles is no different from the prestige lumpen and other "fragmentary" subjectivities might have, something that Ranajit Guha, among many others, has emphasized.[14]

This is, indeed, the most complicated claim I am making here since the revolt in Jesi, as the radical negativity in Bataille, are not to be homologated to the conventional notion of "event" as a rupture that seems to interrupt the sequential representation of time, but only to confirm it as a preexistent disposition in which every single event, every single rupture, should be inscribed. The immanent character of the revolt implies a new relation to history and not only the inversion of the necessity/contingency binomial, neither of the causality/accident metaphysical pair, since the revolt is not an event that happens in history, but a radical dislocation of the historical time, that is to say, a dislocation of the historical form of time, the main consequence of which is the possibility of a *formless historicity* (not subsumed to its archeo-teleological disposition). In this sense, any attempt to rationalize the revolt, to give a positive or negative account of it, to subsume it to a principle of reason is already a reduction of its immanent character, a sort of "teleologization" that is also a "theologization" of the event. The revolt is neither singular nor plural; it implies a multiplicity that is inherent to it and not derivative, a sort of singular-plural character that avoids any account that might fetishize it. If the constellation of events associated with '68 are to be thought according to this logic, that is to say, according to this *phenomenology of the revolt*, then what defines them is their particular relation to temporality, one that is *immanent* and *imminent* at the same time, as this "imminence" is what radically secularizes the notion of miraculous event, turning it into a profane potentiality, a possibility of the real.

Obviously, there is much to be done in comparing and contrasting Bataille and Jesi's works, starting by the crucial role festivity plays in both, as expenditure and ritual, since both the French and the Italian thinkers were concerned with the mythological dimension of life rather than with the anthropological indirect knowledge of the myth. Nonetheless, in this text I want to refer to their particular understanding of the revolt as a negativity without reserve, to take Derrida's notion, and negativity as a revolt, not only different from the orthodox and modern notion of revolution, but also different from the contemporary notion of the event that still is snared by an exceptionalism that reinscribes its occurrence within an unproblematized understanding of historical time. In fact, the revolt, understood as the suspension of the historical time, can no longer be thought of as the negation nor as the realization of a particular plan, whether we are referring to the so-called plan of nature or about our historical destiny. The classical Marxist demand that denounces any given revolt for their hypothetical lack of strategic rationality does not matter any longer here, since the very logic of the revolt cannot be subsumed or capitalized by the principles of a strategic or transformational action. As in Rancière's *Proletarian Nights*[15] during the revolt, the actors do not perform a previously given role, they do not embody the sacrificial libretto of a story organized according to identities and positions already given and easy to be recognized; on the contrary, they emancipate themselves from those pregiven positions in an almost ritual act—an act that implies the dissolution of their preassigned identities in a collective and circumstantial convergence (in the city, at the streets) that might be thought of as oriented to an experience of *jouissance without guilt*.

In other words, as Walter Benjamin would have put it, the very suspension of the sacrificial structuration of historical time brought about by the revolt is already a suspension of guiltiness as a demanding mechanism that extorts the living in the name of an equivalential notion of restitution and justice.[16] In this sense, the revolt in Jesi, as the atheological inner experience in Bataille, interrupts the time of progress and modernization, but also the very principle of reason that informs that time, deactivating the hegemonic logic and the identitarian organization of the political, and disclosing, at the same time, how hegemonic and calculative political thinking are always fed by the time of the guilt, which is the time of philosophy of history.[17]

'68 as a Negative Event

So, let me come back now to Kristin Ross's seminal intervention. Her main goal is to confront the strategies of depolitization of May '68, as if these events were no more than a generational quarrel, a national crisis, an eventless event, or something that we can explain drawing on social psychology or even on a brief economic crisis. And, I would argue, she is quite right in opposing this depoliticizing strategy, but not because May '68 represents a new, unheard-of type of rebellion, in France and elsewhere, but because '68, far beyond France, became an exemplary historical sign that refers to a series of phenomena that cannot be explained only within a national frame. Ross, in fact, wants to oppose, in the field of political memory, both the ritualistic memorialization of '68 and its opposite but symmetrical dissolution, a dissolution somehow similar to the way some French historians have attempted to dissolve the eventful character of the French Revolution, whether referring to the lack of a strong command during that period (François Furet) or to the alteration of the internal and international markets (Ernest Labrousse). The afterlife of '68, for Ross, is indeed a political problem, in so far as what matters for her are the disputes about the signification of the revolt, the meaning of '68 for our contemporary debates. Hence, it is also today that the events of '68 demand a political stand against every strategy oriented to monumentalize them, but also, against any attempt oriented to ignore, silence, or forget them. She specifically confronts the normative or sociological reduction of May '68 to a version that seems to respond to a generational crisis, supplementary of the mass-media image of these events as a series of students' manifestations with no workers' involvement and without the brutal repression performed by the French police.

My goal nevertheless is to interrogate three different but interrelated aspects of the '68 revolts, aspects that are not only or primarily of a historical nature but concern our own historical occasion.

1. What do we mean by depolitization and repolitization of the '68 revolts?

2. In what sense does has '68 become a historical sign and what is the nature of this sign?

3. How to think about '68, expanding its customary referential frame toward the Latin American series of events occurring during those same years?

Regarding the first question, I would claim right away that we should not take for granted what repolitization means when we have characterized the events of '68 as an exhaustion of the classical overdetermination of politics by ontology, expressed as philosophy of history. If May '68 marks the exhaustion of the modern correspondence between theory and practice, an exhaustion that Reiner Schürmann relates with the ongoing problematization of humanism that would have started with Heidegger and achieved its fully articulated expression by the time of the so-called poststructuralist turn,[18] then this very exhaustion implies the impossibility of invoking a conventional notion of politics and politization as the response to the strategies of depolitization. In other words, what would be the nature of the "politics" that emerges from the very exhaustion of modern political thinking triggered by those events? Up to what point is the real problem here not just opposing depolitization with more politization, but opening instead a radical interrogation about the nature of politics in the context of an historical crisis, an interregnum, that cannot be subordinated any longer to the principle of reason or to the narrative mechanism proper to modern philosophy of history? In fact, what I am contending is precisely this: in so far as the events related to May '68 could be read as a radical disarticulation of politics and ontology, they also trigger the possibility of a radical thinking of the political that is not limited by the superfluous, even if honest, demand to rearticulate (*suture*) ontology and politics in order to rehabilitate a "new" radical stand. To think this disarticulation beyond the "suture" and the political anxiety related to it is the task that should concern us today.

As one can see, this question opens an important discussion, beyond Ross's intervention and recovery of what she called a politics that broaden the scope of classical representation; the question aims toward a discussion about the nature of our historical, globalized, and heterogeneous occasion and about the kind of politics we need in order to oppose, with certain efficacy, diverse forms of domination today. But not just that, since here lies another question, one aimed to the dichotomic structuration of the depolitization and repolitization circle, as if these alternatives were the only ones we can draw on. Of course, it is within this context that Jean-Luc Nancy and Philippe Lacoue Labarthe spoke about a retreat of the political, a retreat that was also a rethinking and a withdrawal, a form of *desistance* from conventional politics and political philosophy.[19] To ignore the events of '68 means not just depoliticizing them, but also repoliticizing them in a conventional, thoughtless way, without assuming how these events make '68 a particular kind of historical sign, one that far from the Kantian reading of the French Revolution, does not confirm, verify, or forecast human progress or humanity's moral disposition, since as a sign, '68 is the sign of a radical disarticulation between philosophy and history, a disarticulation that interrupts the very logic of modernity's grand politics.[20] In other words, to simply politicize '68 is to forget its singularity in the name of a political command that subsumes the immanence of the revolt to the strategic and calculative will to power.

Here then our second question, what is the nature of a historical sign as the one related to the events of May '68? If we agree in understanding these events as a historical sign, a series of events that is not to be reduced to the regularity of things, events that interrupt the continuum of historical temporality, then, what is the nature of this sign? As I have anticipated, I consider the Kantian reading of the French Revolution as a very illustrative counterexample, precisely because Kant was able to read the Revolution as a sign that confirms, verifies, and forecasts his own conception of historical progress and human's moral predisposition. However, that conception of history and human predisposition does not seem pertinent today, and not because it has been refuted or replaced by another one, but rather because the riots of '68 mark its radical exhaustion, its disarticulation. So, how are we to read this historical sign in a time of disarticulation when, situated in the interregnum, we cannot draw on the old understanding of politics and history, progress and meaning? As one can see here, the line that goes from Benjamin to Bataille and Jesi seems relevant again: If the revolt is a historical sign, it is a negative one that discloses history as dislocated from the sovereign principle that commands it. As a sign, it discloses history as the place in which sovereign exceptionality and the exception from sovereignty are always (nonexceptionally) at work. Certainly, Benjamin's "real state of emergency" is exceptionless, in so far as it is the opposite of the exceptionalist conception of history as a continuum to be interrupted by an event that still happens within its sequential disposition.[21] In other words, Benjamin's notion of the "real state of emergency" implies a profane conception of history that distinguishes it from the theological notion of miracle, in as much as Bataille's notion of negativity resists radically any attempt to subsume it to the system, and as much as Jesi's notion of the revolt prevents any calculative, strategic, principial, political utilization.

Let me put it another way, among the series of events related to '68, in France and elsewhere, we should mention not only the riots of May, but also the general student mobilization in other European countries; the student movements in Latin America that led to the most important university reforms in those years; the student and political movements in America; and so on. But we should also consider Vietnam, the Israeli-Palestine Six Days War (the Intifada of 1967), and the end of the dollar-gold convertibility as part of Nixon shock policies that led to the end of the Bretton Wood's system, producing a general deregulation of the economy that triggered, eventually, the ongoing neoliberal globalization. So, '68 as a negative event or series of events does not say anything about a new political foundation, a new revolutionary time, because it also signals to the deregulation of classical sovereignty, and its mutation in what today we might call the sovereignty of capital. Then, why do the May '68 events matter if, as we know, those events also generated a sort of metamorphosis of sovereignty and power? They matter because as events they disclosed the policing role of sovereignty, at the political and at the philosophical levels, producing a suspension of the commanding principle of reason and power that organizes the narratives about this historical constellation, granting to it a form (spatial and temporal) that inscribes it within the archeo-teleological (sacrificial) structuration of time. In this sense, the constellation of events related to May '68 needs to be rethought beyond the distinctive self-referentiality characteristic of many approaches that inscribe it within the logic of the archive and the monument, pointing instead toward its worldly consequences.

The Mexican '68

In fact, the '68 constellation, understood not as a Kantian sign of human progress but as a dislocation or disarticulation, discloses too the new strategies of control and domination that are associated with the intensification of biopolitical mechanisms of control and vigilance in its aftermath. Here, I would like to introduce my third and final argument by referring to the Mexican '68, which is a paradigmatic case that shows both sides of this disarticulation: the undecidability of the event and the intensification of control and domination that followed it.

The Mexican '68 took place from early May to the bloody night of October 2nd, and culminated with the execution of hundreds of students by the Mexican army, days before the Olympic Games in Mexico City. Besides its inner complexity, this constellation of events has been reduced to a single incident, mostly defined by the killing of the students in *La plaza de Tlatelolco*. As such, this unfortunate and isolated "excess" has become a referential point both for academic discourses and for political narratives interested in consecrating it as a sacrificial turning point in Mexican history. Even if we do not have time to analyze the whole series of discourses produced around these events, I will mention here a few different scholarly approaches that contribute to expanding and resituating the conventional narrative about the Mexican '68.

First, Sam Steinberg's *Photopoetics at Tlatelolco*[22] seems crucial as it attempts a demonumentalization of '68 that has become a mythical and foundational moment for the sacrificial logic of contemporary Mexican politics. In fact, his study is concerned not only with the repression of the students and the rationality of the State justifying that repression, but also with the process of shaping and limiting the "archive" and the historical narratives about these incidents. Steinberg, in other words, interrogates the relationship between archive and event, showing their cobelonging to a particular, salvific and sacrificial conception of history. His interrogation of the logic of monumentalization, which feeds and organizes official discourses and commemorations, shows how the Mexican '68 has been systematically neutralized (preempted) not only by the use of brutal force, but by the configuration of what Guha called a "prose of counterinsurgency."[23] Thanks to this, Steinberg reopens in a clever way the problematic dimension of this constellation and shows how we still dwell in the same disjointed temporality, a dislocation that the conventional academic discourses and the political narratives of monumentalization have been trying to suture and normalize from the beginning.

Steinberg's book is important because it not only reopens the question about how '68 should be read, punctuating by that gesture history in a different way, but also because in doing so it discloses the inner complicity between the violence that characterized the original contention of the revolt and the violence that limits its memory and shapes the visual, literary, and cultural discourses about these events until today.

Another important and recent intervention is Susana Draper's *1968 Mexico: Constellations of Freedom and Democracy*.[24] Similar to Steinberg's, her approach not only situates the Mexican '68 in the cultural, philosophical, and political global context, but also questions the reductionist logic that feeds official accounts of it. Draper complicates the masculine and salvific narrative about the Mexican 1968 beyond the providential version that assigns almost exclusive leadership to male students and dismisses the ebullient cultural and political background of these events, focusing mostly on the bloody night of October 2nd. Against the grain of this exceptional narrative, her interrogation of cultural practices, women's participation, and diverse theoretical elaborations of that period reopen a necessary discussion not only about the limits of historical archives and narratives but also about the temporality of this constellation. The word *constellation* as a key word in the book could not be more pertinent, beyond its Benjaminian resonance, as it implies a decentering effect that disarticulates the unilateral logic feeding conventional accounts and their complementary monocausality.

Particularly telling in this regard is the chapter 3 of her book titled "Where are the Women of '68? Fernanda Navarro and the Materialism of Uncomfortable Encounters."[25] Far from a simple (liberal) claim of recognition and fair representation of women in the events of Mexico '68, Draper, by way of an intelligent use of Navarro's work and Althusser's aleatory materialism, questions the patriarchal inclination of official and nonofficial versions of these events as another evidence of their adscription to the exceptionalist logic. If this constellation expresses a dislocation regarding official discourses, it also expresses a deidentification process regarding the performative role State narratives have had in shaping the idea of a good citizen, complicating the heteronormative and patriarchal representation of political subjects. As we said regarding Jesi's notion of the revolt, the revolt not only differs from the exceptional logic of the miraculous event, pluralizing this event in an immanent and imminent relation to history, but also dislocates the subject of the political by opening a process of deidentification and desubjectification the main consequence of which, then and now, is unveiling the necessity of a radical interrogation of patriarchalism and its manifold reproduction in the constitution of archives, narratives, and the sacrificial version of history.

Draper's contributions, in other words, are not to be read just as a plea to widen the archive and its representation; on the contrary, her intervention is timely and necessary in so far as the deidentification process proper to the revolt questions not only the exceptional character of the Mexican '68's official narratives, but the reproduction of a heteronormative and male-focused version whose consequences are important not only in the past but today. After all, the revolt also discloses the inherent violence of the process of sexuation that characterizes any form of domination (beyond gender domination) and its "reproductive" narratives.

Finally, my third reference is the crucial reading of these historical events elaborated by Gareth Williams in chapter 5 of his 2011 book titled *The Mexican Exception: Sovereignty, Police, and Democracy*.[26] Williams, indeed, develops an alternative genealogy of Mexico '68 that incorporates the sovereign logic of the revolutionary State apparatus as a crucial aspect of these historical events. His reading of '68, on the other hand, is fed by the 1971 inaugural account written by Luis González de Alba and titled *Los días y los años*.[27] Certainly, González de Alba's testimonial account could be considered as a *phenomenology of the revolt*, far away from what Guha termed as the prose of the counterinsurgency. By the same token, in his book, Williams, following the skeletal narrative presented by González de Alba, relates the student protests of July to October of '68 with the pending situation of the railroad political prisoners of the late 1950s, whose repression and incarceration would have marked a radical turn within the Mexican revolutionary party-State policy. Let us remember that by February 25, 1959, the railroad workers strike started, triggering in the short time a national movement that claimed better conditions of labor for the workers. This movement almost inaugurated the new administration of Adolfo López Mateos as the entering president of Mexico and who, instead of opening a negotiation process, responded with systematic violence, murder and imprisonment of the movement's leaders. The continuity between this national strike and the '68 events become apparent when the '59 strike is understood as one of the first and most important social mobilization against the so-called revolutionary government.[28]

So, the conditions for these protests are not to be found only in the students' agenda, as they also come from a social memory of resistance against the State repression and expropriation of the revolution's social meaning. The revolt, even if immanent, never takes place in an empty social space; rather, it happens as an explosion of many accumulated energies and social fights that decenter the disciplining (counterinsurgent) character of official discourses.

Williams, at the same time, shows us how the brutal repression of these protests that led to the infamous assassination of hundreds of students in the Plaza de Tlatelolco, makes of the Mexican '68 not only a negative sign of history—the history of the Mexican revolution and its expropriation by the Institutional Revolutionary Party (PRI), the perfect party-State system that commanded the country through the twentieth century—but also closed the window opened a few months before October by the student protests, since those protests actually questioned not only the repressive character of the government and its use of the Granaderos army to control the civil population, but were actually questioning the whole State apparatus of control and police repression that defines the sovereign relation the State privileged with the civil population since the beginning of the century. Williams in fact tells us that the government of Gustavo Díaz Ordaz, the president and final person responsible for the "Night of Tlatelolco," as the former, prerevolutionary government of Porfirio Díaz, were regimes of absolute control and total detachment from society. Despite this sovereign power and control, nonetheless, the revolts of the Mexican '68 disclosed the exhaustion of the Revolution, the most important political and cultural "discursive device" supporting the social contract that perpetuated the PRI at the presidential Office. Therefore, the brutal repression of these revolts marked a turning point in the configuration of a State apparatus and its policies of control and administration, disclosing the exhaustion of the revolutionary official rhetoric while opening a new logic related to the brutal implementation of neoliberal control and precarization of life. As we see here, the '68 events in Mexico appear as a disarticulating moment preceded by the historical articulation of the revolutionary agenda and the State-party during the aftermath of the Mexican Revolution and continued by the neoliberal and repressive orientation of the Mexican State from the 1970s through today.

Williams's reading of the '68 revolts makes two things absolutely clear. first, the nature of these events generated a radical suspension of the sovereign principle informing conventional politics, and, as such, the revolts suspended sovereignty and its force, opening the social to the possibility of something other than political relation, to a "passive decision" that always differs from the decisionism of politics and its multiple strategies of depolitization and repolitization. But second, Williams also shows the Mexican '68 as a disclosing moment (a confrontation with the Real), in which the fetish of the Revolution is put in question, radically. And this is something the conventional progressist intelligentsia is not willing to accept, as the revolution keeps feeding the fantasies of many people who do not understand the immanent and imminent logic of the revolts: the general suspension of any calculative, strategic thinking, as a temporary enactment of radical democracy.

I hope with these short references I have made the case for the relevance of expanding '68's self-referentiality; about the need to question our conventional notion of historical events; and about the disarticulation triggered by this constellation; a disarticulation in which we are still situated, and which demands from us something other than the classical restitution of the political. *The phenomenology of the revolt* not only interrupts *the prose of the counterinsurgency* but also opens the possibility of a *formless historicity*, one that is not to be reduced to the archeo-teleological disposition of time according to a sacrificial, subjective, and guilt-ridden conception of history and its supplementary hegemonic and calculative logic. In as much as this remains a possibility, it is the possibility of a jouissance without guilt from which we only have the image that comes to us not from the myth but from the festivity of the revolt.

One last thing seems pertinent here. The actuality of the '68, which is what brings us together, is not to be reduced neither to a conventional historiographical narrative nor to a politicizing celebration, since what the '68 inaugurates for us, in a rather decisive way, is the need to formulate another understanding of the political, an infrapolitics liberated from the sacrificial structuration of historical temporality. It is this possibility what links, indeed, the historicity of the '68 revolts and the social revolts that have disrupted Latin America and the world in recent years.

Notes

1. Kristin Ross, *May '68 and Its Afterlives* (Chicago, IL: University of Chicago Press, 2002).

2. Bataille's confrontation with Hegel started already in the 1930. See, for example, Georges Bataille, "The Critique of the Foundations of the Hegelian Dialectic," and "The Notion of Expenditure," in *Vision of Excess. Selected Writings, 1927–1939*, trans. and ed. Allan Stoekl (Minneapolis: University of Minnesota Press, 1985), 105–15 and 117–29. These early texts are from 1932 and 1933,

respectively. One should also keep in mind the extent to which Bataille's reaction to Hegel's dialectic is also a reaction to Kojève's version of it. See also his "Hegel, Death and Sacrifice," *Yale French Studies* 78 On Bataille (1990): 9–28. This is a piece originally published in 1955.

3. Georges Bataille, *Inner Experience*, trans. Leslie Anne Boldt (Albany: State University of New York Press, 1988). Originally written in 1943.

4. For a general elaboration on the French sacrificial tradition of political thought see Jesse Goldhammer, *The Headless Republic: Sacrificial Violence in Modern French Thought* (Ithaca, NY: Cornell University Press, 2005).

5. In order to understand the general scope of Bataille's project, one should pay attention to his three volume *La Part maudite*, published in English in two: Georges Bataille *The Accursed Share*, vol. I, trans. Robert Hurley (New York: Zone Books, 1991), and *The Accursed Share*, vols. II and III, trans. Robert Hurley (New York; Zone Books, 1992).

6. Jacques Derrida, "From Restricted to General Economy: A Hegelianism without Reserve," in *Writing and Difference*, trans. Alan Bass (Chicago, IL: University of Chicago, 1978), 275.

7. Derrida, "From Restricted to General Economy," 259.

8. What I mean by "fights beyond recognition" is a "politics" that differs from the ontological determination of history that, starting with Hegel, finds in Kojève a symptomatic expression. Let us recall here how for Kojève the end of the Second World War was not only the end of history (its anticipated fulfillment), but also the end of politics in so far as the social struggles that mobilized history in the past appear now reduced to a "fight for symbolic recognition," dissolving by this postulation the master-slave dialectic into the diplomatic and mercantile exchange between Europe and its former North-African colonies. See Alexandre Kojève, "Colonialism from a European Perspective," *Interpretation* 29, no. 1 (Fall 2001): 115–30. The understanding of historical quarrels beyond the logic of recognition is something that could also be read in Fanon's interventions, something we unfortunately cannot elaborate properly here but something that would complicate, for sure, the reading of the Martinican as a partisan promoter of violence.

9. Walter Benjamin, "Capitalism as Religion," in *Selected Writings*, vol. 1, *1913–1926* (Cambridge, MA: Harvard University Press, 1997), 288–91.

10. "Acerca de la imposibilidad de decir yo. Paradigmas epistemológicos y paradigmas poéticos en Furio Jesi," in Agamben, Giorgio. *La potencia del pensamiento* (Buenos Aires, Argentina: Adriana Hidalgo Editora, 2007), 137–54.

11. Furio Jesi, *Spartakus: The Symbology of the Revolt*.

12. Reiner Schürmann, *Wondering Joy: Meister Eckhart's Mystical Philosophy* (Great Barrington, MA: Lindisfarne Books, 2001).

13. Jesi, *Spartakus*, 46.

14. Ranajit Guha, *Elementary Aspects of Peasant Insurgency in Colonial India* (Durham, NC: Duke University Press, 1999).

15. Jacques Rancière, *Proletarian Nights: The Workers' Dream in Nineteenth-Century France*, trans. John Drury (New York: Verso, 2012).

16. Walter Benjamin, "Capitalism as Religion," and "Critique of Violence," in *Selected Writings, Volume 1, 1913–1926* (Cambridge, MA: Harvard University Press, 1997), 288–91 and 236–52.

17. Werner Hamacher, "Guilt History: Benjamin's Sketch 'Capitalism as Religion,'" *Diacritics* 32, no. 3/4, Ethics (Autumn–Winter, 2002): 81–106.

18. Reiner Schürmann, *Heidegger on Being and Acting: From Principles to Anarchy* (Bloomington: Indiana University Press, 1987). Of course, Schürmann was aware of the American origin of the notion "poststructuralism."

19. Jean-Luc Nancy and Philippe Lacoue-Labarthe, *Retreating the Political*, trans. and ed. Simon Sparks (London: Routledge, 1997).

20. See the series of texts collected in Immanuel Kant, *Political Writings*, ed. Hans Reiss and trans. H. B. Nisbet (New York; Cambridge University Press, 1991). See also the seminal essay of Michel Foucault, "What Is Enlightenment?" in *The Foucault Reader*, ed. Paul Rainbow (New York: Pantheon Books, 1984), 32–50.

21. In the Fragment VIII of his "On the Concept of History," Benjamin says: "The tradition of the oppressed teaches us that the 'state of emergency' in which we live is not the exception but the rule. We must attain to a conception of history that accords with this insight. Then we will clearly see that it is our task to bring about a real state of emergency, and this will improve our position in the struggle against fascism," 392. Walter Benjamin, "On the Concept of History," *Selected Writings, Volume IV, 1938–1940* (Cambridge, MA: Harvard University Press, 2003), 389–400. Contrary to the common, messianic, understanding of this, the real state of emergency is exceptionless in so far as it refers to a profane conception of history and not to a theological notion of miraculous event (as in Schmitt's exceptionalism).

22. Samuel Steinberg, *Photopoetics at Tlatelolco: Afterimages of Mexico, 1968* (Austin: University of Texas Press, 2016).

23. Guha, *Elementary Aspects*.

24. Susana Draper, *1968 Mexico: Constellations of Freedom and Democracy* (Durham, NC: Duke University Press, 2018).

25. Draper, *1968 Mexico*, 127–55.

26. Gareth Williams, *The Mexican Exception: Sovereignty, Police, and Democracy* (New York: Palgrave Macmillan, 2011). Williams, in the chapter titled "'Under the Paving Stones, the Beach!': Chance, Passive Decision, Democracy, July–November 1968," 117–52, develops one of the most radical approaches to the events of '68, never falling prey to the exceptional narratives and complicating historically the genealogy of these events bringing to the discussion the whole logic of the revolutionary State apparatus and the logic of sovereignty feeding it through the twentieth century.

27. Written in prison during 1971, this testimonial account still represents an indispensable document that portrays the series of incidents in a way that is not so much affected by the normative logic of the official narratives that proliferate

later. Luis González de Alba, *Los días y los años* (Ciudad de México: Ediciones Cal y Arena, 2018).

28. See Fernando del Paso, *José Trigo* (México: Siglo XXI, 2002), the novel that, originally published in 1966, presents a sort of continuity between the Mexican Revolution, the Cristeros war, and the series of events related to the 1959 workers' strike.

Afterword

Ends of Thinking in the Computational Age

EWA PLONOWSKA ZIAREK

"To Think What We Are Doing . . ."

This volume presents a retrospective rethinking of the cross-Atlantic travels of French Theory and philosophy between Europe, US, and, to a lesser extent, Latin America. Certainly, these travels have not been one-way journeys, but rather back-and-forth unpredictable trajectories of displacement, interrogation, and often unexpected inventions of new possibilities of thinking. Perhaps we can call these cross-Atlantic engagements acts of intellectual hospitality, which, as Julia Kristeva suggests, entails an intellectual exercise of freedom and a performance of interpretive grafting: "Isn't the whole idea of a 'transplant' or 'graft' meant to generate unexpected consequences, the very opposite of cloning?"[1] Although these topics are not the main areas of analysis in this collection, consider, for example, rich questions that arose from these sometimes hospitable, sometimes agonistic encounters in feminisms, critical race studies, queer and gender theory, decolonial and postcolonial studies, political theory, to name just a few new areas that emerged in the aftermath of May 1968.

For me, the most important question this volume raises is how to respond intellectually, philosophically, and artistically to the transformative events of the past, in particular, to the occurrences of intellectual and political struggles. Indeed, divergent essays gathered together as one volume represents a collective, though by no means unified, attempt to think through the political, artistic, and theoretical ramifications of the political events of 1968 in France, the US, Mexico, and elsewhere. Which of these events are regarded as exemplary and which are marginalized, and for what reasons? This is neither an exercise in what Badiou calls "fidelity to the event," nor an attempt to create a unified genealogy for intellectual tradition by finding a common origin, as Jane M. Gaines rightly points out in her essay in this volume. On the contrary, the task of thinking is to respond to the enduring performative force of the past event anew, and in so doing, to reinvent and renew its significance.[2] In this reversed perspective, rather than finding a common origin in the event, critical and artistic responses enable its survival as the futural possibility of new beginnings, to refer to Hannah Arendt's famous formulation of a new beginning as a condition of relational freedom. According to Arendt's reflection on the decline of revolutionary traditions in the West, legacies of events as new beginnings are fragile and depend on ongoing critical remembrance and interrogation. As she writes in *On Revolution*,

> experiences and even the stories which grow out of what men do and endure, of happenings and events, sink back into the futility inherent in the living world . . . unless they are talked about over and over again. What saves the affairs of mortal men from their inherent futility is nothing but this incessant talk about them, which in turn remains futile unless certain concepts, certain guideposts for future remembrance, and even for sheer reference, arise out of it.[3]

This is precisely one of the tasks of this collection: to continue conversations, remembrance, and thinking about the events of 1968 as revolutionary events of freedom, as occurrences that still have performative power to inspire us to act, create, and think in the present. I believe that the tenor of this volume as a whole resonates with Arendt's warning that "failure to remember and, with it, failure to understand" the events of the past results not only in the loss of public freedom but also in the abandonment of the fundamental task of thinking and interpretation, which Arendt defines as "the comprehensive understanding of reality and coming to terms with it."[4] In the context of Arendt's work, thinking in the broadest sense of the word entails not only "inheritance" of political, aesthetic, and intellectual struggles for freedom, but also critical confrontation with unprecedented dangers: for

Arendt, the terrifying novum of totalitarianisms; in our times, genocides, ever new forms of racisms, imperialism, biopolitics, and technological dominations. As we shall see, one of these tasks of thinking in the broad spectrum of interpretative humanities and sciences entails an interdisciplinary reflection on the unforeseeable consequences of the computational turn.

Although this collection does not engage with Arendt, it nonetheless shares an Arendtian insight that understanding of reality does not entail an "adaptation" to the status quo. A term originating in evolutionary biology, adaptation to the environmental changes, or epigenesis, is frequently applied to explain social and psychological shifts, ranging from politics and new media to thought itself. For instance, by drawing on evolutionary epigenesis, Katherine Hayles describes the changes in thought produced by new technologies precisely in terms of cognitive adaptation to the new technological environment and digital media—the process she calls technogenesis.[5] By contrast, this collection collectively argues that coming to terms with the altered conditions of our existence, in particular with the unprecedented new forms of power, entails ongoing interrogations: putting into question ourselves, our modes of inheriting dominant and suppressed histories, our relations to others, and our diverse practices, including artistic, political, and intellectual activities. Indeed, as Arendt claims in the "Prologue" to her book, *The Human Condition*, this task of thinking is at once extremely demanding and "very simple," since it entails "nothing more than to think about what we are doing" from the perspective of "our newest experiences and our most recent fears."[6]

Historical remembrance, critical interrogations of what we are doing, cultivation of imagination, and envisioning of alternative ways of being in the world constitute some of the central tasks of culture and interpretative humanities. However, these modes of intellectual and imaginative engagements with the world, politics, and culture are more and more frequently considered, in the West and increasingly across the globe, as unprofitable and unmarketable. As funds for humanities in public higher education are drastically cut, are we not confronted today with the institutionalized attempts to suppress historical remembrance and interpretation, or to abandon critical thought altogether, in order to facilitate adaptation to the neoliberal universities? In place of critical thinking, the expanding administrative class in the institutions of higher learning and education more generally demands "adaptation" to new learning environments. One of the main methods of such institutional adaptation is the imposition of the ever more invasive "data regimes" or what Jerry Muller calls "the tyranny of metrics,"[7] which requires more and more data, definitions of "successful" quantitate outcomes, and the assessments of their success in the form of new data. Indeed, as Hayles points out, data, computation, and digital technologies more generally are crucial for administrators because they enable them to "see how present trends point to future possibilities, how outcomes will be judged . . . They clearly understand that digital technologies, in broad view, imply transformation not only of the humanities but of the entire educational system."[8]

This replacement of thinking by adaption to the data about present and predictable future trends is evident in the most mundane details of our professional lives. For example, we are told to report our professional, intellectual, and pedagogical activities—that is, reflective accounts of what we are doing as scholars and teachers—in quantitative rather than in qualitative or "narrative" terms so that our "outputs" can be standardized into numerical data applicable to all disciplines across the university. We are witnessing substitution or at least supplementation of intellectual judgments by metrics, such as citation indexes. This trend is so widely spread that the 2020 MLA convention program felt the need to offer a special session on how academic analytics works and what its effects are. We are told to tailor (or eliminate, as the case might be) graduate and undergraduate programs, research and teaching, according to the emerging market trends diagnosed by the algorithmically processed data. In these Kafkaesque "reports to the academy" there is neither room nor time to reflect on the stakes of education in democratic cultures, since the "optimization of performance" on the basis of data is the new benchmark of neoliberal university.

I propose to regard these transformations of interpretative humanities and academic institutions at large, so well documented by the slew of publications on the endangered "future of the humanities," as the manifestations of the increasingly global algorithmic condition of effective computationalism, or what other scholars have called "algorithmic culture,"[9] "the black box society,"[10] "metadata society," and cultural logic of computationalism.[11] In these conditions, the dominant end of thinking, understood in the double sense of a goal and termination, consists in the increasing "datafication," or transformation[12] of diverse human activities into calculable data.[13] As Daniela Aghostino succinctly puts it, "Datafication has been broadly defined as the process through which human activities are converted to data which can then be mobilized for different purposes."[14] Inspired by Foucault, David Golumbia similarly argues that "thinking" according to the cultural logic of computationalism either converts diverse human and nonhuman activities into algorithmically processed data or disregards them altogether if they fail to conform to algorithmic rules of calculation. Different from computer sciences, computationalism is driven by the Leibnizean premise "that mathematical calculation could be made to stand for propositions that are themselves not mathematical."[15] Paradoxically, the tasks of interpretation, engagement in the debate, and the Arendtian call for thinking about what we are doing are nowhere more urgent than in a culture that aims for their replacement by the increasingly automated algorithmic processing of Big Data. So the question we might what to address to this collection as a whole, or at least I would like to pose it in this "Afterword," is how traditions of critical theory, shaped by transatlantic movements between Europe and the Americas, can help us to sustain thinking about what we are doing in the context of this unprecedented computational turn.

The Computational Ends of Event Processing

As we have seen, what animates thinking in this book is aesthetic, philosophical, and political responses to the events of May '68. To better understand some of the differences between interpretative humanities and algorithmic processing of data, let us consider for a moment how the problem of events is formulated and solved in the context of ubiquitous computationalism. Toward that purpose, I would like to refer for a moment to the exemplary case of Complex Event Processing, or CEP. Enabling tracking and processing of high volumes of events in real time, CEP refers to computational tools, including a modeling and computer languages (for example, Rapide), developed for the first time by computer scientists at Stanford between 1989 and 1995 under the direction of David Lukham. As Lukham points out in his retrospective article of 2019, these computational technologies and analytic principles are now widely used in such domains as air traffic control, military command and control systems, radar tracking, algorithmic trading on electronic markets, as well as "automated robotic manufacturing systems." In fact, CEP can be deployed by any organization interested in monitoring events in real time, for example, tracking their volume, synchronization or nonsynchronization, patterns, causality, conformity and nonconformity with the model required by its system. Working on clouds of events, which are already partially preprocessed by IT systems, CEP can not only count the volume of the events as they arrive, but also detect "aberrant" events that "are not related as they should be," establish and monitor event causality even when temporal sequence of arriving events is out of order, for instance, when causes arrive before their results. CEP can also create new events or "detect absent events."[16]

Of course, CEP industrial applications constitute a crucial breakthrough in automated production and in those technological domains, such as air control, traffic systems, or medical devices, where precision and accurate information in real time is of paramount importance. However, as we have seen in Lukham's article, the application of CEP is far wider as it includes increasingly automated military/industrial/financial systems, social media, as well as new "smart" devices tracking and providing feedback on the biodata of their users, such as heart rate, brain activity, posture, or even orgasms. Lukham, for example, suggests that a relatively simple algorithmic application to real event processing can measure the volume of tweets on a given subject matter in a given time frame. CEP, or at least its ontological assumptions about standardization and calculability of events, can easily become a new social norm, tracking increasingly wider ranges of datafied human activities at the very moment of their occurrence.

Consider the following quotation from the 2016 collaborative article providing a retrospective overview of the scholarship about the implementation of Complex Event Processing working in tandem with predictive analytics. Written by the researchers from Germany and Brazil on the computational tools invented in the US, and thus evidencing yet another mode of trans-Atlantic scientific exchanges, this article might give us a glimpse into an exemplary approach to the problem of event and the task of research in algorithmic culture.

> As ever new sensor solutions are invading people's everyday lives and business processes, the use of the signals and events provided by the devices poses a challenge . . . of handling the large amount of data. With the help of complex event processing and predictive techniques, added value can be created. While complex event processing is able to process the multitude of signals coming from the sensors in a continuous manner, predictive analytics addresses the likelihood of a certain future state or behavior by detecting patterns from the signal database and predicting the future according to the detection.[17]

The problem for research is neither the meaning of an event nor "the invasion of people's everyday lives" by new forms of "smart" surveillance. Rather the challenge for thought is the continuous, "effective and efficient" processing of the unprecedented *magnitude* of registered events in real time—that is, "in the course of the events happening"—by computational means. The governing assumption here is that the events extracted by sensors "invading" people's lives are interdependent, and that their correlations form a coherent pattern. By tracking events already partially processed by IT, the automated Complex Event Processing aims for the standardization and monitoring of events. The calculation of patterns emerging from these standardized events, in turn, allows CEP to work in tandem with predictive analytics in order to monitor future events: their increased or decreased volume, possible disorders, or nonoccurrence of desirable events. As other scholars point out, these applications of predictive analytics are tantamount to the engineering not only of the past events (histories) but of future itself: "After predicting the future at first, this future is than carefully shaped."[18] Consequently, in the industrial/military/financial systems, Big Data is both a challenge and a new "treasure" and not only because it saves costs and increase profits.[19] What is far more at stake is the large-scale coordination of datafied human behavior with standardized events.

Between Thinking and Algorithmic Calculations: Early Critiques of Computationalism in Poststructuralist Theories and Computer Sciences

In the United States, the breakthrough in Computational Event Processing technologies occurs in computer sciences at the height of the poststructuralist turn in the humanities, that is, in the 1980s and '90s. And yet, despite this historical "correlation," there was very little critical reflection on the computational turn in poststructuralist theories at that time. It could be argued that this is still the case in the humanities today with the exception of the emergence of the specialized domains of scholarship, such as Digital Humanities, Science and Technology Studies, new media studies, or critical code studies, to name just a few. Provoked by the disclosures of the nefarious political activities of Cambridge Analytica, discriminatory uses of predictive policing, or the controversial use of predictive analytics in the judiciary, not to mention the invasions of privacy by social media, public debates are still initiated primarily by investigative journalism rather than humanities. It is as if the computational turn has not been a part of the critical reflection on what we are doing, to refer to Arendt's formulation again. And when it is addressed, the temptation is to interpret algorithmic culture by updating familiar terms, such as calculative thinking (Heidegger, Golumbia), or instrumental rationality (Adorno), general equivalence (Nancy), or technologically intensified biopolitical surveillance.

Although the computational turn has not been a major topic in poststructuralist or postmodernist theories (other than occasional references to cybernetics), partially because its ubiquity emerges post-9/11,[20] nonetheless there are few notable exceptions, such as Deleuze's frequently cited essay, "Societies of Control."[21] Thus, if we are going to enlist theoretical resources in the humanities to reflect on the increasingly global consequences of computationalism, we might begin with these early critiques, which do not target computer programming per se, but rather contest their cultural and sociopolitical deployment either as the paradigm of scientific rationality or as a possible model of justice.

Significantly, one of the first critical voices in this regard comes in fact from computer science itself, namely, from Joseph Weizenbaum's 1976 *Computer Science and Human Reason: From Judgment to Calculation*.[22] A computer scientist and the inventor of the computer interactive program, ELIZA, which could converse in English with a human partner, Weizenbaum gave ELIZA a script allowing the program to play the role of a Rogerian psychotherapist. To his dismay, practicing psychiatrists took seriously the possibility that the computer program could "grow into a nearly completely automatic form of psychotherapy."[23] Often described as a lonely wolf in his field, Weizenbaum critically responds to this desire to automate and formalize more and more spheres of human life and powerfully argues against the unexamined equation of rationality with logicality: "belief in the rationality-logicality equation has corroded the prophetic power of language itself. We can count, but we are rapidly forgetting how to say what is worth counting and why."[24] Counting without understanding—such is Weizenbaum's trenchant diagnosis of the confusion of scientific thinking and intellectual judgment with computationalism. Inspired partially by Arendt,[25] he enlists the help of humanities—in which he all too modestly considers himself to be "poorly" educated—in order to contest this unwarranted equation of rationality with automatic computation.

Weizenbaum's critique of the reduction of scientific rationality to logicality alone precedes David Berlinski's argument that algorithmic calculation also replaces even logical judgment. In his 2000 *The Advent of the Algorithm*, Berlinski traces an intellectual history of mathematical logic leading to the invention of the automated procedure of effective computation, which we call algorithm.[26] Algorithm is a well-defined, automated, finite computational technique consisting of discreet number of steps leading to specific results. Once completed, it does not require further thinking. According to its textbook definition, algorithm is "a sequence of computational steps that transform the input into the output."[27] According to Berlinski, the simultaneous invention of algorithm in the '30s by Gödel, Turing, and Church completes the long quest of mathematical logic aiming to transform Aristotle's syllogisms into automated procedure, replacing logical inference.[28] In Aristotle's syllogism, inference was still a logical judgment. By contrast, the speed and efficiency of algorithmic calculability stems from the fact that algorithms do not think (though their inventors do).

Yet, what happens if the algorithmic model of computation is transferred from quantitative sciences and engineering to social practices, such as jurisprudence, where judgment and its contestations are of paramount importance? This is precisely the question raised by Alan Wolfe's essay, "Algorithmic Justice," included in the famous 1992 collection, *Deconstruction and the Possibility of Justice*.[29] Interrogating complex exchanges between deconstruction and legal studies, this collection contains, among other essays, Derrida's "Force of Law: The Mystical Foundations of Authority." A sociologist and political scientist, Wolfe worries that we are heading toward algorithmic formulations of justice, which dispense with divergent interpretations, reformulations, and contestations of the law. In place of such critical reflection and the creation of new rules, we are left with rule following: "Algorithms are rules designed to be followed with as little interpretive variations as possible . . . Yet if humans are following instructions algorithmically, then they will have no interpretive capacities. . . . and, as a result, will be subject to a faith of following rules without any input into how those rules are formulated and applied."[30] Like Weizenbaum before him, Wolfe stages a political, intellectual, and ethical conflict between algorithmic and interpretive cultures, between standardization and critical reflection on what we are doing. Implicitly, his essay also critiques the demands of social adaptation replacing critical and creative participation in public sphere.

Despite ostensible differences between computationalism and postmodernists and poststructuralist emphasis on undecidability and close reading, Wolfe nonetheless argues that there are hidden affinities between postmodern thinking and algorithmic culture because of their common skepticism regarding coherent meaning and the autonomy of subjectivity. Needless to say, I emphatically reject his claim that poststructuralist thought undermines interpretation, since there are numerous interpretative practices that do not depend on such presumption of autonomous subjectivity. Despite this disagreement, I take very seriously Wolfe's diagnosis of the ever-deepening antagonistic divide between algorithmic rule following and interpretation, which is the central preoccupation of humanities, legal hermeneutics, and qualitative sociology. Today this divide not only separates humanities and sciences, but also fractures humanistic and scientific inquiries from within.[31]

Wolfe's worry that the algorithmic turn in jurisprudence and politics undermines justice resonates with Lyotard's analysis of the crisis of legitimation in his 1979 *The Postmodern Condition: A Report on Knowledge*.[32] It is perhaps indicative of the changing horizon of the times that in the 1980s and '90s, *The Postmodern Condition* (translated into English in 1984) was read primarily either as a postmodern theory of the sublime or as a diagnosis of the crisis of the grand narratives, while its critique of functionalism and of the corresponding notion of society as the self-regulating system was downplayed. However, in the context of the hegemony of Big Data and algorithmic culture, the importance of Lyotard's work lies elsewhere, namely, in his claim that the crisis of legitimation leads to the emergence of the algorithmic modes of governmentality.

For Lyotard the crisis of legitimation is produced by the deepening gap between quantitative knowledge, exemplified today by computational turn, and interpretive knowledge, which reflects "directly or indirectly on values or aims" of a given society.[33] As Lyotard reminds us, science and new technologies cannot legitimate themselves, even if they claim that their legitimation lies in the pursuit of truth for its own sake or in the increased speed and efficiency, because legitimation always implies an interpretation of the social and political contexts in which science works.[34] Since technoscience "is incapable of legitimating itself,"[35] it is even less able to legitimate politics or justice. In this context, the deepening gap between interpretive humanities and quantitative sciences, between thinking and computation, sidesteps the problem of legitimation, and in particular, avoids the question of whether efficiency and measurable outcomes are the only social good worth pursuing. Writing almost twenty-five years after the publication of *The Postmodern Condition*, Frank Pasquale concurs that legitimacy and authority in a datafied world are "increasingly expressed algorithmically. Decisions that used to be based on human reflection are now made automatically" and are treated as merely technical matters.[36]

As Lyotard correctly anticipates, the crisis of legitimation leads to a new mode of computational governmentality, which delegates more and more decisions and judgments of administrators to automated algorithmic procedures: administrative functions "are being and will be further withdrawn from administrators and entrusted to machines."[37] As the ongoing debate on the ethics of AI suggests,[38] it is still far from clear how the accountability for decision making delegated to algorithmic processing of Big Data is to be formulated. And what complicates this problem exponentially is the lack of, or restricted access to, governing algorithms mediating social relations. As Lyotard predicts, "Increasingly, the central question is becoming who will have access to the information these machines must have in storage to guarantee that the right decisions are made. Access to data is, and will continue to be, the prerogative of experts of all stripes."[39] Yet what does it mean that debates about justice, interpretation, and public good dwindle down to access? Although these are important mechanisms of public control, open access and data audits will not solve a more urgent issue, namely, the fact that social hierarchies and value judgments do not disappear but rather become translated into "mathematical models that reframe subtle and subjective conclusions as the inevitable dictate of salient, measurable data."[40]

Confronting the Unprecedented Computationalism: Humanities to the Rescue?

As digital technologies and Big Data analytics increasingly mediate social, economic, and political relations on the global scale, it seems that the ground is shifting under our feet. Indeed, according to Shoshana Zuboff, the rise of computationalism is an unprecedented sociopolitical phenomenon, which cannot be understood in terms of familiar categories. As she writes, "The unprecedented is necessarily unrecognizable. When we encounter something unprecedented we automatically interpreted through the lenses of familiar categories, thereby rendering invisible precisely that which is unprecedented."[41] The unprecedented character of the computational turn is also missed when it is described only in terms of new digital technologies and computer programming, as Golumbia and Zuboff in different ways point out. It is not digital and computational technologies per se but their changing conjunction with power and capital that matters.[42] Because of these limitations, the computational turn is "overdescribed" empirically but its convergence with power and capital is "undertheorized."[43]

Another reason for this failure of understanding is the asymmetry in knowledge and power produced by the computational turn. For Zuboff this state of affairs is by no means accidental since it constitutes the key feature of the new form of capital, which she calls surveillance capitalism. Similarly, in his *The Black Box Society: The Secret Algorithms that Control Money and Information*, Pasquale argues that the unequal distribution of knowledge is the main characteristic of "the black box society," operating according to the logic of algorithmic secrecy and digital surveillance. In a well-known and contested formulation, Pasquale points to the two meanings of the black box: first of all, it refers to the plethora of recording devices, used in cars, planes, sensors, cameras, and ubiquitous "smart" technologies harvesting data usually without users' awareness or consent.[44] Second, it refers to the secret algorithms processing these data—the algorithms to which we do not have authorized access, or which we simply cannot understand because we lack of technical expertise.[45] "With so much secrecy so publicly in place" on the side of government, corporations, social media, finance institutions, and so forth, corporate actors obtain "unprecedented knowledge of the minutiae of our daily lives, while we know little to nothing about how they use this knowledge to influence the important decisions that we—and they—make."[46]

Zuboff concurs: "surveillance capitalists know everything *about us*, whereas their operations are designed to be unknowable to *us*. They accumulate vast domains of new knowledge from us but not for us."[47] This is the case because surveillance capitalism, invented first by Google, extracts more or more "collateral" data, the byproduct of the billions of users' interactions with smart applications and internet searches, for example, the information about frequencies, timing, wording of the search, spelling, pages visited, the number of clicks on the adds, and so forth. Some of this data about users' behavior is reinvested for the purposes of improving Google services, but most of it constitutes lucrative "behavioral surplus" used not merely for matching advertising with user profile information (UPIs), but primarily for the fabrication of new, more accurate "prediction products," which anticipate our actions, and which are in turn traded "in a new kind of marketplace for behavioral predictions."[48]

Despite these asymmetries of knowledge, Zuboff argues that we need to confront the unprecedented power of surveillance capitalism just as the earlier generations of scholars, such as Adorno or Arendt, had to confront the unprecedented rise of totalitarianism. Whether or not we agree with Zuboff's diagnosis of the computational turn, I concur with her key insights about the limits of empirical descriptions and existing terminologies. I also think that we should heed her call for the creation of new theories. Yet, I would like to insist that the confrontation with the unprecedented character of the computational turn is impossible without the resources of interpretive humanities.

And conversely, intellectual reconstructions of the multiple genealogies of datafication and algorithmic practices—some of which I briefly address in this "Afterword"—provide in my view a more urgent framework for rethinking politics, including some of the key ideas explored in this volume: infrapolitics suggested by Moreiras, revolutionary politics of "dislocation and disarticulation" analyzed by Sergio Villalobos-Ruminott, or the critical, sometimes ludic practices, such as hacking, pillage, and piracy, proposed by Peter Consenstein. These genealogies also introduce a new critical perspective to rethink the enabling potential of the arts and artistic practices (ranging from experimental poetry, graphic novel to film, among so many others analyzed in this collection). And perhaps, as Negrete puts it in her analysis of Duras and Lacan, the passion for the unsayable and the experimental can offer new possibilities of resistance in the face of the daily onslaught of the information glut. Defined by Alison James as the mediation between singular expression and the generality of meaning, the matters of artistic style can be deployed to question the new aesthetic practices of the visual presentation of data.[49]

Consequently, rather than abandoning interpretations for the sake of algorithmic processing of empirical data, we need to acknowledge that the humanities create a certain surplus of knowledge in their own way. In contrast to the expropriation of the surplus capital, this knowledge can and should be widely shared in public. As this collection demonstrates all too clearly, interpretative traditions and the potential of the humanities might be useless for data processing and trading, but precisely because of their noninstrumental character, they can offer resistance to a datafied world and enable us to find new intellectual resources, including in digital technologies themselves, in order to experiment with the possibilities of being and thinking otherwise.

Notes

1. Julia Kristeva, *Hatred and Forgiveness*, trans. Jeanine Herman (New York: Columbia University Press, 2010), 10.

2. In thinking about performativity of the past, I am inspired, among others, by José Esteban Muñoz, *Cruising Utopia: The Then and There of Queer Futurity* (New York: New York University Press, 2009), 19–21.

3. Hannah Arendt, *On Revolution* (London: Penguin, 1990), 220.

4. Arendt, *On Revolution*, 217, 220.

5. Katherine Hayles, *How We Think: Digital Media and Contemporary Technogenesis* (Chicago, IL: University of Chicago Press, 2012), 10, 102.

6. Hannah Arendt, *The Human Condition*, 2nd ed. (Chicago, IL: University of Chicago Press, 1998), 5.

7. Jerry Muller, *The Tyranny of Metrics* (Princeton, NJ: Princeton University Press, 2018).

8. Hayles, *How We Think*, 5.

9. Ted Striphas, "Algorithmic Culture," *European Journal of Cultural Studies* 18, nos. 4–5 (2015): 395–412; Paul Dourish, "Algorithms and Their Others: Algorithmic Culture in Context," *Big Data & Society* 3, no. 2 (August 2016): 1–11.

10. Frank Pasquale, *The Black Box Society: The Secret Algorithms That Control Money and Information* (Cambridge, MA: Harvard University Press, 2015).

11. David Golumbia, *The Cultural Logic of Computation* (Cambridge, MA: Harvard University Press, 2009). Golumbia defines computationalism as the dominant cultural logic of computation rather than computation per se.

12. Daniela Aghostino, "The Optical Unconscious of Big Data: Datafication of Vision and Care for Unknown Futures," *Big Data & Society* 6, no. 1 (February 2019): 1–10.

13. For a persuasive argument that datafiction cannot be separated from narrative and interpretation see, among others, Paul Dourish and Edgar Gómez Cruz, "Datafication and data fiction: Narrating data and narrating with data," *Big Data & Society* 5, no. 2 (July 2018): 1–10.

14. Aghostino, "The Optical Unconscious of Big Data," 2.

15. Golumbia, *The Cultural Logic*, 14. I disagree with Golumbia's claim that computational logic corresponds to the absolutist leader, although I do agree with him that it profoundly undermines democracy.

16. David Lukham, "What's the Difference between ESP and CEP?" published on the website *Real Time Intelligence and Complex Event Processing* (2016).

17. Cyril Alias et al., "Investigating into the Prevalence of Complex Event Processing and Predictive Analytics in the Transportation and Logistics Sector: Initial Finding from Scientific Literature," *MCIS Proceedings* (2016): 1.

18. Atanu Basu, "Five Pillars of Prescriptive Analytics Success. Executive Edge," *Analytics Magazine* (2013): 8–12.

19. Basu, "Five Pillars of Prescriptive Analytics Success," 2.

20. Shoshana Zuboff, *The Age of Surveillance Capitalism: The Fight for a Human Future at the New Frontier of Power* (New York: Public Affairs, 2019), 9–13.

21. Gilles Deleuze, "Postscript on the Societies of Control," in *Negotiations, 1972–1990*, trans. Martin Joughin (New York: Columbia University Press, 1997).

22. Joseph Weizenbaum, *Computer Power and Human Reason: From Judgement to Calculation* (San Francisco, CA: W. H. Freeman, 1976).

23. Weizenbaum, *Computer Power and Human Reason*, 5.

24. Weizenbaum, *Computer Power and Human Reason*, 16.

25. Arendt's definition of logicality points precisely to the replacement of thinking and judgment by automatic process transferred into the realm of politics.

26. David Berlinski, *The Advent of the Algorithm* (New York: Harcourt, 2000).

27. Thomas H. Cormen, et al. *Introduction to Algorithms*, 3rd ed. (London: MIT Press, 2009), 5, 13.

28. In Berlinski genealogy, Gödel's "primitive recursive functions," which allow us to calculate infinite mathematical series in terms of finite and simple rules, Alan Turing's "Turing's machine," Church's lambda calculus with its mechanical rules of application, abstraction, and conversion is a result of the long search for automated calculation replacing decision and judgment.

29. Alan Wolfe, "Algorithmic Justice," in *Deconstruction and the Possibility of Justice*, eds. Drucilla Cornell, et al. (New York: Routledge, 1992), 361–86.

30. Wolfe, "Algorithmic Justice," 366.

31. For example, some Digital Humanities scholars want to replace interpretation with the transposition of big data processing and new data analytics into literary studies. Replacing "close reading" of individual texts, the methodology of "distant reading," for example, aggregates texts into big sets of textual corpora. For the debates on the interpretation versus patterns of data in Digital Humanities, see among others, Hayles, *How We Think*, 23–79, and Benjamin Mangrum's excellent article "Aggregation, Public Criticism and the History of Reading Big Data," *PMLA* 133, no. 5 (2018): 1207–24. For a critical analysis of "data-driven rather than the knowledge-driven" science, see Rob Kitchin, "Big Data, New at This Technologies and Paradigm Shifts," *Big Data & Society* (2014): 1–12. As Kitchin shows, the epistemological conflict between theories versus theory free empiricism of data is also characteristic of sciences and social sciences. For a philosophical critique of Big Data, see Petter Törnberg and Anton Törnberg, "The Limits of Computation: A Philosophical Critique of Contemporary Big Data Research," *Big Data & Society* (2018): 1–12.

32. Jean-François Lyotard, *The Postmodern Condition: A Report on Knowledge*, trans. Geoffrey Bennington and Brian Massumi (Minneapolis: University of Minnesota Press, 1984). Wolfe also refers to Lyotard, but regards him as his opponent rather than a fellow traveler.

33. Lyotard, *The Postmodern Condition*, 13–14.

34. Lyotard, *The Postmodern Condition*, 13.

35. Lyotard, *The Postmodern Condition*, 40.

36. Pasquale, *The Black Box Society*, 8.

37. Lyotard, 16.

38. For a useful overview of different ethical positions in the ongoing debate about ethical implications of algorithmic processing of Big Data, see Brent Mittelstadt, et al., "The Ethics of Algorithms: Mapping the Debate," *Big Data & Society* (2016): 1–21.

39. Lyotard, 14.

40. Pasquale, *The Black Box Society*, 10.

41. Zuboff, *The Age of Surveillance Capitalism*, 12.

42. To illustrate this point, Zuboff argues that capitalism appropriates and ruins early promises of digital technologies to increase access to knowledge and participatory democracy, Zuboff, *The Age of Surveillance Capitalism*, 20, 67.

43. Zuboff, *The Age of Surveillance Capitalism*, 6, 66.

44. These two meanings of the black box underscore for Pasquale the "colonization" of the public sphere and democracy "by the logic of secrecy" and surveillance. Subjected to this joint operation of surveillance and secrecy, we become "qualified selves" (Zuboff, *The Age of Surveillance Capitalism*, 4)—profiled, ranked, labeled, and ultimately classified either as "targets" or as "waste" (Zuboff, *The Age of Surveillance Capitalism*, 33). By contrast, Ziewitz argues that this image of inscrutable and powerful algorithms is one of modern myths surrounding algorithms. See his editorial essay, Malte Ziewitz, "Governing Algorithms: Myth, Mess, and Methods" in *Science, Technology, & Human Values* 41, no. 1 (2016): 3–16. For a useful methodological approach to formulating data politics, see Evelyn Ruppert, Engin Isin and Didier Bigo, "Data Politics," *Big Data & Society* (2017): 1–7.

45. Pasquale, *The Black Box Society*, 3.

46. *The Black Box Society*, 9.

47. Zuboff, 11.

48. Zuboff, 8.

49. For the discussion of aesthetics involved in visual presentation of data, see, for example, Helene Ratner and Evelyn Ruppert, "Producing and Projecting Data: Aesthetics Practices of Government Data Portals," *Big Data & Society* (2019): 1–16.

Contributors

Jan Baetens is professor of literary and cultural studies at the University of Leuven, where he mainly teaches word and image issues and practice-based classes on cultural policy. He has published widely in various fields: contemporary French literature, history of photography, and visual narrative of so-called minor genres such as novelization and comics. Most of his work is published in French, some of which has been translated into English. Among his recent books in English are: *The Graphic Novel*, coauthored with Hugo Frey (Cambridge University Press, 2014); *Novelization: From Film to Novel* (Ohio State University Press, 2018); and *The Cambridge History of the Graphic Novel*, coedited with Hugo Frey and Steve Tabachnick (Cambridge University Press, 2018). With Michael Kasper, he authored *Correspondance: The Birth of Belgian Surrealism* (Peter Lang, 2016), which contains an edited translation of the key text of Belgian Surrealism, the twenty-four tracts of the mail art journal "Correspondance." Two new books are scheduled for 2019: The *Film Photo Novel* (Texas University Press) and *The Dark Cities* (Penn State University Press). A published poet and author of some fifteen collections of poetry, he was awarded the triennial award of the Francophone Government of Belgium in 2007. He also has a special link with Buffalo, thanks to Dr. Jean-Jacques Thomas, who helped publish his work in *SubStance* and who always encouraged him in the context of the journal *FPC/Formes Poétiques Contemporaines*. In 2009, he participated in the *Cityscapes/Urbanités* conference, organized by Dr. J.-J. Thomas. In 2014, he was invited to give a seminar on novelization and a lecture on constrained writing by the Poetics Center.

Vincent Broqua is a professor of North American literature and arts at the University of Paris 8. He is also a writer and a translator. His work focuses on experimental writing and art from Gertrude Stein to contemporary poets, on artists' writings, translation studies and artistic research. He published many translations of U.S. poets: David Antin, Caroline Bergvall, Tracie Morris, Anne Waldman, Rosmarie Waldrop . . . His publications include *A partir de rien: esthétique, poétique et politique de l'infime* (2013), *Récupérer* (2015), Photocall. Projet d'attendrissement (2021) and *Malgré la ligne droite: l'écriture américaine de Josef Albers* (2021). He is the cofounder of Double Change and co-editor of the multilingual online journal *Quaderna*.

David R. Castillo is director of the Humanities Institute and professor of Spanish at the State University of New York at Buffalo. He has authored *Awry Views: Anamorphosis, Cervantes, and the Early Picaresque* (Purdue University Press, 2001), *Baroque Horrors: Roots of the Fantastic in the Age of Curiosities* (Michigan University Press, 2010), and *Undeceptions: Cervantine Strategies for the Disinformation Age* (Juan de la Cuesta Hispanic Monographs, 2021), and coauthored *ZombieTalk: Culture, History, Politics* (Palgrave, 2016), *Medialogies: Inflationary Media and the Crisis of Reality* (Bloomsbury, 2016), and *What Would Cervantes Do? Navigating Post-Truth with Spanish Baroque Literature* (McGill-Queens, forthcoming 2021). Castillo has also coedited *Reason and Its Others* (Vanderbilt University Press, 2006), *Spectacle and Topophilia* (Vanderbilt University Press, 2012), and *Writing in the End Times* (HIOL, 2019).

Peter Consenstein is a professor of French at Borough of Manhattan Community College and a member of the faculty of the PhD Program in French at the CUNY Graduate Center, specializing in contemporary French poetry, translation, and the group Oulipo. He published a book-length study titled *Literary Memory, Consciousness, and the Group Oulipo* (Rodopi, 2002), as well as numerous articles and chapters on the Oulipo and various poets. His current projects include the translation of *Son blanc du un* (*Blank Sound of One*) into English, a book of poetry by Dominique Fourcade, and his translation of *Petit traité invitant à la découverte du jeu subtil de GO* (*A Short Treatise Inviting the Reader to Discover the Subtle Art of Go*), by Georges Perec, Jacques Roubaud, and Pierre Lusson will be published 2019 by Wakefield Press.

Jonathan Culler (BA, Harvard; BPhil and DPhil, Oxford) was Fellow in French at Selwyn College, Cambridge, then University Lecturer and Fellow in French at Brasenose College, Oxford, before moving to Cornell University in 1977, where he succeeded M. H. Abrams as Class of 1916 Professor of English. Former president of the American Comparative Literature Association, chair of the New York Council for the Humanities, and secretary of the American Council of Learned Societies, he is a fellow of the American Academy of Arts and Sciences and of the American Philosophical Society. He is the author of *Flaubert: The Uses of Uncertainty* (1974) and numerous books on contemporary critical theory, French and English, including *Structuralist Poetics* (1975), *On Deconstruction* (1983), and *The Literary in Theory* (2006). His *Literary Theory: A Very Short Introduction* (augmented edition, 2011) has been translated into twenty-six languages. His latest book is *Theory of the Lyric* (2015).

Jane M. Gaines won the Society for Cinema and Media Studies Distinguished Career Award in 2018. Her first two books—*Contested Culture: The Image, the Voice, and the Law* and *Fire and Desire: Mixed Race Movies in the Silent Era*—both received the Katherine Singer Kovacs prize for Best Book in Film and Media Studies. A Radcliffe Institute for Advanced Study Fellowship and an Academy of Motion Picture Arts and Sciences Scholarly Award supported her recent book *Pink-Slipped: What Happened to Women in the Silent Film Industries?* (2018) as well as the Women Film Pioneers Project digital archive published by Columbia University Libraries (2013). Professor Emerita of Literature and English at Duke University, where she founded the program now titled Moving Image Arts, Gaines was also Luce Distinguished Professor at Vassar College as well as Kersten Hesselgren Honorary Chair at the University of Stockholm. She is a cofounder of "Visible Evidence: Strategies and Practices in Documentary," now in its twenty-fifth year, and this year's conference pays tribute to her seminal article in the panel "Political Mimesis @ 25." Her essay on the Arab Spring documentaries recently appeared in Aline Caillet and Frédéric Pouillaude, eds. *A Documentary Art: Aesthetics, Political and Ethical Issues* (Presses Universitaires de Rennes, 2017). Presently she is working on a Comparative Media project in which she considers the Megauploads 2012 litigation over online "piracy" in contrast with motion picture film print "piracy" 1897–1907.

Lucile Haute is an artist and researcher in art and design. She is associate professor of design at the University of Nîmes (France) and associate researcher at the École Nationale Supérieure des Arts Décoratifs of Paris (France). Her work deals with hybrid narrative forms (text, performance, installation, video), artists' books, and printed and digital art publishing. Using methodologies of research-creation, she studies and realizes hybrid multimedia publications using web technologies. She coedited a volume of *Sciences du Design* journal dedicated to digital editions (Presses Universitaires de France, 2018) and a volume of *Formules* journal dedicated to the crossing between literature, performance, and technology (Presses Universitaires du Nouveau Monde, 2020). She contributed to the journals *Back Office* 3: *Writing the Screen* (2019) and *Azimuths* 51: *Research* (2020), both bilingual. She is editor in chief of the journal *Hybrid*, edited by the Presses Universitaires de Vincennes.

Alison James is professor of French at the University of Chicago. Her research and teaching focus on twentieth- and twenty-first-century French literature, with a special interest in experimental literature, theories and representations of everyday life, and questions of fact and fiction. She is the author of *Constraining Chance: Georges Perec and the Oulipo* (Northwestern University Press, 2009), of *The Documentary Imagination in Twentieth-Century French Literature* (Oxford University Press, 2020), and of articles and book chapters on topics ranging from autobiography to the poetics of the list. She has edited or coedited journal issues on "Forms of Formalism" (*L'Esprit créateur* 48, no. 2 [2008]), on the playwright Valère Novarina (with Olivier Dubouclez; *Littérature* 176, 2014). With Christophe Reig, she coedited a volume on documentary practices in literature and the arts: *Frontières de la non-fiction: littérature, cinéma, arts* (Presses Universitaires de Rennes, 2013).

Émile Lévesque-Jalbert is a French Canadian who earned his BA in literature at the Université Laval in Québec City and his master's at Miami University in Ohio. He is now a second year graduate student in the French section of the Department of Romance Languages and Literatures at Harvard.

Alberto Moreiras is a professor of Hispanic Studies at Texas A&M University. He has also held regular appointments at the University of Wisconsin–Madison and Duke University, in the United States, and at the University of Aberdeen, in Scotland. He is the author of the following books: *Interpretación y diferencia* (Madrid, Spain: Visor, 1991), *Tercer espacio: literatura y duelo en América Latina* (Santiago, Chile: ARCIS/Lom, 1999), *The Exhaustion of Difference: The Politics of Latin American Cultural Studies* (Durham, NC: Duke University Press, 2002), *Línea de sombra: El no sujeto de lo político* (Santiago, Chile: Palinodia, 2008), and *Marranismo e inscripción, o el abandono de la conciencia desdichada* (Madrid, Spain: Escolar y Mayo, 2016). He is the coeditor, with Nelly Richard, of *Pensar en/la postdictadura* (Santiago, Chile: Cuarto Propio, 2002). He has also published many essays on Latin American literature, Hispanic intellectual history, critical theory, and political thought.

He is coeditor of *Journal of Spanish Cultural Studies*, *Res Publica: Revista de pensamiento político*, and *Política común: A Journal of Thought*, and of the University of Texas Press Book Series "Border Hispanisms." His works in progress include three books, respectively, on infrapolitics, posthegemony, and contemporary politics.

Fernanda Negrete is the author of *The Aesthetic Clinic: Feminine Sublimation in Contemporary Writing, Psychoanalysis, and Art*, forthcoming with SUNY Press (October 2020). Her essays on aesthetics, French women's literature, psychoanalysis, and contemporary art and music have appeared in *ARTMargins*, *Mosaic*, *CR: The New Centennial Review*, *Humanities*, *Samuel Beckett Today/Aujourd'hui*, and *S: Journal of the Circle for Lacanian Ideology Critique*, and in the edited volume *Deleuze and the Schizoanalysis of Feminism* (Bloomsbury 2019). She coedited the special issue *Beckett Beyond Words* with James Martell for *Samuel Beckett Today/aujourd'hui* (October 2018). At the State University of New York at Buffalo she is assistant professor of French for the Department of Romance Languages and Literatures, and executive director of the Center for the Study of Psychoanalysis and Culture.

Michel Pierssens is an emeritus professor of French literature at Université de Montréal, and has taught in various French, American, and Canadian universities. His publications deal mostly with the relationships between literary and scientific cultures in the nineteenth and twentieth centuries, for which he initiated the field of *épistémocritique*. He cocreated and coedits a number of journals, both in print or online (*SubStance*, *Épistémocritique*, *Histoires Littéraires*).

Jean-Jacques Thomas is University of Buffalo Distinguished Professor and Melodia E. Jones Endowed Chair at the State University of New York at Buffalo. He teaches contemporary French literature, linguistics, semiotics, and poetics. He has published several books on theory or literary criticism: *Lire Leiris* (Paris: P.V., 1972), *La Langue La poésie* (Lille, France: Septentrion, 1989), *La Langue volée* (Berne, Switzerland: Lang, 1989), *Poétique Générative* (Paris: Larousse, 1978), *Poeticized Language* (University Park: Pennsylvania State University Press, 2000), *Oulipo: Chroniques des années héroïques* (1978–2018) (New Orleans: PUNM, 2019), and *Perec en Amérique* (Brussels: Impressions Nouvelles, 2019). He has published translations of important US books into French (*Zoosemiotics* by Thomas Sebeok [Brussels: Degrés, 1978], *Semiotics of Poetry* by Michael Riffaterre [Paris: Le Seuil, 1983]), and, solo or in collaboration, he published special editions of journals or specialized volumes: *Poética*

Generativa (Buenos Aires: Hachette, 1981, 1989), *Michel Leiris* (*SubStance* 11/12, 1975), *Pierre Alfieri* (*SubStance* 123, 2010), "Forme et Informe dans la création moderne et contemporaine" (*Formules* 13, 2009), "Oulipo@50" (*Formules* 16, 2012), "Formes: Support et espace" (*Formules* 19, 2015), "Le Lisible" (*Formes Poétiques Contemporaines* 12, 2016). He is executive editor of the European international journal *Formules* (PUNM). With the help of the Buffalo-based team of *Formules*, he prepared the manuscript of this volume.

Sergio Villalobos-Ruminott is from Chile. He studied sociology and philosophy, and completed his PhD at the University of Pittsburgh (2003). Currently he is a professor of Latin American Studies at the University of Michigan, Ann Arbor. *La desarticulación. Epocalidad, hegemonía e historicidad* (Santiago, 2019), and *Asedios al fascismo. Del gobierno neoliberal a la revuelta popular* (Santiago, 2020) are his two most recent books. He has published numerous journal articles, including "Mito, destrucción y revuelta: Notas sobre Furio Jesi" (*Diálogos mediterráneos*, Brazil, 2018), "Comunismo Sucio" (*Nierika*, México 2018), "Acerca de la posibilidad de una democracia salvaje" (*Pensamiento al margen*, Spain, 2018), "Anarchy as the Closure of Metaphysics: Historicity and Deconstruction in the Work of Reiner Schürmann" (*Political Comun* 13, Michigan, 2017). He has also translated into Spanish works by John Beverley, Gareth Williams, and William Spanos.

Ewa Plonowska Ziarek is Julian Park Professor of Comparative Literature at the State University of New York at Buffalo, a senior research fellow at the College of Fellows at Western Sydney University, and a visiting faculty in the Institute for Doctoral Studies in the Visual Arts, University of Maine. Most recently she coauthored with Rosalyn Diprose *Arendt, Natality and Biopolitics: Toward Democratic Plurality and Reproductive Justice* (2019), a book awarded Book Prize of Symposium: Canadian Journal for Continental Philosophy. Her other books include *Feminist Aesthetics and the Politics of Modernism* (2012); *An Ethics of Dissensus: Feminism, Postmodernity, and the Politics of Radical Democracy* (2001); *The Rhetoric of Failure: Deconstruction of Skepticism, Reinvention of Modernism* (1995); and coedited volumes, such as *Intermedialities: Philosophy, Art, Politics* (2010); *Time for the Humanities* (2008); and *Revolt, Affect, Collectivity: The Unstable Boundaries of Kristeva's Polis* (2005). Her interdisciplinary research interests include feminist political theory, modernism, feminist philosophy and psychoanalysis, and critical race theory. Her work has been translated into Spanish, Italian, Hebrew, French, Polish, and Romanian.

Index

Prepared by Jean-Jacques Thomas

absolute, 46, 54, 121, 130–131, 133, 139n9, 146, 181; Absolute, 110; absolute difference, 126, 128–131, 137; Absolute Knowledge, 129, 131, 169; absolute rationality, 130
absolutely, 55, 58, 63, 122, 124, 135, 162, 181
Acker, Kathy, 25, 28, 37n21
Actes de la recherche en sciences sociales, 9, 19n10
act, 81, 84–86, 89, 122, 138, 148–149, 153, 153, 156n33, 174, 184n18, 187, 188
action, 173, 198
activate, 163
active, 161
activism, 76, 84, 85, 86, 87, 91n11, 163
activist, 18, 66, 76, 84, 86–87, 96, 159, 163; "activist" New Formalism, 96
activity, 48–49, 60, 61, 63n28, 65, 88, 189–190, 192–193
actor, 127, 173, 198
Adorno, Theodor W., 95, 99, 106n38, 194, 198
aestheticization, 14, 16, 17
aesthetic, 23, 26, 44, 70–71, 74, 90, 96–97, 99, 101–103, 188, 191, 199, 202n49

aesthetics, 14, 39, 72, 76
aestheticism, 105n21
affordance, 96, 98, 101–104
Afro-Brazilian, 88
Afrocyberfeminism, 83
Afterimage, 80n46
Agamben, Giorgio, 83, 91n17, 171, 183n10
Agee, James, 101
Aghostino, Daniela, 190, 200n12, 200n14
agrégation, 160
Aix-en-Provence, 161
Alemán, Jorge, 129–130, 138n8, 140n33, 141n36, 141nn38–41
algorithm, 39, 45–47, 49, 129, 194–195, 197–198, 200n9, 201nn26–27, 202n44; commercial algorithms, 18; facial recognition algorithms, 84
algorithmic, 40, 190–191, 193–197, 199, 201n38; algorithmic culture, 192, 196; "Algorithmic Justice," 195, 201nn29–30; algorithmic modes of governmentality, 196; algorithmic secrecy and digital surveillance, 198
algorithmically, 190, 195–196
Alias, Cyril, 200n17

210 / Index

Althusser, Louis, 27, 68–69, 72, 74–75, 77n9, 78n27, 79n36, 79n38
Althusserian, 74
America, 53, 60, 177
American, 43, 54, 61, 62n3, 82, 85–87, 161–162, 184n18; American comics, 7–9, 12, 20n21; American comics code, 7; American critical thought, 53; American Cultural Center of Tours, 161; American experimental poet, 44; American poetry, 29, 36, 37n26, 95; American popular studies, 14; American Satanist Church, 86; American university, 58; American way of life, 161; American writer, 42
Americanism, 159
Americas, 191
amour, 5
analysis, 44, 47, 50n2, 57, 63n28, 64n31, 68–69, 71, 73, 79n28, 135, 137, 149, 154n8, 156n30, 159
analyst, 61, 129, 152–153
analyze, 41, 45, 70, 136, 151, 178
ancestorfuturism, 88
Andrews, Bruce, 23
Angermuller, Johannes, 54, 55, 62n4, 62n6
Anglo-American literary studies, 61; Anglo-American context, 94
Anglo-Saxon, 160
Ann Arbor, 163
Annaud, Jean-Jacques, 147, 154n12
anthropological, 16, 127, 129; onto-anthropological, 169, 173
anthropology, 123, 126–127, 129, 130, 133, 140n29; "philosophical anthropology," 127; "transcendental anthropology," 140n33
anti-aesthetic, 71
anti-Americanism, 8, 12–14, 17
anticapitalist, 86

anticapitalistic, 88
anticomics, 8, 11
antigraphic, 8
antihistoricism, 73
antimodel, 112
anti-ontological, 110
anti-ontology, 110
anti-photo-novel, 7–8
antirealism, 71–72
antirealist, 70–71
antithesis, 75
anti-vietnam War, 70
antivisual, 13
antiwar, 67, 72
Antigone, 141n42
Antin, David, 23, 31
anxiety, 28, 48, 50
AOC média, 92n31
apparatus, 68–69, 75, 78n18, 78n21, 82, 84, 97, 102
appear, 45–46, 67–68, 70, 75, 83, 85, 91n13, 110–111, 114, 116n11
apropos, 127
arche, 60; *arche* and *telos,* 60
Archives of the Paris Police Prefecture, 90n2
archontic, 137
Arendt, Hannah, 3, 5n4, 27, 188–189, 193–194, 198, 199nn3–4, 200n6, 201n25
Arendtian, 189, 191
Aristophanes, 146, 148
Aristotle, 136, 142n43, 143n74, 195
Aristotelian, 103
Arles, 81
Armantrout, Rae, 34
Armstrong, Philip, 115n3
Arnaud, Noël, 103
art, 10–12, 19n8, 19n17, 23, 28–29, 33–34, 43, 46, 49, 51n6, 71, 96, 99, 102, 106n37, 106n41; Cartoon Art, 19n2; comics arts, 9;

performance art, 43; graffiti art, 28; visual arts, 9, 14
Artaud, Antonin, 161
Artemis, 125, 130
article, 24, 26, 28–29, 31–32, 42, 49, 76, 78n16, 94, 109
articulation, 47, 54, 127, 132, 138n8, 170–171, 175, 181; disarticulation, 168, 170–171, 175–176, 178, 182, 199
artist, 24, 33, 83–84
artistic, 24, 29–30, 40, 42, 46, 49, 72, 89, 93, 99
artwork, 99
Atelier Populaire, 81
Atlantic, 65, 93, 102; Atlantic Ocean, 81
attention, 6n1, 42, 44–45, 54, 84; attention merchants, 1, 6n1; pay attention, 54
attentiveness, 50
Atwood, Margaret 2, 6n3
audience, 12, 15, 54, 70, 76, 82, 85; audience participation, 18
Audin, Michèle, 41
Aufhebung, 169–170
Augst, Bertrand, 78n21
Auschwitz, 120–122
auteur theory, 12–13, 17, 69; auteurism, 14
author, 10–11, 14–16, 25–26, 33–35, 39, 40–44, 46, 54
authorial intentions, 94
authoritarian, 28
authority, 28, 31, 99
avant-garde, 9, 42–45, 69, 145; our avant-garde, 54
avow, 113, 117n16; disavowed, 116nn10–11; unavowable, 113–115, 115nn2–3, 117n20
avowal, 113
avowedly, 70

"*a-wall*," 149

bad, 8; "bad" (read American), 12; bad taste, 14
Badiou, Alain, 3, 119, 124, 126, 128, 131–137, 138n1, 140nn17–19, 142nn44–69, 143nn70–73, 153n3, 154n6, 188
Badiouan, 137
Baetens, Jan, 4, 19n11, 20n21, 20n23, 24, 42
Balibar, Étienne, 3, 67–68, 72, 74–75, 77n7, 77n9, 77n9, 78n27, 79n36, 79n38, 119, 126–130, 140nn29–32
Balibarian, 127–128, 130
Balzac, Honoré de, 101
Bambach, Charles, 79n32
bande dessinée, 12–13, 18n2, 19n3, 19n10, 19n17, 20n19
Barnard, Suzanne, 154n6
Barthes, Roland, 8–11, 13, 16, 19n17, 20n18, 20n25, 24, 26–27, 31, 35, 36nn12–13, 54, 59, 63n30, 74, 79n35, 93, 95, 99, 104n1, 106n43
Bartlebooth, 49, 50
Bassano, Roberta, 19n13
Basu, Atanu, 200nn18–19
Bataille, Georges, 3, 27, 33, 38n36, 111, 161, 167–174, 177, 182n2, 183n3, 183n5
Baudelaire, Charles, 101, 161
Bay-Area Language, 25
Beaty, Bart, 12, 19n8
Beaux Arts, École Nationale Supérieure des, 81
Beck, Julia, 6n3
Beckett, Samuel, 155n25
become, 40, 47, 55–57, 68, 70, 75, 81, 83–84, 86–87, 121, 123, 127–128, 130, 135–136, 145, 147, 149–150, 152, 156n30, 161–162,

become *(continued)*
  167–169, 175, 178, 180, 192, 197, 202n44; "become the new woman," 135; "the becoming-citizen of the subject and the becoming-subject
become *(continued)*
  of the citizen," 127–128; "woman-becoming," 135
Bee, Susan, 37n23
begin, 53, 55, 65, 66, 68, 76, 112, 126, 142n43, 148, 167, 194
beginning, 83, 120, 123, 128, 131–132, 138n8, 140n33, 145, 150, 152, 154n32, 160, 168, 179, 181, 188
Beinecke Library at Yale, 31
being, 40, 45, 48, 50, 57, 110–113, 120–121, 123, 127, 129, 131, 134–135, 137, 138n8, 142n43, 148, 151, 153n4, 155n22, 157, 162, 169, 171, 189, 196, 199; "being-in-the-world," 74
Being, 110, 112, 132, 142n43, 184n17
belief, 83, 87, 89, 194
believe, 45, 49, 59, 83, 86, 124, 134, 150, 156n32, 157, 158, 160, 164, 165, 188
Bell, David, 163
Bellanger, Aurélien, 164
Bellamy, Dodie, 23, 26, 28–29, 36n4, 36n8–11, 36n15, 37n16–18, 37n24, 38n40
Benjamin, Walter, 6n4, 27, 28, 35, 171, 174, 177, 183n9, 184nn16–17, 184n21
Benjaminian, 2, 179
Bennington, Geoffrey, 79n41, 201n32
Bens, Jacques, 40–41, 51n5, 51n7
Berge, Claude, 40, 50n2
Berkeley, 160
Berlin, 83
Berlinski, David, 194–195, 201n26, 201n28

Berri, Claude, 147
Bersani, Jacques, 19n9
Bernstein, Charles, 23–24, 27, 30, 36n3, 36n15, 37n23, 37n29–31
Bibliothèque Nationale, 49
Big Data, 191, 193, 196–197, 200n9, 200nn12–14, 201n31, 201n38, 202n44, 202n49; Big Data analytics, 197
Bigo, Didier, 202n44
"Bitch" and "Witch," 85
Blamey, Kathleen, 79n30
Blanchot, Maurice, 5, 26, 109, 110–115, 115nn1–2, 115n8, 116nn9–10, 117n16, 117nn19–22
Blanchotian, 111, 115n7
body, 16, 27, 33–34, 48, 76, 111, 112; body-based feminist performance, 43; "perverted body," 133
Bök, Christian, 43, 44, 51n14–19
Boltanski, Luc, 9, 19n10
Boone, Bruce, 25–28, 31–32, 36n15, 37n33, 38n34
Bonifazio, Paola, 18n1
book, 9–10, 13–16, 20n28, 21n34, 39, 42, 45, 109–110, 117n16, 122, 128, 131, 136, 141n34, 151, 153n, 159, 157, 179–180, 189, 191; booklet, 129; bookstore, 160; CGT book workers, 162; notebook, 140n33; textbook, 9, 195
both, 53, 56, 70, 73, 76, 82, 85–86, 89, 90, 113–114, 120–121, 124, 127–128, 130, 131, 135, 138, 138n8, 142n43, 146, 149, 151, 160–162, 164, 172–174, 178, 193
Bourdieu, Pierre, 164
bourgeois, 68, 71, 135, 146; bourgeois novel, 26; bourgeois realism, 72; carriers of bourgeois ideology, 68
Bowling Green tradition, 14
Boy George, 28

Braffort, Paul, 40
Braidotti, Rosi, 83, 91n15
Brée, Germaine, 161
Bretton Wood, 177
British, 69, 70; British feminist critique, 78n20
Brooks, Cleanth, 94, 105n4
Broqua, Vincent, 4, 38n39
Brown, Marshall, 94, 105nn6–7
Browning, Elizabeth Barrett, 97
Buffalo, 24, 29, 53, 65–66, 72, 76; Buffalo campus, 76; *Buffalo News*, 6n3; Buffalo, New York, 76; Program in Comparative Literature in Buffalo, 53; SUNY Buffalo, 76–77; The State University of New York, Buffalo, 76, 156n30; The SUNY Buffalo French Department, 77; the University of Buffalo, 69; (University of Buffalo) administration building, 67; (University of Buffalo) building, 45, 47, 65, 66; (University of Buffalo) University ROTC building, 76, 77. *See also* poetics
Burger, Mary, 37n17, 38n40
Butler, Judith, 97, 141n42

caesura, 131
Cahiers du cinéma, 68–69
Cahiers, 68–70, 72
Caille, Bernadette, 90n2
Calafat, Marie-Charlotte, 19n14
CalArts, 42
call, 54, 57–58, 61, 66, 70–73, 76, 85, 86–88, 122–124, 127, 130, 133–134, 137, 146, 148, 155n21, 169–171, 175–178, 187–190, 193–194, 197–198; so-called, 53, 60, 158, 169, 170, 173, 175, 180
camera, 68–69, 72, 74–75; camera-pen aesthetics, 14
Camera Obscura, 78n17, 78n21

Cambridge Analytica, 121, 193
Campbell, Eddie, 20n28
campus, 65–67, 69, 72, 76, 160, 163; campus newsletter, 80n46
Camus, Albert, 26, 161
Canadian, 25
Cantin, Lucie, 153n4
capital, 99, 130, 135, 138n8, 177, 197, 199, 200n20, 202nn41–44
capitalism, 47, 90n1, 131–132, 134–135, 138n8, 169, 171, 183n9, 184nn16–17, 197–198
capitalist, 16, 47, 68, 81, 85, 87, 89, 101, 132, 138n8, 198; capitalist discourse, 124, 126, 128, 129, 130, 137, 139, 140n33; capitalist symbolization, 136; outside the capitalist system, 69; "Western capitalism," 132
capitalize, 47, 173
Cartesian-Hegelian subject, 138n8
Casanova, Carlos, 141n34
Cassous-Noguès, Pierre, 163
Catholic, 86
Cavarero, Adriana, 141n42
Cavell, Stanley, 24
CELEG group, 9
censored, 18; censorship, 8, 10, 17
center, 55, 56, 57, 60, 127–128, 149, 150, 156n30; American Cultural Center of Tours, 161; at the center of capitalist discourse, 139; Center for Twentieth Century Studies (University of Wisconsin-Milwaukee), 69, 78n18; decenter, 179, 181; "pierced at its center by a hole," 151; Center for Twentieth Century Studies, 69
central, 47, 55
centralized classification, 17
Centre National de la Recherche Scientifique, 49
Centre Pompidou, 83, 91n11

Centre Pompidou Experiment, 40, 50n3
CEP (Complex Event Processing), 191
Cerisy-la-Salle, 9
Certeau, Michel de, 98
c'est moi, 124
CGT, 162
challenge, 41, 43, 68–69, 71, 73, 89, 112, 114, 192–193
change, 54, 67, 82, 89, 113, 139n9, 162, 189, 197; a radical change, 168; the changing horizon, 196
Charlie-Hebdo, 164
Chiesa, Lorenzo, 153n3
Chinoise, La, 69
Christian, 86, 117n20
Christianity, 133
Christology, 117n20
Church, Alonzo, 195, 201n28
cinema, 8, 17, 68–69, 72, 78n18, 78n26; countercinema, 69–72
cinematic, 69–71
cinematographic, 68
cinephilia, 14
Cinéthique, 4, 68, 69, 72
citizen, 41, 125, 127–128, 179; "citizen *polités*," 125; *citizen-subject*, 3, 129, 140nn29–32; *subjet-citizen*, 129; "the becoming-citizen," 127, 128
citoyen, 41
Citton, Yves, 89, 92n31, 102
City Lights, 160
Civilization III, 45
claim, 42, 55, 58–61, 63n28, 67, 71, 73, 85–88, 114, 124, 126, 128, 132, 134, 136, 138n8, 152, 156n26, 170, 172, 175, 179–180, 189, 195–196, 200n15; reclaim, 86–87
class, 25, 47, 48, 49, 50, 68, 82, 90n6; class struggle, 32, 70; expanding administrative class, 189; working-class, 70

classic, 44
classical, 56, 58, 77n9, 78n27, 160, 173, 175–177, 182; classical Hollywood, 71; classical poetry, 41; classical works, 12
classics, 28, 160–161
Clinton, Hillary, 85
CNU, 17
Coda Press, 163
code, 39, 41, 45; encode, 44; critical code studies, 193
codification, 69
Cold War, 168
Colebrook, Claire, 143n73
collective, 2, 84–85, 89–90, 91n11, 132, 139, 162, 167, 174, 188; collective amnesia, 159; collective hacking, 4; editorial collective, 162; radical collective, 3; this special collective moment, 157
collectively, 89, 189
Collins, Georges, 115n4
Collins, Jim, 21n34
Columbia University. *See under* university
Columbia Revolt. *See under* revolt
comics, 7–14, 16, 19n8, 20n21, 20n28; comics art, 9; comic books, 13; comics strips, 11
common, 59, 75, 86, 114, 120, 124, 127, 130–131, 135, 137–138, 138n8, 169, 184n21, 188, 195
commonality, 139
commonplace, 55, 145
commun, 58
Commune, 41
communicate, 46
communication, 9, 79n28, 81, 99, 111, 133
Communications, 9, 16
communism, 3, 124, 131–132, 136–137; Badiou's communism, 137,

143n73; "communism as egalitarian symbolization," 135; "communism of nonequivalence," 124
communist, 123–124, 128, 131, 134–135; "communist desire," 132; Communist Party, 8, 18n1, 70
communitarian, 82
community, 25, 31–33, 36n3, 36n5, 37n29, 65, 88, 90, 98, 109–115, 115nn2–3, 116nn9–11, 117n20; community life, 18; Harlem community, 65; minimal community, 113
Comolli, Jean-Louis, 78n16, 78n26
Comparative Literature and Society, Institute for, 66
computation, 190, 194–196, 200n11
computational, 187, 191–197, 200n15; computational turn, 189, 191, 193–194, 197–198; computational governmentality, 196
computationalism, 190–191, 193–195, 197, 200n11
computer, 40
concept, 24, 28, 40, 42, 55–56, 60–61, 69, 71, 73–74, 79n39, 113, 127, 132, 155n20, 161, 184n21, 188; concept of existence, 136; concept of hegemony, 139; concept of "the letter," 151; concept or essence, 130
conception, 28, 30, 33, 59, 169, 170–171, 176–178, 182, 184n21
conceptual, 27, 29, 33, 43, 44, 46, 51n17, 56, 68, 72, 88, 120; conceptual art, 4
conceptualism, 33; postconceptualism, 33
conceptuality, 120
conceptualization, 138
conceptualize, 31, 83, 88, 114; reconceptualise, 41

condition, 35, 43, 60–61, 70, 87, 123, 125, 130, 132, 136
Conley, Tom, 159
Conley, Verena, 159
connect, 44–45, 67–68, 88; interconnectedness, 120; reconnect, 164
connection, 65–67, 72–73, 82, 85, 111, 122, 151, 157, 163, 165; interconnection, 122–123
Conseil national des universités, 17
Consenstein, Peter, 4, 199
constellation, 179
constrain, 82
constraint, 40–46, 49, 73, 98, 102–104, 107n60, 149, 154n14, 164; preexisting constraints, 40
construct, 25, 27, 41, 86
constructedness, 31
construction, 34, 57, 65, 80n46, 86, 147, 153, 155n21; deconstruction, 162, 195, 199, 201n29
contemporaneity, 111, 112, 165
contemporarily, 48
contemporary, 10, 16, 40, 44, 46, 49, 53, 73, 75, 81, 82–84, 88–89, 157, 160, 163, 165n1, 171, 173–174, 188, 178, 200n1, 201n31; "contemporary capitalism," 134, 135; contemporary women, 135
contest, 110, 114, 160, 194, 198
contestation, 110, 111, 112, 114, 195; contestation of the law, 195
context, 11, 14, 42, 70, 72, 81–84, 88, 94, 96, 98, 103, 150–153, 168, 175–176, 179, 191, 196, 200n9; recontextualization, 83
continental, 23, 24, 55
Continental Theory, 7, 23, 24, 26, 28, 29, 35, 160, 163; Continental philosophy, 67, 69, 73

control, 47, 48, 59, 83, 84, 89, 91n16, 127, 130, 178, 181, 191–192, 197–198, 200n9, 200n21; "Societies of Control," 194
converses, 30
conversion. *See under* version
"coopérant," 161
Coopern Dennis, 25
Copjec, Joan, 154n15
Cormen, Thomas H., 201n27
Cornell, Drucilla, 201n29
Cota, Gabriela Méndez, 143n73
counter, 139
counterculture, 9, 161
counterexample, 176
counterinsurgent, 181; "counterinsurgency," 178, 180, 182
counterintuitive, 119
counterintentionally, 126
counterpart, 130
course, 54, 56, 67, 77, 128–129, 131–132, 134–136, 139, 145, 158, 160, 163, 170, 176, 184n18, 192, 193
Cratylism, 104
create, 45–46, 48, 58, 88–89, 125, 132, 149, 162–163, 188, 192, 199; how scientists create innovations, 165
creation, 12, 49, 59, 89, 123, 195, 198; research-creation, 89, 92n31
creative, 49, 157, 195
creativity, 46, 50, 162
creature, 146
Crenshaw, Kimberlé, 82, 91n7
crisis, 73, 89, 120, 122–123, 131, 167, 174–175, 196; "crisis in the symbolic organization of humanity," 132; crisis of "capitalist discourse," 126; crisis of civilization, 123; crisis of legitimation, 196
Cristeros war, 185n28

critic, 10, 11, 15, 18, 27, 29, 42, 45, 72, 114
critical, 30, 32–33, 35, 42, 46, 53–54, 56, 61, 66, 70, 83, 88, 94–95, 103, 127, 145, 155n16, 162, 188–189, 193–195, 199, 201n31; critical code studies, 193; critical race studies, 187; critical theory, 23–24, 28, 37n23, 95, 191; critical thinking, 18; new-critical ideal, 97; postcritical reading, 102; theoretico-critical pathways, 141n34; uncritical, 46
critically, 194
criticism, 7, 32–33, 42–43, 54, 62n1, 62n3, 62n5, 63n28, 69, 117n16, 201n31; feminist and queer criticism against sexuation, 154n15; New Criticism, 4, 94, 99, 102
criticize, 56, 60, 72, 170
critique, 10, 29, 34, 42–44, 45–49, 53–57, 60–61, 67, 71, 73–77, 78n18, 104n1, 107nn55–57, 110, 120, 123, 126, 168–169, 182n2, 184n16, 193–196, 201n31
Critique, 100, 106n44
Cronin, Paul, 77n3
Culler, Jonathan, 4
cultural, 14, 32, 42, 56, 60–61, 68, 82–83, 94, 101, 161, 181, 194, 200n11, 200n15; cultural discourses, 179; cultural history, 16; cultural logic, 190; cultural practice, 13, 179; cultural production, 7, 18, 72; cultural studies, 16–18, 93–94
culturally, 11, 14
culture, 8–11, 14, 19n15, 19n17, 20n21, 20n26, 21n 34, 29, 34, 39, 42, 56, 67, 70, 77n5, 77nn11–14, 78nn15–16, 78nn23–25, 83, 86, 88, 96, 146, 156n30, 160, 168, 189, 190, 191, 195, 196, 200n9; algorithmic culture,

192, 194; bourgeois culture, 71; counterculture, 9, 161; culture industry, 9, 12; culture wars, 162; *digitalculture*, 91n20; fan culture, 16–17; high culture, 11; mass culture, 9–10, 12, 14; media culture, 7; nature/culture, 56; permaculture, 88; popular culture, 7–9, 18; print culture 18; subculture, 11; subculture of consumption, 11; US culture, 12–13; Western culture, 56
Cusset, François, 36n1, 53, 55, 58, 60, 62n2, 62n7, 63n22, 63n29
cyber-artist, 83
cyberfeminism, 83, 91n15; Afrocyberfeminism, 83, 91n12
cybermagic, 86
cyber-spiritual, 86

Dada, 161
Dadaism, 29
Dadaist, 162
Dahlstrom, Daniel, 142n43
Da-sein, 140n33
Davidson, Michael, 29, 37n26
Davis, Angela, 82, 90n6
day, 44, 85, 128, 160–161, 164, 178; day after day, 160; day-to-day existence, 41
dead end, 70, 73
De Alba, Luis González, 180, 184n27
death, 131, 132, 133, 141n42, 143n73, 170; death drive, 130, 131, 133, 135, 148; death of the author, 26, 33, 35
debate, 17, 43, 45, 68, 69, 70, 72, 93, 94, 99, 167, 174, 191, 193, 197, 201n31, 201n38
De Baecque, Antoine, 20n26
Debord, Guy, 13, 20n22, 20n23
deconstruct, 112

deconstruction, 56, 69, 113, 114, 162, 195, 201n29
deconstructive historian, 75, 79n40
découverte, 41, 51n6
De Beauvoir, Simone, 82, 90n5
De Kosnik, Abigail, 18, 21n35
De Lauretis, Teresa, 78n18
Deleuze, Gilles, 24, 27, 36n1, 54, 62n2, 81, 83–84, 89, 90n1, 91n16, 91n18–19, 105n3, 160, 162, 194, 200n21
Deleuzian, 88
Del Paso, Fernando, 185n28
De Man, Paul, 95
democracia, 143n73
democracy, 2, 112, 114, 124, 132, 179–180, 184nn24–26, 200n15; *non-equivalential democracy*, 3; participatory democracy, 202n42, 202n44; radical democracy, 182
Democratic Society, Students for a (SDS). *See under* students
democratic, 121, 190
demonstrate, 49, 55, 61, 73, 82, 136, 150, 157, 199
demonstratio, 132
demonstration, 55, 68, 84, 85, 158
demonumentalization, 178
Department of French and Romance Philology [Columbia University], 67; Department of French and Italian [University of Wisconsin-Madison], 161; Milwaukee French Department, 69
de-production, 87
Derrida, Jacques, 4–5, 24, 27–28, 35–36, 36n1, 53–61, 62n2, 62n8–14, 63n15–18, 63n23–28, 75, 79n41–45, 95, 102, 105n3, 107n58, 109, 111–115, 115n4, 116nn12–15, 117nn16–18, 154n8, 162, 169, 173, 183nn6–7, 195

desideratum, 132
design, 7, 83, 91n11, 98, 103, 106n33
desire, 46, 48–49, 84, 88, 95, 102, 111
désœuvrement, 110
desorceleur, 88
destroy, 56, 75–76, 120–121, 145–146, 149, 153n2
destruction, 87, 120, 135–138, 142n43, 145, 170
destructive, 49, 140n33
De Toledo, Camille, 164, 165n3
détournement, 45
détruire, 145, 146, 148
Devij, Faisal, 88, 92n30
Diacritics, 162, 184n17
dialectic, 110–111, 115n7, 129, 182n2, 183n8
dialectical, 170
dialogic, 11
Diaz, Gustavo Ordaz, 181
Diaz, Porfirio, 181
Dickinson, Emily, 98
diegetic, 11
differ, 171–172, 179, 181, 183n8
différance, 58–59
difference, 39, 54–55, 58–60, 62n8, 63n27, 69, 74, 82–84, 89, 91n15, 111, 123, 126, 128–129, 130–131, 136–137, 139n9, 142n43, 149, 155n16, 156n33, 158, 168, 172, 183n6, 191, 195, 200n16; "anthropological difference," 127; indifference, 121; outside a system of differences, 55
différend, 111
different, 40, 42, 45, 55–56, 60, 119, 129, 146, 149, 151, 153n4, 158, 160, 164, 168, 172–173, 175, 178–179, 190–191, 197, 201n38; indifferent, 110, 121, 151
differential, 77

differentiate, 169
differently, 75
digital, 18, 46, 50n2–3, 90, 200n5; digital communication systems, 17; *digitalculture*, 91n20, 91n23; Digital Humanities, 193, 201n31; digital media, 189; digital surveillance, 198; digital technologies, 190, 197, 199, 202n42; digital turn, 17; postdigital, 83
digitization, 17
Diogenes, 125
Diogenes Laertius, 125, 140n20
discourse, 24, 30, 34, 54, 56, 62n8, 63n28, 75–76, 94, 96–97, 99, 112, 114, 126–127, 129–130, 138n8, 169, 178; academic discourse, 178; analytic discourse, 126, 129, 140nn23–28, 156n30; capitalist discourse, 124, 126, 128–130, 137, 138n8; discourse of technology, 130; discourse of the hysteric, 129; discourse of the master, 126, 138n8; *discourse* on fashion, 13; official discourse, 178, 179, 181; "pestiferous" discourse, 126
discover, 44, 56, 109, 159, 165
discovery, 41, 56, 60, 148
discuss, 44–45, 83, 86, 120, 128, 145–146, 151, 159, 163–164, 167
discussion, 42–43, 55, 60, 62n7, 68, 76, 110, 145, 176, 179, 184n26, 202n49
disorder. *See under* order
disposition. *See under* position
divide. See under individual
"dividuation." *See under* individual
Dixmier, Michel, 90n2
DIY hacker culture, 88
document, 65, 73, 184n27, 190
documentary, 65, 71–72, 75–77, 78n20, 101

dominance, 49
dominant, 49, 82, 83, 131, 159, 189, 190, 200n11
dominate, 12, 45, 135
domination, 87, 139, 176, 178, 180, 189
Donato, Eugenio, 53, 54, 62n1, 63nn19–21, 161
Dosse, François, 67, 77n6, 79n29
Dourish, Paul, 200n9, 200n13
Draper, Susana, 179–180, 184nn24–25
dream, 57–59, 83, 87, 92nn25–26, 139, 149, 150–152, 154n7, 156n26, 158, 184n15; dream factory, 8; navel of the dream, 155n24
Drury, John, 184n15
Dubois, W. E. B., 27
Dubrow, Heather, 95, 105nn10–12
Duras, Marguerite, 5, 15, 21n30, 21n31, 26, 145–153, 153nn1–2, 154n9, 154n11, 155n16, 155n19, 155n25, 156n27, 156n30, 199
Durasian, 155n20
Durassien silence, 5, 21n31
Dyer, Richard, 16, 21n32

earlier, 60, 89, 114, 126, 158–159, 198
early, 54, 58–59, 69, 75, 138n4, 160, 178, 182n2, 193, 194, 202n42
East Coast, 23, 160; East Coast writers, 25
Easthope, Anthony, 24, 36n2
ecofeminism, 87
ecofeminist, 87
École Nationale Supérieure des Beaux Arts, 81
École Normale Supérieure, 75; *normaliens*, 160
ecological, 87–88, 90
economic, 8, 21n34, 83, 123, 174, 197

economics, 47
economy, 45, 47, 58, 168–170, 177, 183nn7–8
écriture, 26, 36n12, 102
Éditions du Seuil, 8, 159
effect, 53–54, 56, 60, 74, 76, 148, 152–153, 179, 190
effective, 70, 75–76, 84, 119, 122, 164, 190, 192, 194
effectively, 59, 71, 77, 146
effectiveness, 86, 87, 90
efficacious, 40
efficacity, 56
efficacy, 176
efficiency, 195, 196
efficient, 84, 192
effort, 73, 76
egalitarian, 136; egalitarian symbolization, 131–132, 135–137, 138n8
egalitarism, 137
Egginton, William, 6n2
Egregor, 90
egregor, 89, 90
eigentlich, 137
Eigner, Larry, 37n23
einai-noein, 142n43
Eisenstein, Sergei, 76
element, 54, 110, 112, 148, 154, 155n24, 158–159
elementary, 112, 183n14, 184n23
ELIZA, 194
Elkin, Lauren, 42, 51n9
empirical, 56, 60, 63n28, 73, 76
empiricism, 60, 63n28
empiricist, 68
encode, 44
Encore, 151, 154n5, 154n10, 154n13, 156nn28–29, 156n32
encounter, 7, 12, 18, 53, 67, 88, 110, 132, 146, 148, 179, 187, 197
end, 41–42, 50, 51n9, 57, 60, 70, 73, 76, 84, 88, 121, 123, 125, 126,

end *(continued)*
  128, 130–131, 133135, 138n8, 140n33, 141n35, 147, 150–151, 159, 168, 177, 183n8, 190–191; ending, 111; endless, 41, 47; endlessly, 44; open-ended, 60
endanger, 67; endangered biodiversity, 89
Engels, Friedrich, 132
English, 54, 67, 96, 148, 151, 161, 183n5, 194; English Department, 30, 94; English translation, 62n8, 145, 196
environment, 158, 189
environmental, 45, 87, 89, 189
envision. *See under* vision
Ephesians, 125, 130
Ephesus, 125
epigenesis, 189
epistemological, 165, 183n10, 201n31
epistemology, 160, 162
Epron, Benoît, 21n34
equivalence, 119–124, 129, 131–132, 134, 136–137, 138n2, 138n8; general equivalence, 119, 120, 121, 122, 123, 124, 132, 134, 138n8, 194
equivalent, 120–122, 124, 134, 149, 155n21, 194; nonequivalent, 124
equivalential, 139; nonequivalential, 137
erase, 71
erasure of female authors, 34
Erinnerung, 169
Eros, 148
escape, 56, 57, 58, 59, 69, 87, 110; inescapable, 48
escapism, 7
Esposito, Scott, 42, 51n9
essay, 27–28, 30, 59, 74, 113, 119, 136, 153n, 160, 184, 187–188, 194–195, 202n44; essay-poem, 35; essayistic writing, 16

Esteban Muñoz, José, 199n2
ethic, 57
ethical, 100, 101
ethics, 57, 110, 112
Ettinger, Bracha L., 156n33
Eugenio Donato Chair of Comparative Literature, 2
Europe, 81, 86, 88, 132, 163, 183n8, 187, 191
European, 41, 49, 83, 177, 183n8; European avant-garde, 29; European cultural form, 13
Eurydice, 44
event, 55, 60, 66–68, 72–74, 76, 77n4, 81–83, 121, 147–148, 150–151, 157–158, 160–161, 167–168, 170, 172–182, 184n21, 184n26, 185n28, 187–188, 191–193, 200nn16–17
except, 67
exception, 70, 114, 120, 130–131, 177, 184n21, 193–194; exceptionless, 177, 184n21, 177
exceptional, 179, 180, 184n26
exceptionalism, 173, 184n21
exceptionalist, 177, 179
exceptionality, 177
exceptionally, 177
exist, 40–41, 49, 60, 84, 110, 120, 127, 131, 138n8, 146, 150, 158–159, 161–162, 165, 167, 198; "a bourgeois and dominating feminism exists," 135; preexist, 40, 172
existence, 39, 41, 74, 120–121, 125, 130–131, 136, 138, 138n8, 150, 152, 189; coexistence, 146; *conceptual existence*, 68; inexistent, 146; literal existence, 87
existential, 120, 125, 130, 137, 138n8; existential experience, 125; existential facticity, 130; existential *jouissance*, 130

existentialism, 82
Existenz, 137
experience, 28, 32, 34–35, 75, 86, 90, 113; proof of experience, 63n28
experiential, 75
experiment, 27, 40, 43–44, 50n3, 51n17, 51n19
experimental, 29, 35, 36, 42, 43–46, 49; experimental literature, 4; experimental writing, 25, 28
experimentalism, 44–45
experimentation, 32, 42–43, 45, 48–49
exploration, 24, 31, 162, 169; freedom of exploration and curiosity, 162
explore, 27, 37n17, 38n40, 53, 54, 82, 88, 156n27, 163, 199; exploring love, 146; exploring the unconscious, 156n30

Facebook, 88, 121, 122
fact, 40, 42, 45–47, 55, 58, 61, 79n28, 83, 113, 120, 124–125, 133–134, 137, 138n8, 147, 152, 156n31, 167–169, 171, 173–175, 178, 181, 191, 194–195, 197
factical, 136, 137
facticity, 130, 136, 137
faction, 160
factor, 159
factually, 132
Fairfax, Daniel, 78n26
"faisons table rase," 159
fake news, 1
Fanon, Frantz, 27, 183n8
Father, name of the, 133, 135, 137, 139
Favret-Saada, Jeanne, 88
Faye, E., 156n31
fecundity, 56, fecundity of structuralism, 59
Felski, Rita, 102, 107nn55–57
female, 34, 146; female minorities, 82

feminine, 146, 153n, 154n6, 156n33; feminine *amour*, 149; feminine castration, 155n20; feminine jouissance, 152
femininity, 34, 85, 134; "a feminity we will call premature," 134
feminism, 28, 83, 91n13, 135, 143n73, 187
feminist, 33, 42–43, 70, 78n20, 82–83, 85–86, 87, 91n13, 141n42, 154n15; feminist avant-garde, 69; feminist-Marxist, 85; feminist theory, 82
Ferrari, Jérôme, 164
fifty years, 73, 74, 158, 162; since 1968, 68
film, 8, 11, 13, 19n17, 21n30, 28, 65, 67–68, 70–71, 73–76, 79n31; film journal 10; film novel, 7; film photo-novel, 7, 10, 15, 19n11; film practice, 69, 70, 72; film theory, 67, 69, 70, 72–75, 78n22; filmmaker, 68, 72
find, 40, 49, 53–55, 59, 65, 67–68, 70, 72, 74–75, 77, 85, 114, 131–134, 140n33, 145–146, 151–152, 159, 161, 164, 167, 180, 183n8, 188, 199, 200n17
Fink, Bruce, 154n6
Fiore, Quentin, 20n24
first, 67, 69–70, 74, 78n17, 82, 85, 87
follow, 40, 42, 47, 67, 69, 72, 76, 85, 89, 109, 111, 120, 129, 138, 140, 148–151, 157, 160, 168, 172, 178, 180, 192, 195, 196
follower, 42
"Fond sans fond," 111
"foolish and nasty," 14
force, 84, 87, 89, 112
Forest, Philippe, 36n14
forget, 69, 73, 79n30, 83, 87

form(s)s: 4–5, 7–8, 11, 13, 16, 19n17, 26, 32, 35, 41, 43, 45–46, 49, 57, 59–61, 68–71, 73–75, 77, 83–85, 87, 93–104, 105nn6–7, 105n13, 105n21, 106nn22–38, 107n52, 107nn58–59, 107n61, 110–112, 117n16, 117n20, 128, 130, 140n33, 141n35, 156n30, 158, 161–164, 168–170, 173, 176–177, 180, 189–190, 192–194, 197; European cultural form, 13; *formes de vie*, 106n44; formless, 59, 104; *formless historicity*, 173, 182; forms of theory; 17; radical form, 4; the new form of the One, 135; "the utopia of form," 104

formal, 42–43, 47, 69, 86, 94–95, 104

Formalism, 29, 33, 35, 93, 94, 95, 96, 98, 99, 102, 103, 105n8, 105n10, 105n14, 105nn17–19, 106n39; new formalism, 5, 94, 96, 99; "New Formalism," 95, 96, 99, 105n14, 105nn17–18

formalist, 32, 37n33, 94, 95, 96, 99, 105n4

formalistic, 43

formality, 45

formalize, 194

formally, 72

format, 10, 18

formation, 49, 70, 122

former, 12–14, 29, 53, 65, 75–76, 95, 96, 160, 169, 181, 183n8

formula, 85, 154n15, 156n32

formulate, 63n28, 67, 70, 75, 147, 182, 191, 195, 197, 202n44

formulation, 56, 70, 97, 128, 170, 188, 193, 195, 198; reformulation, 124, 125

Formules, 51n11, 52n34

Foster, Hal, 33, 34, 38n37

Foucauldian, 73, 101

Foucault, Michel, 4–5, 24, 27, 36n1, 54, 61, 62n2, 63n30, 64n31, 73, 77, 79n28, 79n30, 89, 94, 96–97, 99, 105n3, 105n5, 160, 164, 184n20, 190

Foulipo, 42, 43, 51n12–13

found, 40, 49, 53, 54, 55, 65, 67, 70, 72, 74

foundation, 45, 57, 64n31, 69, 70, 133, 140n29, 177, 182n2, 195

foundational, 47, 48, 66, 72, 73, 74, 168; foundational moment, 178

founder, 49

Fournel, Paul, 40, 50n3

Fradinger, Moira, 141n42

framework, 33, 32, 53, 61, 199

France, 9, 13–14, 17–18, 19n9, 25, 49, 54, 65, 69, 70–71, 81, 87, 93–95, 102, 157–160, 162, 168, 170, 174, 177, 184n15, 188

France-Soir, 8

Francophone, 76

French, 7–8, 12–14, 16–17, 18n2, 19n15, 35, 39, 41, 53–55, 58, 62n8, 66–70, 72–74, 76–77, 77n6, 77n9, 78n27, 79n36, 79n38, 82, 87, 99, 102, 148, 157, 159–160, 162–164; French and the Italian thinkers, 173; French History, 62n7, 63n22, 81, 95, 97, 105n3, 105n15; French intellectual life, 159; French-language, 145; French philosophy, 4–5; French Revolution, 174, 176; French sacrificial tradition, 183n4; French society, 158; French studies, 161; French Theory, 4, 17–18, 24, 29, 36n1, 53, 62n2, 161, 187; French writer, 170; the French police, 175; the French tradition of partisan though, 168. *See also* Department (of French)

Freud, Sigmund, 55, 69, 133, 146, 149–152, 154n7, 155nn17–18, 155n22, 155n24, 156n26, 160
Freudian, 129, 133, 138n8, 148, 159
Frey, Hugo, 20n21
friend, 112–114
friendship, 112–114, 115n4, 116nn12–15, 117nn16–18
Fruchter, Norm, 76
Frye, Northrop, 160
Fumetti, 4
fundamental, 40, 47, 61, 112–113, 120, 136, 148–149, 188
fundamentally, 137
Furter, Loraine, 91n11
futural, 188
future, 11, 18, 40, 49, 51n4, 57, 59, 75–76, 79n39, 112–115, 123, 134–135, 158, 162, 164–165, 188

Gaia, 87
Gaines, Jane, 3, 4, 78n21, 79n31, 79n37, 80n47, 188
Gaité Lyrique, La, 83, 91n12
Gallimard, 159
game, 39–43, 45–47, 49, 82, 138, 161, 178
gamer, 45–46, 51n21, 51nn23–25, 52nn26–27
gameplan, 46
gamespace, 45–46
Gamma-Rapho-Keystone, 90n2
Gardner, Jared, 20n28
Garréta, Anne, 39, 41
gay, 27, 32
Gefen, Alexandre, 106n41
gender, 28, 34, 37n21, 38n39, 41, 69, 97, 149, 180; gender studies, 95; gender theory, 187
general, 43–44, 48, 55, 120, 122–123, 136, 139n9, 160, 163, 168, 170–171, 177, 182, 183n4, 183n5–7. See *also* equivalence
generality, 199
generalize, 122
generally, 127, 134, 189, 190
generation, 43, 137, 162, 164, 198; a new generation of graduate students, 163
generational, 162, 175; a generational quarrel, 174
generationalism, 47
Genette, Gérard, 54, 58–59
genre (type of writing, media, etc.), 12, 95; subgenre, 10
Germany, 171
Ghera, Serge, 10, 19n12
Giff Wiff, 9
GIFRIC, 155n24
Gil, Gilbert, 88
Girard, René, 54
Glassman, Deborah, 77n6
Gledhill, Christine, 79n37
global, 86, 179, 194, 197; global algorithmic condition, 190; global climate change, 120; global warming, 2
globality, 46, 120
globalization, 17, 177
globalize, 176
Glück, Robert, 25, 27–28, 32–33, 36n5, 36n15, 37n17, 37n19–20
Go (game), 41, 51n6
God, 133, 137, 153n3
god, 130, 146; "god trick," 83, 91n13
Godard, Jean-Luc, 69–71
Gödel, Kurt Friedrich, 195, 201n28
Goldhammer, Arthur, 77n7, 77n9, 78n27
Goldhammer, Jesse, 183n4
Goldsmith, Kenneth, 42, 43, 51n12
Golumbia, David, 190, 194, 197, 200n11, 200n15

good, 13, 14, 41; good (French), 12; good literature, 12
goods, 48
Gómez Cruz, Edgar, 200n13
González de Alba, Luis, 180
Gordon, Peter E., 79n32
Gorin, Jean-Pierre, 70
Gorton, Kristyn, 155n16
Grahn, Judy, 28
Gramsci, Antonio, 160
Granaderos, 181
Grangaud, Michelle, 41
graphic, 84; antigraphic, 8; graphic language, 82; graphic literature, 16; graphic narrative, 7–10, 12, 14, 16–18; graphic novel, 14; graphic novelist, 17; graphic storytelling, 16
Greek, 154n8, 160
Grégoire, Ménie, 11, 19n16
Grenier, Robert, 37n23
Grieveson, Lee, 78n22
Groensteen, Thierry, 11, 20n19
Grosz, Elisabeth, 26
ground, 46, 59, 111, 112; regrounding, 114
groundless, 113
groundswell, 67
group, 8–9, 17, 39, 40–45, 47–49, 54, 65, 70, 85, 87–88, 112, 124, 146, 162, 167
Grundwesen, 132
Guardian, 44
Guattari, Félix, 27, 81, 90n1, 91n19
Guha, Ranajit, 172, 178, 180, 183n14, 184n23

hack, 39–42, 45–50; "Trans Hackmeeting," 92n28
hacker, 45–49, 51n20, 51n23, 52n28–33, 88
Halpern, Rob, 25, 35, 36n4, 37n33
Halsberghe, Chistophe, 116n9

Hamacher, Werner, 184n17
Hamilton, David, 15, 21n30
"Hanoi Jane," 70
Hanson, Susan, 115n8
happen, 54, 67, 79n31, 87, 88, 111, 113
happy, 61, 64n31
Harari, Josué, 54, 62n5, 161
Haraway, Donna, 83, 91n13
Harlem, 65
Harris, Kaplan, 37n22
Harris, Paul, 163
Harryman, Carla, 25, 37n23
Harvard, 24
Harvey, Sylvia, 67, 70, 77n5, 77n11–14, 78n15–16, 78n23–25
hashtag, 83, 85, 86, 89, 91n21
Hatfield, Charles, 20n28
have-nots, 47
haves, 47
Hayles, Katherine, 189–190, 200n5, 200n8, 201n31
Heath, Stephen, 78n18
Hegel, Georg Wilhelm Friedrich, 75, 110–111, 116n15, 128, 168–171, 182n2, 183n8
Hegelian, 111, 127, 129, 131, 168–169, 182n2; Cartesian-Hegelian, 139
Hegelianism, 131, 170, 183n6
Hegelo-Marxian, 129
hegemonic, 174, 182
hegemony, 31, 122, 137, 138n8, 141n34; hegemony of big data, 196; hegemony theory, 122
Heidegger, Martin, 55, 73–76, 79n34, 79n39, 79, 41–45, 110, 120, 125, 136, 137, 138n4, 138n8, 140n22, 140n33, 141n35, 142n43, 143nn73–76, 175, 184n18, 194
Heideggerian, 130; Heideggerian-Althusserian theory of ideology, 74
Heinich, Nathalie, 164

Hejinian, Lyn, 23, 25, 30–31, 34–35, 36n6–7, 37n22–23, 37n25, 37n27, 38n38
Heraclitus, 125, 140n22
Heraclitean, 125, 129, 130, 131
Herman, Jeanine, 199n1
hermeneutical, 126, 143n74
hermeneutics, 60, 61, 137, 196; "hermeneutic revival," 102
Hermodorus, 125
heterosexuality, 82
heterotopian, 46
hex, 85
Hicks, R. D., 125
Hill, Leslie, 114, 117nn19–20
Hirano, Keiichiro, 91n19
historian, 72–73, 75–76, 79n40, 158, 164, 174
historical, 10, 17, 32, 41–42, 46, 56, 61, 65, 68, 71–76, 77n9, 78n18, 78n27, 79n37, 79n39, 94, 96, 98, 103, 127–128, 136–137, 141n34, 142n43, 158, 163, 168, 170–182, 183n8, 189; historical "correlation," 193; "historical hypothesis," 119, 124; metahistorical, 168
historically, 11, 33, 65, 101, 112, 184n26
historicism, 94–96; antihistoricism, 73; New Historicism, 94, 96–97, 105n18; new-historicism/cultural-studies, 94; old historicism, 94
historicist, 95; antihistoricist, 95; new-historicist/cultural studies turn, 94
historicity, 58, 75, 77, 79n39, 95, 182; "formless historicity," 173, 182
historicize, 47
historiographical, 182
historiography, 73, 78n18
history, 9, 16, 30, 39, 40, 46, 53, 56–57, 60, 68, 73–75, 95–96, 103, 106n41, 113, 127–128, 137, 140n33, 153n4, 154n15, 157–158, 160, 163–165, 167–182, 183n8, 184n17, 189, 193, 201n31; "French History"; 158; history of mathematical logic, 194
Hoens, Dominick, 155n23
Hoggart, Richard, 9, 19n5
Hold, Jacques, 149, 150, 151; Jacques Hold (Jacques Lacan's uncanny namesake), 152, 155n23, 156n33
hole, 82, 147, 149, 150, 156n30; "hole" (*trou*), 149; hole-word, 150, 151–153, 155n21
Hollywood, 8, 71; Hollywood Mosfilm, 71
homosexual, 33
Honig, Bonnie, 141n42
Horkheimer, Max, 9, 11n4
Houellebecq, Michel, 164, 165n2
Houghton Library (Harvard University), 117n16
Howard, Richard, 19n7, 20n25, 79n35
Howe, Susan, 23, 29, 30, 31, 37n28
Hugo, Victor, 161
human, 46, 49, 111, 123, 128, 139n9, 140n33, 151, 169, 176, 189–190, 192–196, 200, 200n20, 200nn22–24, 202n44; human dignity, 120; human progress, 176, 178; human rights, 163; Human Sciences, 53, 62n8; nonhuman, 190; *Posthuman*, 143n73; "*sciences humaines*," 159, 163
humans, 58, 120, 146
humanism, 57, 58, 59, 175
humanist, 59
humanistic, 93, 196
humanities, 1–2, 5, 6n2, 6n3, 13, 24, 79n28, 189–191, 193–194, 196, 198–199; Digital Humanities, 193, 201n31; Humanities Institute, 2; Humanities to the Rescue, 1–2, 6, 197

humanity, 89, 120, 128–130, 132, 176; "symbolic organization of humanity," 132
Hurley, Robert, 183n5
Husserl, Edmund, 75
Huysmans, Karl-Joris, 164
hybridization, 85, 88
hyperstition, 88

IBM Selectric, 162
iconophobia, 13–14, 17
iconophobic, 13
idea, 10, 12, 16, 18, 65–66, 68, 70, 72–74, 93, 98–101, 103–104, 124, 127–128, 131–133, 136–137, 148, 150, 158, 162–165, 179, 187, 199
ideal, 145, 151; "life without an ideal," 134; new critical ideal, 97
idealism, 75; luxurious idealism, 32
identification, 84, 119, 128–130, 138n8, 142n43, 179–180
identify, 23, 29, 32, 35, 61, 88, 111, 123, 148
identity, 34, 43, 47–49, 76, 111; identities as difference, 47; identity politics, 47
ideologeme, 127
ideologic, 159
ideological, 17, 42, 43, 45, 68, 69, 72, 75, 123
ideologically, 25
ideology, 10, 29, 37n23, 68, 69, 70, 71, 74, 75, 78n16, 78n26, 79n30, 153n
image, 7, 11, 13, 17, 19n17, 45, 72, 74, 82, 133, 148, 153, 160, 175, 182; *Afterimage*, 184n 22; images d'Épinal, 19n17; this image of inscrutable and powerful algorithms, 202n44
imagery, 72
imaginary, 15, 69, 80n46, 150

imagination, 54, 84, 89, 165, 189
imaginative, 62n3, 189
imagine, 59, 125, 129, 135–136, 168
imposition. *See under* position
impossible. *See under* possible
Indes Savantes, Les, 21n31
individual, 8, 16, 83–84, 89–90, 111, 124, 136, 201n31; *dividu*, 84; "dividuation," 84
individualization, 84
individually, 86, 89
inform, 44, 59, 168, 169, 174, 181
information, 41, 47–48, 50, 63n28, 81, 192, 197–199, 200n10
informational silo, 1
infrapolitics. *See under* politics
infrastructure, 89
Inquisition, 86
inspire, 40–41, 43–44, 49, 88, 135, 188, 190, 194, 199n2
Instagram, 85, 88, 89, 90, 91n21
instance, 55–56, 59, 61, 84, 121, 126, 129–130, 138, 142n43, 146, 148, 152, 153n4, 154n6, 154n15, 156n30, 189, 191
Institute for Comparative Literature and Society, 66
Institutional Revolutionary Party (PRI), 181
insurrection, 83, 89; Transcontinental Crossroads of a Critical Insurrection, 3
insurrectional, 171–172
institute, 172
Institute for Comparative Literature and Society, 66
institution, 33, 181, 189–190, 198
institutional, 9, 17, 67, 160, 162, 189
institutionalization, 36
institutionalize, 189
intellectual, 18, 54, 62n2, 67, 89, 134, 138n8, 158–160; the intellectual

"revolution," 159; the intellectual stars of the day, 160
intellectualism, 2
intellectualization, 14, 16, 17
intellectually, 161, 187
intelligence, 42
interdisciplinarity, 17
interdisciplinary, 26, 95, 189
interest, 30, 44, 47, 60, 67, 75, 87, 120, 124, 125, 131, 162–163, 164, 178, 191
interesting, 119, 131, 140n33, 148, 155n16, 158, 164, 171
intermedial, 19n3
intermodal, 49
internal, 174
international, 54, 81, 85, 163, 168, 174
Internationale, The, 159
internationally, 81
internet, 47, 83, 90n3, 198; postinternet, 81
interpret, 43, 57, 60
interpretation, 57, 58–59, 61, 90, 128, 136, 142n43, 143nn74–78, 149, 150, 170, 183n8, 188–189, 191, 195–197, 199, 200n13, 201n31; divergent interpretations, 195; misinterpretation, 26
interpretive, 187
intersect, 54
intersection, 45
intersectionality, 82, 83, 91n7
intersubjective, 111
Intifada of 1967, 177
invent, 40, 60, 192, 198; reinvent, 46, 49, 154n6, 156n31
invention, 46, 69, 132, 134, 187–188, 194–195
inventiveness, 42
inventor, 194–195
inversion. *See under* version

invisible. *See under* visible
ipse, 111
Irigaray, Luce, 141n42
Irma, 151, 155n22
Isin, Engin, 202n44
Israeli-Palestine Six Days War, 177
issue, 45, 46, 68, 78n18, 82, 84, 124–125, 143n73, 154n15, 163, 197
IT, 191
Italian, 8, 12, 18n1, 41, 85, 161; Italian thinkers, 171, 173
Italy, 15, 126, 140n23
Ivy League, 69

Jablonka, Ivan, 165n1
Jacquier, Nicholas, 86
Jakobson, Roman, 59
James, Alison, 5, 42, 51n11, 199
Japanese, 41
Jean, Raymond, 160
Jenkins, Keith, 79n40
Jesi, Furio, 3, 171
Jetty, The, 9
jeu, 57, 62n8–14, 63n15, 63n17–18, 63n23–24, 63n26, 63n28
Jeudi, 39
Jigsaw puzzles, 49
Johns Hopkins. *See under* university
Johns Hopkins University Press, 162
Joris, Pierre, 115n2
Jouet, Jacques, 103–104, 107n64, 107n66
Joughin, Martin, 200n21
jouissance, 130–131, 147, 151–152, 154n6, 154n10, 174, 182
journal, 28, 37n22, 68, 69
journalism, 16
Joyce, James, 155n25
Junior Year Abroad of Michigan-Wisconsin, 161
juridical, 135
jurisprudence, 195, 196

just, 54, 59, 73–74, 76, 120, 122, 125, 128, 132–134, 137, 148, 151, 157, 161, 170, 175–176, 180, 187, 193, 198; unjustly, 160
justice, 48, 85, 87, 112, 174, 194–197, 201n29
justify, 178

Kafka, Franz, 101
Kafkaesque, 190
kakoi, 125
Kant, Immanuel, 96, 106n37, 176, 178, 184n20
Kantian, 99, 127, 176
Katamari, Damacy, 45
Kazi-Tani, Tiphaine, 91n11
Keats, John, 44
Kelly, Mary, 34
Kerényi, Károly, 171
Kehre, 128
Killian, Kevin, 23, 25, 27–28, 31, 36n4, 36n8–11, 36n15, 37n16–18, 37n24, 38n40
kind, 50, 70, 72–73, 76, 79n28, 88–89
King, Stephen, 26
Kitchin, Rob, 201n31
know, 54, 58, 60, 66, 68, 76, 88–89, 111, 122, 124–125, 128, 134, 146, 150–153, 156n32, 161, 177, 198; well known, 65, 147, 154n15, 158, 198; unknown, 54, 149, 150, 151, 153, 200n12; best-known, 104; unknowable, 198
knowledge, 48, 61, 64n31, 73–74, 79n28, 83, 94, 96, 129, 131, 155n16, 161–162, 169, 173, 196–199, 201n32, 202n42; "knowledge and jouissance," 154n6; "knowledge-driven," 201n31
knowledgeable, 54–55
Kojève, Alexandre, 116n9, 170, 183

Kolbowski, Silvia, 34
Koselleck, Reinhardt, 79n39
kreitton, 125
Kristeva, Julia, 26–28, 30, 35, 37n28, 187, 199n1
Kruger, Barbara, 34
Kuhn, Annette, 79n33

Labarre, Nicolas, 19n3
Lacan, Jacques, 5, 27, 63n30, 69, 126, 140nn23–28, 141nn36–42, 145–149, 151–153, 153n3, 154nn5–7, 154n7, 154n10, 154n13, 154n15, 155n25, 156nn27–32, 159–160, 199
Lacanian, 69, 127–129, 134, 138, 138n8, 143n73, 153notes, 153n4, 162
Laclau, Ernesto, 138n8
Lacroix, Romain, 91n11
Lacoue-Labarthe, Philippe, 184n19
Lana Del Rey, Elizabeth Woolridge Grant, 85, 91n23
language, 17, 23–32, 34–35, 37n22, 39, 41, 43–44, 47, 49, 56, 59, 63n28, 72, 93–94, 96, 103, 113–115, 145, 147–149; English language, 67; French Language, 68, 145; graphic language, 82; language-based hack; 42, language poet, 24; Language Poetry, 4, 23–24, 34; language turn, 29; Language writer, 25, 28–32, 35; Language writing, 23–25, 28–29, 31–35, 37n22, 37n23, 37n33, 38n34; West Coast Language, 25
L=A=N=G=U=A=G=E, 4, 24
Laporte, Roger, 109, 117n22
Latin, 160
Latin America, 3, 167–168, 177, 182, 187
Latin American, 175

Latin Quarter, 157
Latour, Bruno, 97
Lauterbach, Ann, 36n3, 37n29
Lautréamont, 161
law, 39, 84, 114, 129, 134, 195; Law, 133, 155n23, 195; law of profit, 120, 124; phallic law, 149
Lawler, Louise, 34
Leblanc, Gérard, 69
Lefebvre, Henri, 16, 21n33
left, 33–34, 58, 122, 126, 133, 137, 139, 146, 162–163, 195; left and right, 8; Left Bank of Paris, 158; "left out," 72; left-wing, 35; New Left, 37n22, 80n46; revolutionary left, 169
leftism, 32
leftist, 16, 70
Lehman, Robert, 99, 106n37
Leibnizean, 191
Leighton, Angela, 102, 105n21, 107n59
Leiris, Michel, 162
Le Lionnais, François, 39, 40, 49, 51n4
Lenfest Center for the Arts, 77n2
Lentricchia, Frank, 54, 62n3
lesbians, 82
Le Thor, 141n35
letter, 146, 149, 151, 152, 153, 153n4, 155n25, 160; a veritable rupture in French letters, 164
Letter to Jane, 70, 71, 72
Lévesque-Jalbert, Émile, 5
Levinas, Emmanuel, 110
Levine, Caroline, 5, 93, 96–103, 106nn22–29, 106nn31–32, 106nn34–36, 107n61
Levine, Sherrie, 34
Levinson, Marjorie, 96, 105n17, 105n20
Lévi-Strauss, Claude, 4, 26, 53–57, 59–60, 63n28, 63n30

Lévy, Sydney, 161
L'Excelsior, 160
Lezra, Jacques, 141n34
liberal, 132, 179; neoliberal, 177, 181; the neoliberal universities, 189–190
liberate, 83, 182
liberation, 83, 85, 119; "liberation of life," 120
liberatory, 119
libertarian, 16
life, 85, 88, 92n30, 98, 100–101, 119–120, 122, 125–126, 128, 134, 136, 140n33, 141n42, 143n73, 150, 154n14, 156n30, 158–159, 161, 173, 181, 194; afterlife, 174; "civilizational life," 123; factical life, 136, 137; "new idea of collective life," 132; stupid life, 135; suture of life and politics, 127, 128, 129, 130, 138; "true life," 124, 131, 132, 133, 136, 137
lifelong, 147
lifestyle, 101
lignes de fuite, 81
liminal, 53
limit, 40, 44–45, 56, 82, 84, 120–121, 126, 129–130, 138n8, 147, 151–152, 158, 164, 175, 178–179, 198, 201n31; unlimited, 120–122, 129–130, 132, 138n8; illimitation, 121, 130; unlimitedness, 137
limitation, 88, 113, 197
L'Infini, 159
linguistic, 29–31, 93, 102, 113; nonlinguistic, 112; sexual-linguistic constitution of the subject, 33
linguistically, 93, 99
linguistics, 13, 29, 160
lipogram, 103–104, 107n67
lipogrammatic, 103
listserv, 28
literal, 87, 137

literally, 29, 86
literariness, 99
literary, 9, 12–14, 21n34, 26, 28–30, 35, 38n44, 39, 40–43, 46, 49, 61, 68, 93–95, 98, 99–102, 104, 105n14, 106n37, 145–146, 155n25, 160, 164, 179; "literary community," 113–114; literary history, 165; literary studies, 201n31; spatio-literary, 111
literature, 12–16, 20n28, 26, 39–42, 44, 46, 49, 50n2–3, 51n4, 86, 93, 96–97, 99–104, 113, 148, 152, 154n14, 156n30, 159–160, 163, 164, 165; "literature-world," 164; paraliterature, 9; scientific literature, 200n17
logarithm-type programing, 41
logic, 129, 140n22, 153n3, 170–174, 176–182, 183n8, 184nn26–27, 190, 194–195, 198, 200n11, 200n15, 202n44
logical, 194, 195
logicality, 194, 201n25; rationality-logicality, 194
logically, 60, 148, 152, 194
Lol. *See under* Stein
look, 49–50, 58, 68, 70, 82, 85, 88, 121, 125, 129–130, 136, 159, 164–165
López Mateos, Adolfo, 180
Lorde, Audre, 82, 90n4
love, 5, 134, 145–153, 153n, 153n1, 153n3, 154n6, 155n23, 156n32, 160; in love with counterculture, 161; "Lol V. Stein as a kind of 'anagram of LOVe,'" 156n30; "ravishing" love scene, 150
lover, 149–151
low, 11, 27; low-brow, 18; lower-class, 25; low culture, 67

Lowood School, 96
Lukács, Georg, 27
Lukham, David, 191, 192, 200n16
Lula, Luiz Inácio, 88
Lusson, Pierre, 41, 51n6
Lyotard, Jean-François, 196–197, 201nn32–35, 201n37, 201n39
lyrical, 27

Macé, Marielle, 94, 100–103, 106n44, 107nn45–54
machine, 76, 171, 197, 207
machinery, 39, 56, 82
Macksey, Richard, 53, 62n1
made, 10, 12, 14, 17, 59, 65, 67, 69, 75–76, 81, 85, 119–120, 126, 150, 162–164, 182, 191, 197; are now made automatically, 196; made in France, 14; made in US, 13; ready-made, 148
Madison, 161
magazine, 7–12, 20n18, 20n20, 81–82
magic, 86–88; #magicresistance, 85; cyber-magic, 86
magical, 79n28, 84, 86–88, 90; #magicalresistance, 85–86
Maingueneau, Dominique, 99, 106n40
Maison Française (Columbia University), 66
make, 54, 55, 56, 58, 59, 60, 61, 70, 71, 72, 73, 75, 77, 83, 87, 121, 122, 123, 126, 127, 128, 129, 130, 134, 138n8, 140n33, 141n35, 146–149, 153, 156n26, 164; love is something one *makes*," 148, "make love not war," 146; meaning-making, 89; "Of the past let us make a clean slate," 159; "the important decisions that we—and they—make," 198; these events make '68 a particular kind of historical sign, 176

maker, 50, 129; filmmaker, 68, 72
"male gaze," 69; male capitalism, 83
Mallarmé, Stéphane, 40, 103–104
Mandel, Tom, 37n23
Mandeville Special Collections (library at the University of California at San Diego), 31
Mangrum, Benjamin, 201n31
manifest, 42, 75, 90, 113, 167
manifestly, 55
manifesto, 39–40, 47–49, 51n20, 51n23, 52n28–33, 132, 165n1
manifestation, 158, 175, 190
Manning, Erin, 89, 92n31
Mao Zedong; "Mao-Spontex," 161
March 22, 66
Marcuse, Herbert, 160
margin, 122
marginal, 17, 18; marginal cinema, 69
marginality, 46, 160
marginalize, 188
Marin, Louis, 54
market, 87, 133–134, 174, 190–191; unmarketable, 189
marketplace, 198
Martinican, 183n8
Marx, Karl, 47, 68–69, 122–123, 132, 141n34, 158
Marx, William, 106n41
Marxian, 120, 129, 138n8, 141n34
Marxism, 123, 129, 159–160, 169
Marxist, 72, 170, 172–173; the official Marxist intelligentsia, 170
Marxist-Leninist, 68
mass, 9, 16, 24; mass cultural production, 7; mass culture, 9, 10, 12, 14, 34; mass media, 8, 82, 175
massive, 81
Massumi, Brian, 89, 92n31

master, 81–83, 90n4, 129, 138n8, 162, 170; "master's discourse," 126, 138n8; master-slave dialectic, 183
mastery, 151
material, 10, 18, 34, 48, 84, 126, 138n8, 139, 162
materialism, 179
materialist, 68, 69, 141n34
materiality of language, 34
mathematical, 39–40, 191, 194–195, 197, 201n28
mathematician, 161
mathematics, 40, 42, 49
Matias, Diana, 77n10
matter, 49, 87, 97–98, 104, 121, 126–127, 148, 158, 168, 173–174, 177, 192, 196–197, 199
may, 54, 57, 60, 67, 73, 76, 82–84, 88–90, 119, 123, 126–131, 136–137, 138n8, 147, 150–152
May, 81, 140n23, 177–178
May '68, 2–4, 6, 65–67, 72–73, 75–76, 77n5, 77n11–14, 78n25–26, 78n23–25, 119, 124–126, 145, 153 n, 157–160, 162–165, 167–168, 170–177; '68, 174
May 1968, 65–70, 73, 75–76, 81, 119, 124–125, 187, 191
McCaffery, Steve, 23, 44
McCormick, John P., 79n32
McLuhan, Marshall, 20n24
McNulty, Tracy, 154n14
mean, 39, 40, 42, 48, 50, 69, 70, 72, 74, 113, 119, 121–123, 126, 129, 131, 133–134, 139, 141, 146, 150–151, 158, 168, 170, 175–176, 183n8, 187–188, 193, 197
meaning, 11, 19n17, 27, 29, 34, 42, 46, 59, 61, 88–89, 93–94, 100–101, 103–104, 120–121, 125, 151, 156n30, 157, 169–170, 172, 174,

meaning *(continued)*
   177, 181, 195, 198–199, 202n44; annihilation of meaning, 121; failure of meaning, 152; nonmeaning, 103; the meaning of an event, 192
meaningful, 44, 97
Méchoulan, Éric, 163
media, 7–8, 13, 81, 85, 87, 90, 92nn30–31, 189, 193, 200n5; intermedia, 19n3; mass media, 82, 175; media saturation, 1, 6n2; remediating, 12; social media, 192, 193, 198; transmedial festival, 83, 91n10, 91n20
mediate, 197
mediatic, 82, 86, 87
mediation, 199
medium, 13, 17, 20n24
Melodia E. Jones Chair, 2
member, 39–44, 46, 48–50, 76, 163
memory, 6n4, 6n5, 147, 150, 174, 179, 180; place of memory, 3
Meschonnic, Henri, 107n62
metaphor, 112
metaphysical, 121, 128, 173; metaphysical ontology, 120
metaphysics, 55, 56, 57, 138n8, 140n33, 142n43; "metaphysics of presence," 75; Western metaphysics, 169
meter, 95, 97
method, 39, 40, 42–44, 46, 48, 53, 68, 83, 189
methodical, 42
methodological, 202n44
methodology, 201n31
Mexican, 178, 180–181, 184n26; Mexican 1968, 179; Mexican revolutionary party-state policy, 180; the Mexican '68, 178–182
Mexico, 160, 179–181; Mexico '68, 180, 184nn24–25

Mexico City, 178
Michallat, Wendy, 8, 18n2
Michaux, Henri, 101
Michigan. *See under* university
Middleton, Peter, 30, 37n28
Midi-Minuit Fantastique, 10
Midwestern, 69
militant, 68, 87, 131, 136–137; different militant factions on campus, 160; "militant function," 68; "militant idea," 131; "militant practice," 68; "militant sacrificial commitment," 169
Miller, Jacques-Alain, 154n5
Miller, Tyrus, 30, 37n32
Milwaukee. *See under* university; department
Milwaukee Conferences, 69
Minnesota, University Presses of, 163
Mitchell, W. J. T., 95, 105n13
Mittelstadt, Brent, 201n38
modern, 10–11, 13, 16, 18, 29, 36n2, 37n26, 37n28, 53, 86, 91n13, 121, 127–128, 139, 158, 160, 162, 168–169, 170–173, 175, 183n4, 202n44; modern poetry, 160; postmodern, 91n19, 98, 101, 105n2, 107n52, 195–196, 201nn32–35; pre-postmodern, 18
modernism, 29, 69–72, 76, 78n24
modernist, 16, 31, 32, 37n23, 74, 101; modernist-materialism, 70; postmodernist, 195, postmodernist theories, 194
modernity, 120, 128–129, 132–133, 137, 139, 161, 176
modernization, 10, 174
Modern Language Quarterly, 94
MOMA poet laureate, 42
moment, 50, 53, 56, 67, 72, 74–76, 88, 124–125, 128, 131, 133, 156n30, 157, 163, 165, 182,

191; disarticulating moment, 181; foundational moment, 178; the crucial moment, 147; the very moment of their occurrence, 192
Monroe, Jonathan, 36n3, 37n29
Montreal, 160–161, 163
Moraga, Cherríe, 90n4
"moral scarecrow," 86
morale élémentaire, 41
morally, 46
Moreiras, Alberto, 3, 141n42, 199
Mori, Bruna, 42, 43, 51n13
Morin, Edgar, 9, 19n6
Morningside Park, 65
Morreale, Emiliano, 19n13
"*motus*," 152
move, 56, 58, 61, 65, 67–68, 87, 89, 98, 100–102, 110, 126, 128–129, 138, 149, 150–151
movement, 23–25, 27, 29, 31–32, 34–35, 36n3, 36n4, 37n22, 37n29, 46, 51n9, 59, 61, 65–66, 67, 82, 85–86, 87, 100, 123, 136, 141n35, 157–159, 161–163, 172, 177, 180, 191; movement of Capital, 130, 138n8; Surrealist movement, 159; the May '68 movement, 145, 146
movie, 8, 9, 10, 11, 14
Muller, Jerry, 189, 200n7
multidimensional, 41
multiple, 47, 75, 84, 87, 199
multiplicity, 47, 48, 68
multivocality/ies, 3, 6n5; multivocal, 3, 6
multilocality/ies, 3, 6n5
Mulvey, Laura, 69, 78n19
Munslow, Alun, 79n40
Musée des Arts Décoratifs in Paris, 9
Musset, Alfred de, 161
mysterious, 85, 151
mystic, 154n15, 155n16
mystical, 171, 183n12, 195

myth, 48, 57, 66, 67, 146, 147, 148, 154n8, 170, 182, 202n44
mythical, 160, 178
mythological, 171, 173
mythologist, 171
mythology, 8, 16, 57, 60, 67

nada es más que nada, 124
nadie es más que nadie, 124
name, 57, 61, 70, 77, 82–83, 90, 111, 114–115, 120–121, 123, 127, 130, 137, 152, 156n30, 158, 164, 168, 174, 176, 187, 193; Name of the Father, 133, 135, 137; the new name of Being, 132
namely, 129, 135, 194, 196–197
namesake, 152
Nancy, Jean-Luc, 3, 5, 109–115, 115n1, 115nn3–7, 116nn10–12, 117nn19–20, 117n22, 119–124, 132, 137, 138nn2–3, 138nn5–7, 139n9, 140nn11–16, 176, 184n19, 194
Narboni, Jean, 78n16, 78n26, 145
narration, 39
narrative, 7–10, 12, 14, 16–18, 25, 27, 33, 38n40, 71, 78n19, 95, 98, 121, 148, 153n4, 168, 175, 177–180, 182, 184nn26–27, 200n13; "narrative," 190; New Narrative, 4, 23–28, 31–35, 36n4, 37n17, 37n20, 37n22, 38n35, 38n36; official narratives, 180; political narratives of monumentalization, 179; the crisis of the grand narratives, 196; the historical narratives about these incidents, 178
narratological, 58
natural, 45, 56, 57, 123; "natural," 122
naturalness, 112
nature, 47, 56, 87, 91n13, 121, 150, 167, 171, 173, 175, 176, 181; nature/culture, 56

Navarro, Fernanda, 179
Nebraska, University Press of, 163
negate, 46, 110, 114, 169
negation, 16, 147, 152, 154n10, 173
negative, 40, 48, 57, 61, 86, 111–112, 124, 164, 173, 177, 181; '68 as a Negative Event, 174; nonnegative, 114
negativity, 110, 168, 169–173, 177; radical negativity, 167
Negrete, Fernanda, 4, 5, 153n1, 199
neo-French, 41
neoliberal, 177, 181, 189–190
neopagan, 87
neopragmatist, 29
network, 17, 81, 82, 83, 84, 85, 88, 157, 162
new, 7, 9, 10, 11, 13, 16, 17, 18, 39, 44, 49, 54, 55, 57, 59, 61, 67, 68, 73, 81, 83, 84, 88, 89, 96, 120, 125, 127, 132–137, 138n8, 140n33, 162–163, 171–172, 174–175, 177–178, 180–181, 187–190, 192–193, 195–199. *See also* criticism; formalism; historicism; ideal; novel; rhetoric; poetry
New German Critique, 162
newly, 40
news, 54, 89; newsletter, 76; newspaper, 8, 10, 41, 162; newsreel, 76; newsstand, 8
New Scientist, 44
New York, 65, 68, 76, 160; New York City, 67, 76; New York financial district, 85; New York University, 82
New Yorker, 161
New York Newsreel, 3, 65–66, 76, 77n1
Nicholson-Smith, Donald, 20n22
Niépce, Nicéphore, 69
Nietzsche, Friedrich, 55, 140n33, 160
Nietzschean, 55, 57, 59, 101

Nixon, Richard, 177
Nobus, Dany, 156n30
noisecracy, 88
nonappropriable, 139n9
nonassertive, 113
nonbrother, 112
noncapturable, 130
noncomparison, 120
nonconformity, 191
nonequivalence, 124
nonequivalent, 121
nonequivalential, 137
nonexceptionally, 177
nonexclusive, 114
nonexpert, 130
noninstrumental, 199
nonlinear, 40
non-Hegelian, 111
nonhierarchical, 83
nonhuman, 190
non-*lieu*, 111
nonlinguistic, 112
nonliterature, 8
nonnegative, 114
nonoccurrence, 193
nonofficial, 179
nonorganic, 103
non-owning classes, 48
nonphallic, 151
nonpoliticity, 130
nonpower, 134
non-produced, 121
nonprofit, 162
nonpublication, 16
nonreified, 30
nonsimple, 128
nonsovereign, 168
nonspecies, 59
nonspecular, 148
nonstrategic, 172
nonsynchronization, 191
nontotalizable, 110

nontransparency of language, 31
nontrivial, 125
nontropic, 83
non- or even antitraditional perspective, 136
normaliens. See under École Normale Supérieure
North-African, 183n8
North America, 13, 44; North American English Departments, 94
nostalgia, 59, 88, 163
nostalgic, 42, 43, 57, 58, 60, 139
notion, 41–42, 45–46, 55–56, 74, 88, 112–114, 117n16, 117n20, 125, 140n33, 172–175, 177, 182, 184n21, 196; Bataille deepens his notion of "inner experience," 169, 182n2; Bataille's notion of radical negativity, 171, 177; Jesi's notion of the revolt, 179; Hegel's notion of negativity, 168; Heideggerian notion of technology, 130; notion of a "true life," 124, 131; notion of a "true politics," 124; notion of expenditure, 168; notion of "general equivalence," 120; notion of poststructuralism, 54, 184n18
Noulipo, 42, 43, 51n13
Nous Deux, 11
nouveau roman, 26. See also novel
Nouvelle Revue Française, La, 159
novel, 39, 41, 46–47, 145–148, 150, 152, 155n20, 155n23, 156n30, 160, 161, 164, 185n28; graphic novel, 199; New Novel, 13, 15. See also nouveau roman
novelist, 161; New Novelists, 10, 161
now, 54, 55, 66, 67, 72, 73, 76, 77, 84, 87, 111, 113, 120, 121, 124, 126, 128, 129, 130, 131, 134, 138n8, 149, 159, 162, 163, 164, 165, 174, 180, 183n8, 191, 196; "it is now too late," 124, 126; The Freudian myth is now liquidated, 133; what now exists in French society, 158
nuclear war, 87

object, 17, 67, 93, 99, 101–103, 106n37, 127, 133, 137, 146, 153n4; an object-cause-of-desire, 149; object of inquiry, 93; *objet*, 149
objection, 68, 72, 99, 102
objective, 33, 73, 83, 91n13, 167, 171, 172
objectively, 73
Objectivist, 31
obscurantism, 89
obscure, 58, 110, 115
obscurity, 89
occult, 86
occultist, 86
œuvre, 40
Offset, 162
O'Hara, Frank, 25
old, 47–48, 56, 103, 125–126, 128, 131–132, 134, 162, 176; "beyond old hierarchical moons," 132; centuries-old, 41, 68; Lacan retakes his old 1968 lines, 126; *love* is an old word, 146; old age, 131; Old Continent, 60. See also historicism
once, 75, 148, 167, 189, 195; "Once More with Feelings," 77n8
online, 81, 88
ontological, 110, 120, 138n8, 169, 170, 183n8, 192, 110; onto-anthropological, 169; onto-theology, 57; ontologico-historical, 128. See also anti-ontological
ontology, 110, 112, 114, 115, 120, 127, 168, 170, 171, 175. See also anti-ontology

ontopolitical, 170, 171
ontopolitics, 170
oppose, 45, 71, 81, 84, 90, 111, 126, 174–176
opposite, 46, 83, 86, 162, 174, 177, 187
opposition, 56, 60, 116n12
oppositional, 23, 69, 70, 126
oppress, 184n21
oppression, 83, 84, 86; oppression of women, 87; women's, 78n20
option, 55, 56
order, 44, 47, 55–58, 60, 67–68, 83, 85–87, 110–111, 114, 123, 129, 131, 134, 137, 146, 153, 170, 175–176, 183n5, 189, 191, 194, 199; disorder, 193; social order, 145; symbolic order, 133; the categorical order of modern thought, 168
organize, 47, 53, 60, 72, 86, 88, 170, 173, 177–178
organizer, 88, 92n27, 162
organization, 42, 70, 132–133, 170, 174, 191
organizational, 162, 167
origin, 55, 57, 59–60, 65–67, 72–73, 75, 76, 111, 146, 157, 184n18, 188
original, 40, 48, 55, 59, 87, 112, 155n17, 179
originally, 53, 63n18, 182n2, 183n3, 185n28
originate, 189
origination, 74, 77
Orpheus, 44
Osman, Jena, 35, 38n43
Oulipian, 40–43, 46, 49, 51n10, 103, 104
Oulipo, 4, 39, 46, 48–50, 50n2–3, 51n4, 51n8, 51n8–9, 51n11, 51n16, 52n34, 102–104, 107n60, 107n65, 107n67, 108nn68–69

oulipotentiality, 102
own, 39, 43–44, 48, 56, 67, 70, 72, 74–75, 82, 88, 109, 110–111, 117n16, 121, 129, 137, 146, 148–149, 151, 154n5, 164, 167–168, 176, 199; created their own activist press, 163; [eigen], 137; his own words, 148; its own mystification, 123; my own trajectory, 157; on his own name, 156n30; our own historical occasion, 175; our own time, 125, 137; own critique, 56; the pursuit of truth for its own sake, 196; their own ends, 121

Palmer, Michael, 37n23
paradox, 26, 73, 88
paradoxical, 75, 84, 88, 89, 121
paradoxically, 88, 191
Paris, 41, 65–67, 70, 81, 83, 91n11, 92n28, 145, 154, 157–159, 162; Paris "uprising," 67, 73
Parisian, 8, 87, 157
Paris Match, 82, 90n2
Parmenidean, 131, 141n35, 142n43
Parmenides, 142n43
part, 56, 58, 65–67, 76–77, 81–82, 86–87, 109, 112, 114, 125, 140, 149, 151–152, 163, 169, 183n5, 193; not part of a repetitive event, 158
Partenie, Caitlin, 154n8
partial, 83, 91n13, 139
partially, 191, 193, 194
particular, 43, 54–55, 57, 60–61, 88, 63n28, 74, 81, 94, 98, 100, 146, 157, 162–163, 170, 173, 176, 178, 187, 189, 196
particularity, 98
particularly, 49, 81, 84, 86, 112, 141n42, 157–158, 160, 163, 179
partly, 157

party, 70, 71, 167; party-State policy, 180, 181
Pasolini, Pier Paolo, 101
pas tout, 127
pas de réponse, mot, 152
Pasquale, Frank, 196, 198, 200n10, 201n36, 202n40, 202n44, 202n45
pass, 57, 58, 83, 111, 169
passage, 57, 58, 111, 150, 152, 155n16, 155n21, 170
passé, 60, 149, "du passé faisons table rase," 159
passion, 18, 109, 115, 115n1, 115n6, 117n22, 199
passive, 181, 184n26
past, 11, 18, 40, 48, 75–76, 79n39, 113–114, 134, 158–159, 163, 165, 172, 180, 183n8, 187–188, 193, 199n2
patriarchal, 8, 69, 136, 179; patriarchal hierarchy, 98
patriarchalism, 180
patriarchy, 83, 85
Pavel, Thomas, 93, 105n2
Peer, Shanny, 77n4
Pellauer, David, 79n30
people, 46, 47, 54, 57, 86–89, 139, 140n33, 170, 182, 192–193; People's Workshop, 81; young people, 162
Perec, Georges, 41, 46–47, 49–50, 51n6, 52n35, 103–104, 162
Perelman, Bob, 32, 36n3, 37n23, 36n29, 36n33
perform, 40, 48, 55, 86, 168, 170, 173, 175
performance, 43, 58, 84, 187, 190
performative, 89, 179, 188
performativity, 34, 199n2
Perloff, Marjorie, 44, 51n16
"pestiferous," 126
"pestiferously," 126

phallocentric, 114
phallocentrim, 114
PhD candidate, 84
phenomena, 30, 174
phenomenological, 13, 54, 62n3, 128; our phenomenological sleep, 54, 62n3
phenomenology, 33, 62n3, 128, 129, 141n35, 143nn74–78; Hegelian phenomenology, 127; *phenomenology of the revolt*, 173, 180, 182
phenomenon, 60, 120, 197
philia, 114
Philology, Romance, 67
philosopher, 24, 73, 86, 125, 131, 141n42, 140nn20–21, 132, 171
philosophical, 30, 61, 67–69, 73–77, 127, 131, 133, 135–136, 160, 164, 168, 177, 179, 191; a philosophical critique of Big Data, 201n31; philosophical anthropology, 123, 126–127, 129–130, 133, 140n29; *philosophical events*, 72, 76
philosophically, 187
philosophy, 23, 24, 29–30, 35, 37n23, 37n26, 56, 67, 69, 73–75, 77, 77n6, 77n9, 78n27, 79nn31–32, 79n36, 79n38, 112, 127, 129, 131, 134, 136, 138n4, 138n8, 154n8, 162, 168, 170, 176, 183n12, 187; philosophy of history, 128, 167–168, 174–176
photo, 90n2; photogramme, 19n17; in photo-novel format, 10; photo-novel, 7–15, 19n11; photo-roman, 9, 19n17, 20n20, 21n31; photoromances, 18n1; *Photopoetics*, 178, 184n22
photograph, 68, 70, 86
photographic, 74
photography, 12, 69, 81
pictogram, 11

picture, 85, 88, 89, 90
picturesque, 161
Pieds nickelés, Les, 14
Pinchon, Pierre, 19n14
Pizzino, Christopher, 20n28
place, 58, 67, 74, 87–88, 90, 111–112, 121, 124, 127, 129, 131, 142n43, 145, 150, 152, 156n30, 163, 172, 177–178, 181, 189, 195; commonplace, 55, 145; displacement, 147, 187; marketplace, 198; replace, 158, 164, 176, 194, 201n31; replacement, 190, 191, 201n25; "so much secrey so publicly in place," 198
Plato, 146–147, 154n8
Platonic, 147
play, 41, 47, 49, 53, 55, 57–59, 63n18, 67, 70, 76, 89, 111, 113, 125, 129, 149, 152, 155n22, 162, 164, 173, 194; downplay, 196; play on words, 39; replay, 158; wordplay, 156
playful, 58, 96, 135
player, 41
Plaza de Tlatelolco, 178, 181; "Night of Tlatelolco," 181
pleasure, 14, 16, 44, 69, 103, 129, 148, 161
Pleynet, Marcelin, 68, 69
plural, 99, 173; singular-plural character, 173
plurality, 75, 99, 100, 101
pluralize, 179
plus d'un, 127
plus-de-jouir, 138n8
"po," 49. *See also* Oulipo
Poe, Edgar Allan, 155n25
poem, 31, 35–36, 44, 95, 97, 104, 105n10, 156n30
poésie, 154n13
poet, 9, 24–25, 29, 31, 35, 41–42, 44; Language poet, 32, 34
poetic, 28, 31, 35, 41, 44, 95, 97, 99, 103, 113
poetics, 25, 29, 30, 35, 36n6, 37n25, 37n32, 39, 51n16, 60–61, 95, 97, 106n38, 183n10, 184n22; Poetics program at Buffalo, 24
Poetics Journal, 30, 34, 37n22, 38n38
poetry, 23–25, 28–32, 34, 36, 36n2, 36n3, 37n23, 37n26, 37n29, 39, 41, 44, 95, 105nn18–21, 148, 156n30, 160, 161; experimental poetry, 199; Language Poetry, 34; New American poetry, 29; US Modern Poetry, 29
politeuesthai, 125
politeuma, 125
politeuo, 125
politic, 122
political, 8, 17, 18n1, 42–45, 48, 68–71, 73, 76–77, 81, 83–89, 109, 119, 121, 123, 125, 128–130, 132–137, 138n8, 157–159, 163, 169, 174–182, 183n4, 184nn19–20, 187–189, 191–192, 197; antipolitical, 125; being-political, 112; biopolitical, 178, 194; ontopolitical, 171; infrapolitical, 130, 137–138, 141nn34–35, 141n42, 142n43; overt political consciousness, 43; political activism, 163; political anthropology, 123; political modernism, 70–72, 76; political rationality, 169; social-political framing, 82; sociopolitical, 194, 197
politically, 126, 168
politician, 125
politicity, 129–130, 138; impolicity, 130; nonpolicity, 130; ultrapolicity, 130
politicization, 119, 131, 175; depolitization, 112, 174–176, 182; repolitization, 175–176, 182

politicize, 125, 160, 182; depoliticize, 14, 174, 176; repoliticize, 176
politics, 41, 47, 65, 69, 86–90, 91n7, 92n26, 112, 114–115, 116nn13–15, 117nn17–18, 119, 120, 123–130, 133–134, 138, 168–171, 175–176, 178, 181, 183n8, 189, 196, 199, 201n25, 202n44; biopolitics, 119, 189; infrapolitics, 119, 123–124, 131, 137, 140n22, 141nn34–35, 141n42, 143n73, 199; "Let infrapolitics be," 119; "mourn politics," 112, 115; *ontopolitics*, 170; politics of poetic form, 35; "true politics," 124
Pollock, Grisela, 156n33
Ponge, Francis, 101
pop, 81, 85
pop singer, 85
Populaire, Atelier, 81
popular, 10, 12–14, 18, 82; popular culture, 8–9, 14, 21n34; popular fiction, 9, 16; popular mass culture, 12
Portland, 85
Positif, 3
position, 24, 26, 31–33, 43–44, 49, 70, 73, 124, 126–127, 133–134, 148–153, 154n7, 155n16, 156n33, 170, 173–174, 184n21, 201n38; disposition, 169, 171–173, 176–177, 182; imposition, 180; predisposition, 176; proposition, 152, 191; transposition, 40, 201n31
positivism, 44
positivist, 44, 61, 64n31
positive, 132, 164, 168–169, 173
positively, 142n43
positivize, 168
possibility, 42, 45, 48, 60–61, 112, 120–121, 123, 129–130, 133, 136–137, 138n8, 173, 175, 181–182, 187–188, 190, 194–195, 199, 201n29
possible, 40, 55, 59, 61, 83, 87, 115, 119, 120, 122–126, 128, 131–132, 134–135, 137, 139n9, 141n34, 150–151, 193–195; impossibility, 74, 111, 131, 135, 148, 175; impossible, 73, 111, 113–115, 134, 138n8, 146, 156n33, 159, 198
possibly, 50, 56, 69, 109; impossibly, 134
post, 85, 89, 90, 122
post-1968, 72, 74, 75, 77
post-'68, 4, 5, 171
post-9/11, 194
post-beat, 35
postcolonial, 95, 187
postconceptualism, 4, 33
"postcritical reading," 102
postdigital, 83
postface, 43
posthuman, 143n73
postinternet, 81
post-Language poets, 35
postminimalism, 4, 33
postmodern, 91n19, 98, 101, 105n2, 107n52, 195, 196, 201nn32–35
postmodernist, 194, 195
post-New York School, 35
postrevolutionary, 70
postscript, 91n16, 91n18
postscriptum, 81, 89
post-structural, 29
poststructuralism, 4, 5, 13, 53, 54, 55, 57, 58, 59, 60, 61, 66, 67, 94, 184n18
poststructuralist, 4, 29, 53, 54, 55, 60, 61, 66, 71, 72, 73, 95, 175, 193, 194, 195
post-truth age, 1
post-World War I, 73
post-War, 8

potential, 39, 40–41, 44, 48–50, 50n2–3, 98, 100–101, 103, 107n67, 146, 199; potential/impotential, 104; potential potentiality, 103, 173
potentiality, 42, 98, 102–103, 107n60, 107n66; Oulipotentiality, 102
Poucel, Jean-Jacques, 42, 51n17, 107n60
power, 24, 27, 28, 50, 61, 71, 82–83, 86, 87, 90, 121, 132, 135, 138n8, 172, 176–177, 181, 188–189, 194, 198, 200n20, 200nn23–24; nonpower, 134; power produced by the computational turn, 197
powerful, 24, 27, 49, 70, 82, 84, 89, 91n13, 125, 202n44
powerfully, 120, 194
Pratt Institute in Brooklyn, 29
practice, 13, 17–18, 40–43, 56, 68, 70, 72, 86, 89, 109, 152, 153n4, 156n31, 168, 175, 179, 189, 195, 199, 202n49; a new practice of truth, 134; film practice, 69–70, 72; modern theoretical practice, 127; the practice of psychoanalysis, 149
practitioner, 42, 43, 44
prayer, 86, 114; #PrayerResistance, 86
predisposition. *See under* position
pre-postmodern, 18
"Pre-potential Literature," 103
prerevolutionary, 70, 181
presence, 54–55, 57, 75, 85, 113–114, 123, 142n43
present, 46, 47, 55, 58, 75, 76, 90, 90n2, 120, 127, 128, 132, 135, 137, 147, 151, 158, 159, 180, 185n28, 187, 188, 190; the ever-present reference, 158
presse du coeur, 7
Prince, Gerald, 161
prise de plaisir, la, 148

problem, 40, 63n28, 73, 75–77, 115, 139, 145–147, 153n4, 154n8, 155n22, 158, 174–175, 191–192, 196–197; unproblematized, 173
problematic, 73, 74, 146, 178
problematization, 168, 170, 175
produce, 40, 42, 46–50, 60–61, 68, 71, 74, 76, 82, 90, 111, 121–122, 131, 138n8, 147, 160, 163, 169, 171, 177–178, 189, 196, 197, 202n49
producer, 123
product, 122, 123, 198; byproduct, 198
production, 7–8, 11, 18, 19n17, 48, 61, 68–69, 72, 81–82, 122–123, 135–137, 140n33, 141n34, 155n25, 192; de-production, 87; film production, 70; reproduce, 145; reproduction, 128, 180
productive, 47, 48, 68, 121, 169; reproductive, 135, 180; unproductive, 170
project, 39, 43, 57, 61, 70, 75, 127–128, 135, 138n8, 147, 183n5
proposal, 124
propose, 45, 68, 75, 83, 84, 110, 111, 112, 113, 120, 136, 149, 152, 155n23, 190, 199
proposition. *See under* position
protest, 65, 72, 84, 114, 170, 180–181
Protestant, 86, 169
protester, 65
Pro-Trump, 86
Proust, Marcel, 41, 99, 106n40, 106n42
Proustian, 99
Provençal courtly poetry, 155n25
psychic, 89
psychiatrist, 194
psychoanalysis, 69, 141n37, 147, 149–150, 152, 153n, 154n7, 155n20, 156nn30–33, 159

psychoanalyst, 152, 156n34, 159
psychoanalytic, 126, 140nn23–28, 155n21, 162
psychoanalytical, 34
psychological, 189
psychology, 174
psychotherapist, 194
psychotherapy, 194
public, 20n20, 21n31, 58, 65, 84–88, 189, 193, 197, 199; public demonstrations, 158; public freedom, 188; public space, 81; public sphere, 7, 195, 202n44; public universities, 161
publication, 7, 10, 13, 18, 54, 73, 81, 90n2, 152, 159, 190, 196; nonpublication, 16; republication, 10
publicly, 117, 198
publish, 9, 13–15, 42, 49, 53, 73, 78n18, 82, 86, 92n31, 109, 131, 145, 147, 159, 162–164, 182n2, 183n5, 185n28; republish, 87; unpublished, 75, 141
publisher, 14, 18
Puyo, Jean-Yves, 20n27

Quake,quake, the witches are back!, 85
queer 35, 44
Queneau, Raymond, 41, 49
quest, 60, 165, 195; quest of the origin, 64n31
question, 43–45, 56, 58, 60, 68, 70, 72–74, 79n41, 83–84, 87–89, 91n13, 109–111, 114–115, 127, 132–134, 137, 138n4, 146, 149, 152, 153n3, 158–159, 165, 167–168, 175–176, 179, 180–182, 187, 189, 191, 195–197, 199
questionable, 136

Rabaté, Dominique, 36n12

Rabaté, Jean-Michel, 156n30
race, 82, 90n6
racism, 8, 47, 82, 189
radical, 7, 12–13, 15, 17–18, 61, 65, 72, 76, 80n46, 120, 127–129, 131, 137, 139, 146, 168–170, 173, 175–176, 180–181, 184n26; radical cinema, 68; radical democracy, 182; radical documentary, 71; radical negativity, 167–168, 170–172; radical policity, 130; radical singularity, 124
radically, 121, 139, 140n33, 173, 177, 182; radically egalitarian, 136
Rainbow, Paul, 184n20
Rajchman, John, 67
Rancière, Jacques, 97, 162, 173, 184n15
rap (singing), 28
Rapide, 191
Rat, The (Buffalo campus newsletter), 76, 80n46
rational, 86, 88; irrational, 172
rationale, 141
rationality, 88, 130, 169, 173, 178, 194; instrumental rationality, 194; irrationality, 89; rationality-logicality, 194
rationalize, 173
Ratner, Helene, 202n49
read, 8, 12, 14–15, 26–28, 30–31, 36, 42, 55, 60, 68, 94–97, 102, 105nn6–7, 109, 110–114, 117n20, 125, 128, 138, 141n43, 147–148, 150, 152, 155n15, 155n21, 155n23, 156n33, 159–160, 170–171, 176, 179–181, 163n8, 196, 201n31; close reading, 195; "distant reading," 201n31; feminist readings of Antigone, 141n42; his most-read novels, 164; I can't read novels anymore, 145; Kantian

read *(continued)*
    reading of the French Revolution, 176; May '68 could be read as a radical disarticulation of politics and ontology, 175; misreading, 26; reread, 53, 73, 138n8
reader, 24, 28, 30, 40, 42, 46, 50, 59, 67, 74, 102, 147, 152, 153, 170, 184n20
Reagan-era, 95
real, 7, 12, 14, 17, 46, 48, 75, 88–89, 123, 127, 129, 132, 153n4, 156n30, 164, 169, 173, 175, 177, 184n21, 191–192, 200n16; *as something real* that resists the signifier, 149; in real time, 191–193; Real, 182; surreal, 162
realism, 10, 70–75; antirealism, 71–72; naive realism, 71
realist, 71; antirealist, 70–71
realistic, 46; unrealistic, 11
reality, 10, 45, 70, 73, 75, 77, 83, 86, 146, 167, 188–189
reason, 46, 60–61, 72, 83, 119, 168–171, 173–175, 177, 188, 194, 197, 200nn22–24; ontological reasons, 138n8
recent, 78n18, 89, 121, 126, 129, 141n42, 159, 171, 179, 182, 189
recently, 67, 87, 153n4, 154n6
reconceive, 72
reconceptualization, 74
reconceptualize, 41, 83
reduce, 55, 59; irreducibility, 58; irreducible, 56, 59
refer, 39, 46, 74, 79n28, 85, 122–123, 125, 127, 130, 140n22, 141n35, 149, 171, 173–174, 178, 184n21, 188, 191, 193, 198, 201n32
reference, 11, 49, 55, 57, 65, 68–69, 74, 76, 110, 117n16, 126, 143n73, 158–160, 168, 180, 182, 188, 194

referent, 132
referential, 13, 175, 178; self-referentiality, 177, 182
reflect, 53, 54, 190, 194, 196
reflection, 47, 83, 113, 127, 139, 164, 188–189, 193, 195–196
reflexive, 190
reflexivity, 69
*réjouissant post*tructuralism, 58
relate, 45, 56, 110, 114, 147–148, 168, 170–171, 175–177, 180–181, 185n28, 191; interrelated, 175
relation, 56, 74, 111–113, 115, 117n16, 121–122, 127, 146, 148, 152, 154n8, 172–173, 179, 181, 189, 197; correlation, 193; historical "correlation," 193; *relation*, 168
relational, 121, 188
relationality, 139
relationship, 40, 43, 46, 50, 88, 122, 141n35, 152, 162, 168, 178
relative, 44, 56, 67, 73, 75, 76, 160
relativize, 129
Renaissance, 131; Renaisssance humanism, 68
rendezvous, 86
Renov, Michael, 80n46–47
repetition, 57, 63n18, 97, 98, 107n46, 115, 133, 140n33, 158; "doomed to repetition," 133
repetitive, 158
represent, 41, 43, 53, 57, 61, 123, 160, 172, 174, 184n27, 188
representation, 32–34, 47, 48, 71, 82–83, 90n3, 106n37, 133, 162, 168, 170, 172, 176, 179–180
representational, 72
representationalism, 70
representative, 160
Republican, 85
research, 10, 16, 17, 40, 61, 89, 122, 137, 192, 201n31; research and

teaching, 190; research-creation, 89; research in algorithmic culture, 192
researcher, 192
resist, 47, 98, 87, 84, 113, 139n9, 145, 149, 177
resistance, 5, 13, 17, 25, 28, 38n44, 82, 84, 86, 88–89, 98, 153, 168, 180, 199; #magicalresistance, 85, 86;#magicresistance, 85; #PrayerResistance, 86
result, 40, 43–45, 54, 61, 63n28, 85, 90, 114, 132, 139, 168, 195; the results of catastrophic calculation, 122
return, 25, 28, 38n37, 41, 50, 68, 72, 74, 76, 93, 103, 111, 126, 132, 147, 155n16; return to the symbolic Father, 139; return to tradition, 133
revolt, 3–4, 16, 65–67, 119, 131, 146, 167–168, 171–177, 179–182, 183n11; Columbia Revolt, 3–4, 65–67, 72, 76, 77n1–2; *phenomenology of the revolt*, 180
révolter, 119, 138n1
revolution, 126, 129, 158, 163, 172–173, 181–182, 199n3–4; French Revolution, 174, 176; Mexican Revolution, 181, 185n28; "Revolution in/through Cinema," 68; the intelectual "revolution," 159
revolutionary, 68, 70, 72, 145, 153, 158, 169, 172, 177, 180, 188; Institutional Revolutionary Party (PRI), 181; postrevolutionary, 70: prerevolutionary, 70, 181; revolutionary politics of "dislocation and disarticulation," 199; the revolutionary State apparatus, 184n26
revolutionist, 130
rewrite. *See under* write

rhetoric, 49, 60; new rhetoric, 49; official rhetoric, 181
rhetorical, 67, 95
rhythm, 5, 75, 97, 101, 106n22
Richardson, Michael, 150
Ricoeur, Paul, 31, 79n30
Riffaterre, Michael, 54
right, 8, 15, 119, 148, 174, 175, 197; copyright, 18; human rights, 18, 163
rightly, 188
riot, 67, 171–172, 176–177; the May '68 riots and protests, 170
ritornello, 41
ritual, 86, 88, 89, 90, 91, 123, 133, 173, 174
ritualistic, 174
Rivette, Jacques, 145
Robbe-Grillet, Alain, 26
Robinson, Josh, 99, 106n38
Rodefer, Stephen, 37n23
Rodowick, David, 78n24
romance, 7, 8, 10, 11, 15. *See also* Department
Romantic, 103, 105n17
Romanticism, 99
romanticize, 49
Ronell, Avital, 26
Rosen, Philip, 78n22
Rosler, Martha, 34
Ross, Kristin, 10–11, 16, 19n15, 174, 182n1
Roubaud, Jacques, 39, 41, 50n1, 51n6, 103, 107n63
Rouselle, Duane, 154n6
Rousseauistic, 57, 59
Roy, Camille, 34, 37n17, 38n41
rule, 18, 41, 44, 121, 126, 133, 184n21, 195–196, 201n28; rules of calculation, 191; ruling class, 48
Ruppert, Evelyn, 202n49
rupture, 95, 131, 158, 164, 172

Russian Formalism, 29

Sade, Donatien Alphonse François, 11, 161
Said, Edward, 95
Saint John, of the Cross, 154n15
Saint-Michel, Serge, 15, 20n29
San Francisco, 23, 25, 160
say, 58, 60, 67, 70–71, 74, 79n28, 84, 88, 113–114, 124–125, 127, 133–137, 138n8, 145–152, 153n2, 156n31, 158, 168, 170–173, 177, 184n21, 194–195
unsayable, 147, 149, 153, 199; *unsayable*, 147
scarecrow, "moral scarecrow," 86
Schmitt, Carl, 112, 116n13, 184n21
Schmittian, 112
Schürmann, Reiner, 175, 183n12, 184n18
Schwartz, S., 156n31
science, 9, 13, 40, 43–44, 49, 53, 55–56, 62n8, 83, 86, 91n13, 134, 160, 165, 189, 191, 193, 196, 201n31, 202n44; Computer Science, 194; Digital Humanities, Science and Technology Studies, 193; humanities and sciences, 196; quantitative sciences and engineering, 195; "*sciences humaines*," 159; 163, *sciences sociales*, 165n1; technoscience, 196
scientific, 13, 18, 39, 42–43, 135, 192, 200n17; scientific inquiries, 196; scientific rationality, 194; scientific thinking, 194
scientist, 44, 165, 191, 194, 195
Scott, Gail, 25, 35, 35n17
Screen, 69
screen, 46, 78n22
screening, 65, 66, 67, 76
screenplay, 14, 15

SDS. *See under* Students for a Democratic Society
search, 54, 64n31, 66, 82, 89, 139, 151, 198, 201
second, 8, 11, 14, 17, 40, 54, 56, 58, 76, 82, 86, 109, 131–132, 136, 169, 176, 182, 198; second-degree, 13; second nature, 47
secondary, 132
see, 40, 42, 46, 49–50, 55, 57, 61, 66–67, 69, 75, 111–114, 116n12, 148, 176–177, 181, 189–192; as seen retroactively, 157; first seen as a tragedy, 158; "what you see is what you got," 71
seek, 55, 57, 60–61, 86, 87, 110, 127, 131, 133, 135–136, 162–163
seem, 43, 45, 54, 56–58, 60–61, 76, 84, 87–89, 112–114, 122–124, 134, 136–137, 145–147, 150, 156n30, 157, 160, 172, 175–176, 178, 182, 197
"Sein," 110
self, 33, 34, 45, 110, 111, 112; dissolution of the self, 33; distinctive self-referentiality, 177, 182; self-aggrandizement, 34; self-avowed, 23; self-awareness, 27; self-consciousness, 111; self-effacement, 34; self-evidence, 75; self-importance, 43; self-imposed, 49; selfish, 132; self-novelization, 14; the heroic self-sacrificial partisanship of the revolutionary left, 169; the order of self- and group-identities, 146; the self-regulating system, 196
semantic, 44
seminal, 67, 68, 184
semiotician, 24
semiotics, 14, 16, 34
sense, 48, 83, 110, 114, 120, 126, 129–130, 135, 137, 151, 163,

167, 169–170, 173–175, 177, 188, 190; "primordial sense of phenomenology," 141n35
senseless, 131
Serra, Hubert, 21n31
Serres, Michel, 54
sex, 33, 82, 85, 90n5, 92n26, 136, 146; gender identities or biological sex, 149; sex scenes, 148
sexual, 25, 136, 146, 148, 153n3, 154nn5–6; sexual-linguistic, 33; sexual revolution, 146
sexuality, 11, 27, 34, 154n6; heterosexuality, 82
sexualized, 33; desexualized, 33
sexually, 33
sexuate, 130, 138n8
sexuation, 154n15, 180
shape, 69, 97, 98, 100, 102, 110, 112, 165, 179, 191, 193; giving shape to meaning, 120
Sheldrake, Philip, 6n5
shoot, 65; shooting of the movie, 8
show, 55, 56, 82, 112, 113, 117n16, 117n20, 141n35, 142n43, 147, 148, 151, 178, 181–182, 201n31
sign, 57, 59, 62n8, 102, 104, 133, 175–177; a Kantian sign of human progress, 178; a negative sign of history, 181; an exemplary historical sign, 174–177
signal, 53, 121, 177, 192
signature, 56, 156n30
significance, 11, 93, 120, 188
significant, 78n16, 146, 154n5, 157
significantly, 74, 194
signification, 55, 59, 60, 96, 107n58, 121, 139n9, 169, 174
signified, 55, 56, 60
signifier, 5, 56, 71, 73, 146, 149, 151, 153, 153n4, 154n15, 156n30
signify, 68, 102, 121

silence, 10, 11, 14, 15, 16, 21n31, 82, 111, 149, 152, 155n19, 174
silent, 15, 127, 150, 152
Silliman, Ron, 23, 32, 37n23, 44, 51n18
similar, 44, 46, 88, 155n16, 158, 162, 174, 179
similarity, 86
similarly, 190, 197
Sims, 45; Sim Earth, 45
singular, 94, 101, 104, 106n37, 123–124, 136, 138n8, 171, 173, 199
singularity, 99, 100–102, 104, 107nn46–47, 107n52, 124, 138n8, 148, 176
Sisley, Dominique, 91n23
Sisyphean, 43
situate, 59, 113
situation, 24, 27, 72, 82, 132, 143n74, 157, 163, 180
Situationism, 162
Situationist, 8, 13, 45, 160
"slasher," 84
Small Press Traffic, 25, 27, 37n22
Smith, Sheridan, 79n28
Snowden, Edward, 83, 88
Socerlid, 9
sociability, 102
social, 26–27, 32, 39, 42–45, 47–49, 56, 61, 70, 76, 81–83, 88, 94–98, 101–102, 124, 135, 138n8, 158, 180–182, 189, 192, 195, 197, 201n31; social contract, 146; social media, 87, 192–193, 198; social network, 84–85; social order, 131, 145; social platform, 85; social-political, 82; social psychology, 174; social sciences, 165n1; social struggle, 183n8; the French, social, intellectual and political scene, 159
socialism, 169
socially, 45

societal, 45, 89
society, 46–47, 57, 81–84, 112, 121, 128, 158, 164, 181, 190, 196, 200nn9–10, 200nn12–13, 200n21, 201n31, 201n36, 201n38, 202n40, 202nn44–46, 202n49; "society of control," 83–84, 89, 91n16, 194; "the black box society," 198; traditional society, 133. *See also* Students for a Democratic Society; Institute for Comparative Literature and Society
Society for Cinema and Media Studies, 67, 77n8
sociological, 41, 127, 175
sociologist, 9, 160, 164, 170, 195
sociology, 16, 162, 196
sociopolitical, 82, 97, 194, 197
Söderback, Fanny, 141n42
solitary, 90, 138n8
solitude, 112, 114; the fundamental solitude of speaking beings, 148
Sollers, Philippe, 159
sonnet, 41, 98, 103
Sorbonne, 9, 66
sorceress, 86, 90
South of France, 81
Soviet, 70, 76
Soviets, 70, 77
space, 40, 45–46, 81, 83, 85–86, 110, 112, 114, 131, 146, 148, 150, 153n4, 157; an empty social space, 181; literary space, 146
Spahr, Juliana, 35, 38n44, 42
Spain, 6
Spanish, 160
Sparks, Simon, 184n19
Spartacist, 171
Spartakus, 167
speak, 59, 75, 113, 126, 128, 130–131, 134, 138n8, 147, 148; Badiou speaks of two errancies, 131; Lacan speaks of feminine jouissance, 152; two positions for speaking subjects, 149
speaker, 59
special, 157, 163, 190
specialize, 193
specific, 152, 195
specifically, 174
specificity, 148, 155n22
specify, 152
spectacle, 43
spectacular, 157
spectator, 148
spectatorship, 69
spectrum, 189
spirit, 41; the spirit of May '68, 126
spiritual, 85–86, cyber-spiritual, 86
spirituality, 84, 86–88, 90
Spring, 65, 83
Stacey, Jackie, 79n33
stage, 50, 115, 151, 195
Stalinist, 160
Stanford. *See under* university
Starhawk, Miriam Simos, 86–87, 92n25–26
stasis, 50
state (v), 44, 49, 67, 89, 124, 131, 136, 145–146, 148, 155n21, 156n30, 156n32
state, 113, 134, 146–147, 168, 192, 197; Mexican revolutionary party-State, 180; nation-states, 47; state control, 17; State of Emergency, 45, 177, 184n21; State narratives, 179; the revolutionary State apparatus, 180, 181, 184n26; the State, 178, 181. State University of . . . *See under* Buffalo; university
statement, 11, 73, 83, 85, 87, 148–149, 154n15, 165
Stein, Gertrude, 29, 31
Stein, Lol V., 149–151, 156n30

Steinberg, Samuel, 178, 179, 184n22
Stengers, Isabelle, 86, 92n25
still, 60, 67–68, 76, 81–82, 86, 88–89, 109, 113–114, 123, 125, 127, 132, 136–137, 140n33, 157, 161, 163, 167, 173, 177–178, 182, 184n27, 188, 193, 195, 197; (*Encore*, "still," "again," "more,"), 151; the magazine that still exists today, fifty years later, 162
Stoekl, Allan, 182n2
story, 10, 11, 27, 45, 46, 54, 65, 67, 68, 148, 173
storytelling, 7, 16, 20n28
storyteller, 9, 28
Strachey, James, 154n7
strange, 60, 61, 65, 74, 76
strangely, 70
Stretter, Anne Marie, 150, 153
Strier, Richard, 95–96, 99, 105n8, 105nn18–19, 106n39
Striphas, Ted, 200n9
structural, 69, 138n8
structuralism, 4, 10, 13, 16, 53–61, 62n5, 63n28, 77n6, 79n29, 93–94, 102; poststructuralism, 13, 184n18
structuralist, 53–55, 57, 59, 61, 62n1, 62n5, 62n8, 63n18–21, 63n28, 63n30, 94–95; poststructuralist, 94, 95, 175, 193, 194, 195
structurality, 55
structurally, 134
structuration, 171, 174, 176, 177, 182
structure, 39–40, 46–48, 53, 55, 57, 59, 74, 76, 94–95, 102, 114, 120, 133, 156n27, 167
structuring, 47
struggle, 27, 28, 32, 47, 49, 65, 70, 82, 111, 183n8, 184n21, 188; intellectual and political struggles, 187
student, 16, 65, 66, 67, 76, 81, 126, 157, 159, 160, 175, 177–181; a new generation of graduate students, 163
Students for a Democratic Society [SDS], 72, 163
study, 24, 28, 60, 61, 62n3, 67, 72, 73, 75, 88, 93, 95, 99, 143n73, 156n30, 178. *See also* center
style, 5, 27, 70, 72, 93–94, 96, 99, 100–104, 106n44, 107nn45–53, 110, 145, 148, 199; self-stylization, 101, 145, 148, 199
stylistic, 101
stylistics, 94, 99–100
subaltern, 48
subject (v), 202n44
subject, 25, 31–34, 48, 56–57, 60–61, 63n28, 74, 87, 89, 123, 128–130, 133, 138, 139, 140nn29–32, 146, 152–153, 153n1, 154n15, 156n30, 156n32, 156n34, 172, 179, 192, 195; a feminine subject, 146; a male subject, 149; for speaking subjects, 149; highly sensitive subjects, 160; subjectless, 34; the becoming-subject of the citizen, 127–129
subjectification, 84; desubjectification, 180
subjection, 123
subjectivation, 134, 136–137
subjective, 43, 45, 165, 169–170, 182, 197
subjectivity, 43, 138, 172, 195
substance, 40
SubStance, 157, 160, 162–163
substantive, 125
substitute, 58, 64n31, 79n30, 121, 126, 129, 134
substitution, 55, 190
substrate, 113
subversion, 40, 138n8, 161
subversive, 84, 86, 87
subversiveness, 84

subvert, 40, 139
succeed, 90
suggest, 44, 47, 54, 55, 70, 73, 109, 111, 112, 114, 117n20, 136, 138, 145, 156n30, 158, 159, 170, 187, 192, 197, 199
Sullerot, Evelyne, 9, 10, 12, 19n7
SUNY. *See under* Buffalo; university
superego, 129–130
superegoic, 130, 137
superfluous, 175
superhero, 12, 13
superimpose, 89
superior, 61
supernatural, 86
superstitious, 86
surface, 56, 88, 92n30, 151
Surrealism, 29, 159
Surrealist, 159, 159
symbolic, 131–133, 135, 137, 138n8, 154n14, 163, 183n8; "a-symbolic vision of Western capitalism," 132
symbolical, 7, 13, 20n21
symbolization, 131, 132, 133, 134, 135, 136, 137, 138n8
symbology, 167, 183n11
syntax, 55
system, 39, 42, 55–57, 60–61, 69–70, 72–73, 77, 78n26, 81, 83–84, 121, 154, 169–170, 177, 171, 190–192; in the industrial/military/financial systems, 193, 196
systematic, 61, 172, 180
systematically, 56, 178
systematize, 61
systemic, 41

tabula rasa, 159
take, 53–54, 58, 60–61, 66–70, 74, 75–77, 78n18, 86, 110–111, 113, 120–121, 125–126, 128–129, 137, 141n42, 149, 152, 171, 173, 175, 196; mistake, 127; retake, 126
talk, 23–24, 27–29, 31, 35–36, 82, 85, 87, 113, 125–126, 130–131, 137, 188; political talk, 125
Tarnac, 92n28
Tarot, 87
teach, 44, 68, 77, 155nn24–25, 161, 184n21, 190
teacher, 84, 190
technical, 18, 49, 89, 102, 121, 137, 161, 162, 196
technique, 45, 49, 95, 99, 150, 192, 195
technofeminism, 91n14
technogenesis, 189, 200n5
technological, 88, 90, 121, 192, 198; Heidegger's critique of the technological gigantic, 120; technological dominations, 189
technologically, 194
technology, 18, 69, 81, 83, 86–87, 89, 123, 130, 135, 138n4, 189–191, 193, 196–199, 201n31, 202n44; digital technologies, 202n42; pure technology of calculation, 122; Sciences and Technology Studies, 193
technoscience, 196
technoshamanism, 88
telos, 60, 110
Tel Quel, 3, 68–70, 159
temporal, 75, 112
temporality, 75
temporarily, 82
temporary, 83, 84
term, 40, 42–47, 55, 56, 60, 82, 84, 88, 90, 111, 119, 124, 130, 132–133; four decades of writing in terms of a reduction of narrative, 148; in his own terms, 168; political

terms, 122, 148, 154, 169, 172, 180, 188–190, 197; updating familiar terms, 194
terminally, 119
terminology, 198
text, 10–11, 13, 26–28, 33, 40–43, 45, 48–49, 60–61, 62n8, 67–68, 75, 94, 101–102, 104, 107n52, 109–110, 115, 140n22, 140n33, 141n42, 143n73, 145, 147–148, 150, 152, 154n8, 155n17, 156n30, 173, 182n2, 184n20, 201n31; French contemporary texts in translation, 163; text-centered, 17
textbook, 9, 195
textual, 96, 159, 201n31
textualist, 93
textuality, 102
theater, 39, 89
Theile, Verena, 95, 105n14
The Internationale, 159
thematic, 57
thematics, 59
thematize, 67, 113, 140n22
thematization, 120
theme, 109, 113, 131, 145
theology, 112
theoretical, 11, 13, 16, 24, 26, 28, 30–32, 35, 44–48, 50, 53–54, 60, 73, 79n28, 127, 136, 179, 188, 194; practico-theoretical, 127; theoretico-critical, 141n34
theoretically, 26, 69, 127
theoretician, 27
théorie, 164
theorist, 10, 24, 26, 74–75, 160
theorization, 26, 33, 69, 72, 74, 138n8
theorize, 69
theory, 10, 12–13, 17–18, 23–31, 33–36, 36n1, 36n2, 37n23, 37n26, 37n28, 45–46, 48, 53–54, 62n2, 62n7, 63n22, 63n29, 65, 67–70, 72–75, 78n18, 78n22, 79n28, 79n37, 82, 86, 91n17, 109, 128, 198, 201n31; between theory and practice, 168, 175; critical theory, 191; French Theory, 81, 161, 187; gamer theory, 51n23–25, 52n1–2; gender theory, 187; hegemony theory, 122, 138n8; literary theory, 164; political theory, 187; postmodern theory, 196; postmodernist theories, 194; poststucturalist theories, 193
Thibaudeau, Jean, 58
thing, 40, 46, 54, 109, 113, 134–135, 137, 141nn34–35, 146–147, 149, 153, 153n4, 163–165, 176, 181–182
think, 24, 31, 35, 55, 57, 68, 70, 72–73, 75, 77, 81, 87–88, 110, 112, 119–120, 123–125, 127–129, 131–133, 135–136, 140n22, 140n33, 142n43, 142, 163, 165, 170, 174–175, 182, 187–191, 193–196, 198–199, 199n2, 200n5, 200n8, 201n25, 201n31; rethinking, 35, 176, 187, 199; unthinkingly, 62n3
thinker, 24, 54, 61, 77, 125, 153n4, 171, 173
third, 111; third nature, 47; third political age, 87; Third World Newsreel, 77n1
Thomas, Jean-Jacques, 162
Thompson, John O., 24, 36n2
thought, 53, 55–56, 60–61, 67, 72–75, 81, 114, 116n12, 120, 124–125, 127–131, 133, 138, 139n9, 140n33, 141n35, 168–169, 171, 173–174, 183n4, 189, 192, 195;

thought *(continued)*
  rethought, 177; thought-provoking, 83; thoughtless, 176
time, 43–44, 46–47, 50, 60, 68–69, 73–76, 77n9, 78n27, 79n28, 79n37, 82–84, 86, 89, 110–111, 113, 117n16, 119–121, 123–125, 128, 131–132, 136–137, 138n8, 140n33, 145, 147, 150–152, 157–159, 162–164, 168–169, 171–178, 180–182, 189–193, 196, 200n16; our own time, 32
timely, 167, 180
timing, 198
Times Literary Supplement, 49
Tintin, 14, 20n27
title, 49, 53, 54, 68, 110
today, 55, 58, 74, 76–77, 87, 88, 113, 120, 122, 124, 131–135, 157, 159–160, 162–165, 174, 176–177, 179–181, 189, 193, 196
Todorov, Tzvetan, 55, 58–59
tool, 49, 56, 77, 81–83, 85, 90n4, 162; computational tools, 191–192
toolbox, 27, 29, 31
topographic, 45
topography, 45
topology, 45
topological, 45
Toronto, 67
Törnberg, Anton, 201n31
Törnberg, Petter, 201n31
totalitarianism, 189, 198
totemism, 60
Tours. *See under* center
tradition, 40, 61, 66, 72–74, 86–88, 114, 133, 141n34, 158, 160, 162, 184n21, 188; French tradition, 168; modern tradition, 128; interpretative tradition, 199; the modern and normative tradition of thought, 169; the French sacrificial tradition of political thought, 183n4; tradition of critical theory, 191
traditional, 40–41, 46, 68, 72, 133, 137, 145; antitraditional, 136; in good traditional departments, 161; return to hierarchical, traditional symbolization, 132; traditional role, 135; traditional sexual difference, 136; Western tradition, 141n42
traditionally, 63n28
transatlantic, 42, 51n11, 53, 93, 191
trans-Atlantic, 192
transcend, 134, 138n8
transcendence, 133
transcendental, 55, 60, 64n31, 127; "transcendental anthropology," 140n33; transcendental idealism of the present, 75
transcontinental, 3, 4; Transcontinental Crossroads, 3
"transference," 153, 156n32
transfer, 195, 201n25
transform, 47–48, 151, 157, 164, 195
transformation, 33, 40, 42, 83–84, 114, 146, 148, 190
transformational, 173
transformative, 146, 187; transformative space, 5; transformative agenda, 18
transgression, 27, 33, 69
transgressive, 35
transition, 162, 169
transitory, 172
translated, 8, 196, 197
translation, 67, 113, 163
transmediale, 83, 91n10, 91n20
transmission, 79n28
transnational, 25, 98
transparency, 32, 129; nontransparency, 31
"transplant," 187
transportation, 200n17

transposition. *See under* position
travail, 110
Tredennick, Linda, 95, 105n14
Tremate, tremate, le streghe son tornate, 85
Tremblay-McGaw, Robin, 35, 36n4
Tribe, Keith, 79n39
Trotskyist, 160
true, 46, 56, 84, 86, 125, 131, 133, 158, 164; "true life," 124, 131–133, 136–137; "true politics," 124
truly, 147
Trump, Donald, 85–86, 88, 91n23
trust, 88, 129, 134–135; entrust, 197
truth, 11, 49, 56–58, 73, 127, 133–138, 147, 150, 169, 170, 196
Turing, Alan, 195, 201n28
Turkle, Sherry, 90n3
turn, 29, 33–34, 53, 55, 57, 59–61, 73–74, 77, 83, 87, 94–96, 113, 119, 121, 127–128, 130, 146, 150, 161, 164, 173, 175, 180–181, 188–189, 191, 193–194, 196–198: a sacrificial turning point, 178
turnover, 84
two, 53, 54, 56, 57, 58, 59, 60, 61, 69, 72, 74, 109, 110, 111, 112, 117n16, 121, 128, 131–133, 140n33, 141n34, 146, 147, 149, 153, 161, 168–169, 172, 181, 202n44; have all developed the question of [...] "the two," 153n3; the story's two lovers, 148; the two errancies, 137; the two initiators at the helm of the magazine, 162; the two meanings of the black box, 198
tweet, 192; retweet, 85
Twitter, 85, 91n22

UK, 16, 70, 71; UK-US cultural studies, 17; UK-US versions of French theory, 18

unadressed, 145
unassailable, 148
unavowable, 113–115, 115n2, 116n9, 117n20
uncanny, 152
uncomfortable, 179
unconcealed, 141n35
unconscious, 5, 138n8, 146, 148, 151–152, 153, 154n7, 155n16, 155n25, 156nn30–31, 200n12, 200n14
uncritical, 46
undecidability, 178, 195
undeniable, 59
underground, 82
underline, 47, 112
undermine, 47, 73, 196
underpinning, 72, 73
underscore, 202n44
understand, 50, 60–61, 110, 120, 126, 131, 137, 138n8, 153, 157, 168, 171, 173, 180, 182, 183n5, 188, 190–191, 198
understandable, 136
understanding, 60–61, 70, 140n33, 141, 160, 168–169, 171–173, 176, 182, 183n8, 184n21, 188–189, 194, 197
"undertheorized," 197
"under the thrall," 67
undetermined, 113, 195, 200n15
unequal, 198
uneven, 77
unexamined, 194
unexpected, 82, 115, 187
unforeseeable, 189
unfortunate, 61, 178
unfortunately, 183n8
Ungrund, 111
unheard, 174
uniform, 161
unify, 188

unilateral, 179
union, 167
uninterpretable, 151
unique, 149–150, 153
United States, 32, 54, 62n2, 85–87, 161–162, 193
unity, 61, 110, 112, 115, 129
universal, 34, 56, 83, 131, 132, 136, 156n30, 170; "new universal symbolization," 135
universalism, 170
universalize, 33, de-universalize, 33
university, 58, 65–66, 122, 127, 160–161, 177, 190; Columbia University, 65–67, 161; Harvard University, 161; Johns Hopkins University, 162; neoliberal universities, 189, 190; Stanford University, 191; university discourse, 129; University of California-Berkeley, 78n17; University of California-Irvine, 161; University of Indiana-Urbana-Champaign, 161; University of Michigan at Ann Arbor, 163; University of Milan, 126; University of Minnesota, 163; University of Nanterre, 66; University of Nebraska, 163; University of Wisconsin-Madison, 161, 162; University of Wisconsin-Milwaukee, 69, 78n18; Yale University, 161
unjustly, 160
unknowable, 198
unknown, 54, 149–151, 200n12
unlikely, 72
unlimited, 138, unlimitedness, 137
unmarketable, 189
unnamable, 59, 150
unpaid, 18
unplumbable, 149, 151
unprecedented, 83, 188, 191, 193, 197–198

unpredictable, 187
unproblematized, 173
unproductive, 170
unprofitable, 189
unpublished, 75
unquestioningly, 72
unravel, 76
unrecognizable, 197
unrepresentable, 115
unrestricted, 168
unsayable, 147, 153, 199
unseen, 150
unspar, 68
unspoken, 45
unthinkable, 76
unthought, 70, 87
untrained, 18
unveiling, 180
unwarranted, 194
unworkable, 70
unworking, 110
uprising, 81; May '68 Paris uprising, 73, 170
uproot, 42
upwardly mobile, 12
Urgrund, 111
US, 12–14, 16–18, 23–24, 28–29, 37n26, 67, 69–70, 72, 81–84, 87–89, 93–94, 97, 187–188, 192
usage, 74
use, 39, 40–41, 45, 47, 54–56, 60–61, 74, 76, 82–88, 119, 122, 137, 158, 164, 167–168, 179, 191–193, 196, 198
useful, 49, 75, 136, 201n38, 202n44
useless, 169, 199
user, 121, 192, 198
usual, 164
usually, 158, 198
utopia, 32, 102, 104, 199n2
utopian, 94, 104
utopianism, 3, 6

utopic, 45

value, 56–57, 96, 98–101, 121–122, 124, 145, 167, 172, 192, 196, 202n44; surplus value, 138n8; value judgement, 197
"vanguard organization," 70
vectoral, 47
Vectoralists, 47, 48, 49
Verbivoracious Press, 42, 51n8
version, 40, 43–44, 47, 49, 58, 66–67, 72, 128, 135, 139, 153n, 168, 172, 175, 179–180; conversion, 139; inversion, 136, 173; "Kojève's version of universal history, 170, 182n2
Vertov, Dziga, 70
Viart, Dominick, 36n12
Vice City, 45
Vichy regime, 8
Victoria, Queen, 97
video, 85, video game, 45, 46, 47
Vietnam, 177; Vietnam War, 70, 163
Vietnamese, 70
view, 24–25, 28, 32, 34, 43, 49, 58, 68, 75, 84, 158, 190, 199; negative view, 164; overview, 192, 201n38; point of view, 142n43, 164, 172; purview of the signifier, 146
viewer, 33, 76
viewpoint, 45
Village, 160
Villalobos-Ruminott, Sergio, 3, 199
vintage American comics, 9
violence, 8, 14, 28
virtual, 48, 49, 161
virtuality, 48
visibility, 81, 89
visible, 9, 12, 16, 82; invisible, 197
vision, 43, 132, 182n2, 200n12; envision, 189

visual, 10, 12–14, 44, 69, 73, 78n19, 81, 82, 179, 199; antivisual, 13; visual artist, 164; visual arts, 9, 14; visual culture: 5; visual turn, 17
Vitali-Rosati, Marcello, 21n34
vocabulary, 61
voice, 81–82, 111, 124; the first critical voice, 194
voice-over, 70
void, 34, 50, 164
Voloshinov, V. N., 27

Waidner, Isabel, 44, 51n17–19
Wajcman, Judy, 83, 91n14
Waldfogel, Joel, 21n34
Waldman, Anne, 35, 38n46
Waldman, Diane, 78n20
Waldrop, Rosmarie, 23, 34, 38n39
Walker, Janet, 78n20
Wall Street, 85
war, 7, 86–87, 113, 120, 146; Cold War, 168; Cristeros War, 185n28; culture wars, 162; Israeli-Palestine Six Days War, 177; "Make love not war," 146; post-War, 8; post-World War I, 73; Second World War, 183n8; Vietnam War, 159, 161, 163
warfare, 86
Ward, Mathew, 20n25
Wark, McKenzie, 4, 42, 45, 46, 47, 48, 49
Wasson, Haidee, 78n22
Watten, Barrett, 23, 25, 29, 32, 36n6–7, 37n22–23, 37n25, 37n27
way, 40, 47, 54–56, 60–61, 67–68, 70, 74, 76, 83, 88–89, 97–98, 100–102, 104, 109, 114, 121, 124–128, 130, 133–134, 137, 145, 151–152, 158, 160, 164, 174, 177–179, 182, 189, 199; a conventional, thoughtless way, 176; a way out, 130; American way of life, 161;

way *(continued)*
  in a way, 156n30, 157, 184n27; indifferent ways, 197; liberatory ways, 119; one-way journey, 187
"weapon in class struggle," 70
website, 85, 200n16
Weimar Philosophy, 79n32
Weizenbaum, Joseph, 194, 195, 200nn22–24
well, 10, 12–14, 16, 40, 43–44, 46, 66–72, 74, 76–77, 122, 125, 128, 159–160, 169, 191–192; so well documented, 190; well-aware, 49; well before 1968, 157; well-defined, automated, finite, computational technique, 194; well-established colleagues, 162; well-known, 9, 48–49, 65, 124, 146–147, 154n15, 158, 198; well-made, 14; well-structured, 18
West, 188, 189
West Coast, 23, 160; West Coast Language, 25; West coast writers, 5
Western, 86, 113; Western capitalism, 132; Western economics, 47; Western metaphysics, 169; Western philosophy, 77; Western tradition, 141n42
white male European, 49; white feminists, 82; white male capitalism, 83
Williams, Gareth, 141n34, 180, 181, 182, 184n26
Williams, Linda, 79n37
Wisconsin. *See* University
witch, 85, 86, 87, 90; "You don't have to call yourself a witch to be a WHITCH," 85
WITCH (Women's International Terrorist Conspiracy from Hell), 85, 86
witchcraft, 88, 91n23, 92n29
witchy, 88

Wittgenstein, Ludwig, 31, 100
wizard, 89
Wolfe, Alan, 195, 196
Wolfson, Susan, 94, 95, 105nn6–7, 105n7, 105n9, 105n16
woman, 7–8, 10, 15, 34, 82, 85–87, 90n4, 90n6, 91n7, 112, 134–135, 149, 151–152, 155n16, 179; a man and a woman, 149; "man" and "woman" are signifiers, 154n15; "nasty woman," 85; the adult woman as mother, 134; women writers, 42; women's oppression, 78n20
Woo, Benjamin, 12, 20n21
word, 11, 13, 17, 24, 28, 34, 74, 114, 121–122, 124–125, 129, 131, 133, 137, 138n8, 143n73, 146, 148–153, 169–172, 174–178, 180, 188; afterword, 16, 187, 191, 199; "hole-word," 151–152, 155n21; key word, 179; wordplay, 156
wording, 198
work, 24, 26, 29–30, 33, 37n21, 38n39, 65, 67, 70, 72, 82, 109, 111, 117n16, 117n20, 134, 137, 142n43, 143n73, 145, 147, 152, 153n1, 154nn6–7, 155n16, 156n27, 156n30, 164, 169–171, 173, 188, 190–193, 196; working-class, 70; work-ethic mentality, 28; workplace, 121
worker, 81, 162, 175, 177, 179–180, 184n15, 185n28
workshop, 25
world, 73–74, 111, 119–121, 124, 129, 132, 135, 137, 138n4, 148, 163, 170, 177, 182, 183n8, 188, 189; authority in a datafied world, 196, 199; "being-in-the-world," 74; "literature-world," 164; "make the world uninhabitable," 130; post-

World War I, 73; Second World War, 183; Third World, 77n1
worldwide, 76
write, 3, 8, 14–16, 23, 24–26, 28–35, 37n22–23, 37n30–31, 37n33, 38n34, 53–54, 56, 59, 72–73, 83, 87, 90n4, 110, 114–115, 117, 145, 147–150, 152, 153, 153n4, 155n25, 156nn30–31, 164–165, 180, 183n3, 184n27, 188, 192, 196–197; rewrite, 26, 41, 147
writer, 10, 14, 23, 25–35, 36n4, 36n8–11, 36n15, 37n16–18, 37n24, 38n40, 54–55, 87, 115, 145, 155n21, 156n27, 156n34, 164, 170
Wu, Tim, 6n1

Xenotext Experiment, 43, 44, 51n17, 51n19

Yale. *See* University

year, 53, 65, 68, 72–74, 76–77, 77n2, 89, 109, 119, 126, 131, 150, 152, 157, 160–164, 168, 175, 177, 182, 196; fiftieth-year celebration, 65; fifty years later, 158, 162
Junior Year Abroad, 161
young, 131, 134, 136, 155n22, 161–163
younger, 162
youngster, 136
Young, Stephanie, 42
YouTube, 85

Zähringen, 141n35
zeitgeist, 84
Ziarek, Ewa, 3, 5
Ziewitz, Malte, 202n44
Zuboff, Shoshana, 197, 198, 200n20, 202nn41–44, 202nn47–48
Zukofsky, Louis, 29, 31
Zupančič, Alenka, 153nn3–4, 154n6

www.ingramcontent.com/pod-product-compliance
Lightning Source LLC
Chambersburg PA
CBHW030534230426
43665CB00010B/895